The Waist-High Culture

The Waist-High Culture

by Thomas Griffith

Harper & Brothers, Publishers, New York

Library of Congress catalog card number: 58-12449

To Caroline, for keeps

Contents

Note

The first third of this book is autobiographical. I have borrowed this form—which is properly reserved to those with imposing names, impressive exploits or eccentric families—because where I came from helps explain where I stand.

To begin in the first person enables me to produce my credentials, requires me to declare my prejudices, and helps me to proclaim my theme. That theme—stated so loosely as to leave myself plenty of elbow room—is about being an American in these times.

Le Castellet (Var), 1957-58

The Waist-High Culture

1. Is Everybody Happy?

We Americans may complain about our country, but rarely abandon it. We move often, but inside our own borders; we travel abroad, but do not emigrate. Americans can conceive of someone giving up citizenship in another nation; so many did in coming here. But give up American citizenship? The idea is unthinkable, and the man who suggests it must be out of his mind. Perhaps it is unthinkable for reasons as plain as a Fourth of July oration—that this is the best of all nations, and if some people abroad do not think so, who cares what they in their ignorance and envy think? Immigrants who came here in their tired, teeming millions felt the special pull of America; they did not leave their native land because they hated it. What was intolerable was not the "old country" but their own place in it.

"Give me your tired, your poor, your huddled masses yearning to breathe free," is Emma Lazarus' moving welcome inscribed on the Statue of Liberty. Noble words, but because of a slight excess of sentimentality in them they did not state the offer quite exactly: America did not want Europe's aged and sick; it wanted Europe's strong and willing arms. Come and pitch in—the work won't be pleasant at first because ditches must be dug, railroad tracks laid, coal mined and steel molded; the hours will be long and the cities congested. You may know nothing better than this all your lives, because you started late and your tongue is incomprehensible and you stink of garlic, but everything will be open to your children. They can be what they want to be, and not because we grant it to them but for an even better reason: they will be free to make their own fortunes. Our offer was not seriously misrepresented—America is not a landscape paved with ready gold; it is a land of opportunity. Who, then, would want to give up a passport to the possible, a citizenship in the future?

We are the children of that past, and we have done well. We are the richest nation in the world, the richest in all history. Let us acknowledge our great merits. Across the largest free surface in the world men travel freely, trade freely, share a common justice and need fear no tyrant's whim. We live in peace, and menace no other nation. We are largely free of civil strife and have come to a common understanding of each other's rights; we stop for traffic lights, pay taxes and honor agreements. We have overcome destitution, its brutality and its degradation. Whoever among us really wants work can generally find it; who is sick will be cared for; and our old are paid simply for being old. We allow workingmen to unite, and the rich to pile up new wealth. Our science is superbly equipped; our medicine prolongs and eases our lives; our schools diffuse learning to millions, and soon a college education will be every child's birthright. As a nation we are moving with tremendous, almost unthinking gusto into a different future. We have become the restless land of the bulldozer and the earth mover.

We should be fully satisfied, but find that we are not—and are puzzled. Once everything seemed conquerable. Overcoming obstacles, organizing successes, plunging ahead: this was the American genius. If something went wrong, we said, "Fix it, and don't stand on ceremony." We liked to talk big and to do big: "The sky's the limit," "We're going places," "We're on the move." But what if that which needs fixing is part of the changing; if what is bad grows along with our growth, as a shadow does; and if it is intertwined inextricably with what we consider good? Then we are at a deeper level of difficulty, and the easy American instinct for "fixing things up" runs into a conflict of choices, becomes bewildered, and hesitates.

It is here we stand today. We have widespread education and almost universal suffrage, but neither of these great reforms fully justifies the high hopes of those who fought so hard for them: we have mediocrity in politics and banality in entertainment. We are the gainers for the marvels of mass production, and acknowledge the necessity of advertising to provide its market, but we are dinned and dulled by its insistence and pervasiveness. We acclaim the theoretical right of everyone to do almost as he pleases, and so must put up with the disorder of our roadsides and the ugliness of our cities. We proclaim that what is not forbidden is permitted, and soon hear a far different proposition argued, that what is not illegal is not wrong. We respect the arts in principle—but reward the illustrator more than the artist, the jingle writer over the poet, the tunesmith over the composer. We talk of high standards, but sentimentally reward the most appealing instead of the most deserving, and too often assign merit not where it belongs but to those who most noisily lay claim to it. Democracy is in fact suspicious of high standards. In each succeeding generation of American history certain questions have been asked with increasing urgency: Though we gain in the ability to gratify our material wishes, are we declining as a culture? And: Is there something in democracy that is inherently hostile to the first rate?

Such questions torment other critics as well as our own, for the questioning spreads beyond our borders, to those who see the New American as the forerunner, in this as in much else, of what is happening more slowly to their own people. They cherish a vision of an elite holding fast against the spreading mass, and the assumption is that the critic who complains and the man who reads his indictment belong to this elite (who else is eligible for membership is never quite made clear). I envy these critics their certainty that they are uncontaminated by the evils they inveigh against, but I have never seen the American elite I wanted, or felt qualified, to join. Does it consist of people who listen only to Bach's *Goldberg Variations* and would not be caught humming a tune unless it were certifiably authentic folk music? And to hold their views, must they keep themselves aloof from 99 per cent of their fellow Americans?

If so, I cannot belong, for I am by origin, by impulse—and sometimes exultantly—part of that society whose trend disturbs me. It may be that we as a people are simply the victims of what we do not know how to prevent, and that the crass and brassy surface of American life does not do us justice; it may be that we are better than the American Image which we as a nation give off. At least, these are not questions which I can answer as an outsider: What is wrong in America I am part of; through me (as through you) travel the currents of our culture. The battlefield is not off somewhere else, and the enemy is not something other, anonymous and massive. The terrain of struggle is my own mind. Through me passes the vulgarity of our times, and the misgivings.

I. One Man's Immersion

2. Every Door Open

Vanity is possible today only to those who close their minds. We are bounced around, like corks on the waves, more than we care to admit. We think we choose, and do not. We cannot really call our minds our own, for we have been told how much our thoughts are controlled by our circumstances, our opportunities condemned by our origins, and even our outlook governed by our gall bladders. We have also, in the age of Freud, been given disturbing intimations of the dark side of our minds, which we would as soon not know about. We have been made smaller by one set of scientists, while another multiplies the complexity of the world.

We are no longer encouraged, like Byzantine princes born in the Purple Chamber, to consider ourselves unique. We are early confronted by teachers trained in the care of difficult children, who show us soothingly back to our places in line. As we grow older, there are psychologists to find our every ambition unworthy, the product of some unrecognized aggression in ourselves. Most of us resent and resist the attempts of scientists to explain us mechanically —to treat our senses as faulty and our knowledge of our own motives as hopelessly deceived. We also resist the patternmakers of society who treat us as one unit in a mass whose predictable comings and goings make expressways possible. The imp of individuality in everyone continually asserts itself—not out of vanity but out of necessity. We may be of planetary insignificance but we cannot

7

live by such long views; we may have needs in common and perhaps should behave accordingly, but we insist that our eccentricities be reckoned in. Our individuality may be a fiction, but it is necessary to act as if it were fact.

And so each of us is engaged in a continual process of isolating, discovering and asserting his individuality. It may be our destiny to be drawn into the flames, but at least we can beat our wings: individuals are we. We cry out our uniqueness, though, being social animals, we do so discreetly. Our claims are modest. We say only that no one else has quite the same intermingling of experience and feeling as we; no one else has seen precisely what I have seen, even if it is not very much; has thought all that I have thought, though I may not be very wise; or feels exactly as I feel.

In these times, the problem is not so much to cultivate our uniqueness as to find it. To do so, all of us must begin by disentangling what has been done to us from what we have done for ourselves, and only what we can be properly blamed for can we properly take credit for. Once we have found our uniqueness, we may also have found the seat of opinions which we have held so long as to call them truths.

Henry Adams was born under the shadow of Boston's State House and christened by his uncle, the minister of the First Church. "Had he been born in Jerusalem under the shadow of the Temple and circumcised in the Synagogue by his uncle the high priest, under the name of Israel Cohen," Adams wrote of himself, "he would scarcely have been more distinctly branded, and not much more heavily handicapped in the races of the coming century." Reading this, perhaps the most famous opening passage in American autobiography, I can remember envying the clearness of his markings, and of finding my own hopelessly unremarkable.

We all carry our past about us, like luggage on our backs, and we cannot, even if we would, remove the stickers showing where we have been. On my own baggage a label reads *7035 19th Avenue Northeast.* Could anonymity be more numerical? Neither a grand house on Boston's Beacon Hill nor the log cabin or remote farm which politically would do just as well, 7035 19th Avenue Northeast sat in an outlying street in Seattle, Washington, in a block whose grassy parking strips and nondescript builders' houses—white Cape Cods and creamy Dutch Colonials—would excite no surprise if set down in a street in Omaha or Knoxville. 7035 was distinguished from the others in the block by being larger and by being known as The Boardinghouse.

It was a place for children whose parents could afford to keep them out of an orphanage but did not want them around; for families of "broken homes" it was called: children of the divorced, the remarried, the widowed or perhaps (though it never occurred to me at the time, we were all so respectable) of those who had enjoyed the fruits but neglected the formalities of marriage. In my own case, my brother who was ten, my younger sister who was four, and I who was eight arrived at 7035 19th Avenue Northeast about one year after an event which, though it is far from the first I remember, is for me most vivid. I hardly remember my mother, and can only take on faith those who described her as lively and bright and pretty. Were they only trying to please me? She had red hair, I know from the snippets in a jar on my father's dresser, saved at the time she had her hair cut short. We were told that she had lasted longer with cancer than anyone else within memory at Providence Hospital. This was cited as an achievement and so accepted by me at the time. Perhaps it was meant to testify to fortitude or to a strong constitution; but now that I reflect back on it, this seems to me only an appalling testimonial to her suffering. Yet the awfulness of cancer was somehow kept from me, and I regret to say I have no memory of my mother's face or voice on those visits to the hospital when I was seven, no memory at all except of a round blue candy tin with a rose painted on its lid, which we were given to play with on the floor. When I see such a candy tin nowadays, I have a sharp image of my mother whose face I cannot remember; and when I see red geraniums, a flower which to this day makes me melancholy, I can think only of them planted, and then neglected, on my mother's grave.

My mother died at three o'clock one morning. My brother and I, but not my three-year-old sister, were at the bedside. But what I vividly remember is the two-mile walk home, just before the summer dawn. We held tightly to Father's hand, one of us on either side of him. His voice was strained as he tried to tell us what

"Mother is dead" meant, that we would never see her again, that she was going away to another place and would be happy there, and that it would be very hard on us all, but that he would try to keep our home together.

I remember this so well because it is the only time in my life I ever felt genuine affection toward us from my father.

He worked for the telephone company. I never knew exactly what he did, but for a long while thought that his job consisted in taking a letter or paper from a desk tray marked *In*, looking through it, crossing out his name on it, and putting it into a tray marked *Out*. It was the only work I ever saw him do. He was a self-made man and proud of it. His mother had been widowed when he was two years old; as a boy back in Pittsburgh he had worked as a Western Union messenger to help support his family. (We would have admired this saga more had it not been invoked so often to illustrate the necessity of work and the virtue of thrift.) He must have had a hard time of it; what little education he got was at night school, but unfortunately he learned only the value of money and missed many of the softening experiences that should be every boy's birthright. He played semipro baseball as a young man, and later liked to play whist, and then bridge; in addition he had total recall of every joke ever recited on the Keith Vaudeville circuit and of dialect music-hall songs, which he liked to repeat over and over as his contribution to parlor entertainment. With this brief catalogue I think I have named everything that ever gave him pleasure. I don't think his children did. We came along in time to exempt him from service in the first World War, and I believe he left the telephone company for a time to make big money in the shipyards—probably the same Scattle shipyards where Jack Dempsey worked.

How my mother and father came together I do not know, but there was one fatal obstacle to a happy marriage. She was Irish and Roman Catholic, and he was an indifferent Protestant—indifferent, that is, until the priest made him promise to rear any children as Catholics, a promise he regarded as made under duress and which he felt discharged from on my mother's death.

And so religion, which enters most children's homes as naturally as the Sunday roast, becomes part of their lives before they understand it and a solace to those who sustain a faith, was to us children the cause of an absurd but deep friction in our home. A few days after my mother died, her brother and sister—as Irish as could be—called on us children and took us to our favorite sweet shop. The way to our hearts was paved in chocolate: chocolate cake, hot chocolate and chocolate ice cream. We promised to continue going to Catholic church. When my father got home that night and heard it all from us, he—in a rage—forbade my aunt and uncle ever to see us again. A typical Popish trick, he called it, taking advantage of innocent children. From then on we were encouraged to go to my father's Protestant church, which he himself did not bother to attend except at Easter. We did not mind: since we went by ourselves, no one knew when we spent our plate money on candy on the way, and the church had a fine basketball court over the auditorium, where we bounced the ball about after Sunday School until an indignant deacon came storming upstairs to say that our thumping was interfering with the sermon below.

Shortly afterward my father began receiving, in a plain wrapper, a weekly paper called *The Fellowship Forum,* which he said was the only newspaper that dared to print the truth. I remember the headlines describing the defiance of the Pope of Rome by a southern Senator, one Tom-Tom Heflin, and the advertisements for books, sent in plain wrappers, written by ex-priests who promised to tell all about the tunnels leading from their quarters to the nunneries, and of what sweet illicit orgies took place at the other end of the tunnel. This was in the early twenties, when the Ku Klux Klan, with the bogus courage of hooded men, was riding the land after dark; I suppose that my father was a member. He later softened his feelings on the subject of religion, or at least became indifferent to it without repudiating his earlier views. Yet, when I too would soften my feelings, I cannot forget the later deaths of my mother's Irish parents. My grandfather, Peter O'Reilly, like many an Irish immigrant, had moved west with the railroad whose tracks he helped lay, settling with his wife (who had been Bridget Murphy back in County Cork) in Tacoma, Washington, the terminus of the Northern Pacific. When these old people lay dying, within a few months of one another, they asked as a final wish to see us, their only grandchildren. My father did not even answer the letter.

For a year after my mother's death, my father held our household together, hiring a succession of housekeepers who lasted only a few weeks, either because they were impossible or because we were. One, who lasted the longest, was a kind soul beneath her pinched bellicosity. She was also gossipy. Soon we children were being told of nightly goings on in the parlor after we had gone to bed: my father was having a visitor; the housekeeper could tell by the cigarette butts with lipstick on them, and the lingering perfume smell of woman. And before we knew it, my father had remarried—where or when I do not know. I only know that our household was broken up, and we were put in the boardinghouse.

We met her later and were told to call her by her first name. She did not ask us to come to live with them, nor even invite us at Christmastime; instead my father brought us presents to be opened among ourselves at the boardinghouse. He also came, alone, to visit us every Monday night. The routine was unvarying: We would drive aimlessly about the darkened city streets for an hour while my brother and father discussed batting averages in great detail, or we reported such small triumphs as a good grade or a teacher's praise, or my father would fill the car's silence with one of his Weber and Fields dialect routines, singing one awful comic song which involved an "r" which he trilled so long that it made my teeth ache.

Then we would stop for an ice-cream cone, which we would eat standing on the curb outside so as not to soil the car's upholstery. This was the pleasant part of the visit. The short trip home from the soda fountain my father dreaded, and we dreaded it even more. Then it was, having postponed it as long as we could, that we had to ask for something beyond the fifteen cents apiece he customarily gave us. "Thanks, Dad," we would begin tactfully, "but—" and then one of us would rush into an explanation of emergency need. We used to hold family councils beforehand, my brother and sister and I, deciding which one thing we might hope to get—a new pair of pants for me (a hurried demonstration where the present britches were worn through) or a new pair of shoes for my sister ("See, Dad, the holes in them?"). I do not think that it can be charged against us children that we preferred asking about clothes to mentioning our cavities. The result was that we all ended with bad teeth. My father just did not like to part with money; he knew how hard it was to get.

If my father did not particularly care for us, he did not particularly dislike us either, and later, when we were earning our own spending money and were no burden to him, I think he even took a muted satisfaction in our progress. We were getting an education and that mattered most to him, for he was convinced that had he had the proper schooling, everything in life would have been easier for him.

I should say more about my father, since in a way I retain an affection for him, but I do not know what more to say, except that his children never held their circumstances against him, as others did who complained of his treatment of the "Catholic side" of our family and deplored his failure to make a home for us. We children knew that at any time he might have done what in disgust he sometimes threatened to do—put us in an orphanage instead of parting so unwillingly with thirty dollars a month for our board and room. And as for making a home for us: after two years at the boardinghouse, we would not have wanted to exchange its anarchy for the confining domesticity of a stepmother who obviously did not want us around.

"Aunt Jessie," who was of course no aunt, ran the boardinghouse. She was a tugboat captain's widow with a large figure, a ruddy, veined face and a commanding presence. That confident manner of hers eventually gave way, but only gradually and after years of assault on her authority by every mischievous device known to inventive children.

There were from a dozen to a score of us boarding at Aunt Jessie's. We ranged in age from six to fourteen, and were about evenly divided between boys and girls. We were gathered together under her roof by the accident of a classified ad advising that she took in children for room and board with "tuition optional and loving care." She had some literary pride about her, and used to complain that other boardinghouse keepers had purloined these distinctive phrases to use in their own ads. She did have a certain gentility about her when, sheathed in black and puffing a cigarette, her formidable figure amply corseted, she climbed up into her lumbering old Buick to go out for an evening's cardplaying. But I remember better a more familiar Sunday scene, when, in house dress and big brown boots laced up to her knees, she would go into the back yard, grab a scurrying Rhode Island Red, cradle it beneath one arm and with her free hand take the chicken by the head and with one authoritative twist end its life. A not very feminine talent, perhaps, but most useful and performed with skill and coolness.

Though she wanted her charges to address her as Aunt Jessie, some stubborn adolescent dedication to fact in my brother made him decide that since she was really not our aunt she must be addressed by her correct name, Mrs. Leisen (soon reduced to a manageable slur, *mizleezen*). It was not long before the other children also gave up calling her Aunt Jessie, and deprived her of one of her few harmless conceits. It was not an easy life she led; sometimes we would come upon her in her back bedroom crying, a tax bill in her hands.

She had some sense of manners, for which I am grateful, and wanted to instill in all of us troublesome urchins a correct knowledge of the use of forks and spoons, of how to sit up straight and not overload our mouths. These arts were most important when a new sucker swam into her net, on those occasions when Mrs. Leisen would invite a parent to dinner, along with his child, to sample the bill of fare and to size up the atmosphere (the "loving care" promised in the classified ad) before placing his child with us. Though I hated the place, as we all did, some queer pride in what was after all our only home made us all want to make a good impression. Children are apt to greet unknown children with that air of suspended suspicion, prepared at any moment to turn to hostility, which can be observed in dogs. But we—particularly those of the old guard who were to sit at the table with Mrs. Leisen and the parent— were encouraged to show what companionable playmates we would make. We always anticipated these affairs, for they brought novelty to our lives, and the meal was better than usual, though it was clearly understood that we should in no way hint at this. Grateful for an adult audience, and eager to show how likable and intelligent we were, we must have been unbearable showoffs. With a sounder commercial instinct, Mrs. Leisen tried to contrive the conversation so that the new child would have a chance to register a success. But children cannot long collaborate in a falsehood. Perhaps an occasional new boy would impress us with his wider experiences and superior wit; if so, we were crestfallen. But, as it usually happened, we would probe until we found him somewhere wanting, and would thereafter be able by sheer force of numbers to claim to have better toys, to be able to spit further, or to have traveled to queerer places. Perhaps we still intended to help Aunt Jessie at this point, but I doubt it.

She was prepared for such conduct, and had a string of code words to deter us. I do not think FHB was one of them, for she would have scorned any signal which the enemy might intercept, and Family Hold Back was too familiar; yet I do recall that when the new child was urged to have a second helping of our favorite dessert, a custard pudding known as Floating Island, it was understood that though we too would be offered more, we must decline. Her style in code words was more like YTTM—which meant You Talk Too Much—which she could deliver out of the side of her mouth while maintaining a public smile. "Ladies Home Journal" meant to take the teaspoon out of your cocoa cup, a social indiscretion she had read about in a magazine.

We stayed seven years at Mrs. Leisen's, and seven more years at another boardinghouse. It would be possible to describe either place as Dickens might have, and to make of my boyhood a tale of horror and pity, full of hurts and scars, but I did not feel sorry for myself at the time. I look back on that little fellow I was with a dispassionate regard, as if he were someone else. I see him now, delivering papers on his bicycle, a tuft of hair in his eyes, a conspicuous nose, a wide grin on his face, exposing bad teeth. He wanted everyone to like him, and, if his heart could be read, was prepared to be endearing. But he had little to offer: he carried papers while other boys spent after-school hours playing football or tennis or going swimming. He was no good at any of these things; he was not particularly agile; he had poor eyesight; and if he read a lot and found classroom study easy for him, these were not talents admired by his fellows. He learned about girls and was healthily curious about them, but shy. Secretly intoxicated by the presence of some girl in his classroom, he would letter her name—*Rose, Rose, Rose*—time after time in his notebook, as if this established a bond with her; or would rush to some spot knowing that she was scheduled to pass by. These activities generated a great deal of excitement in him, but little achievement. He had no money, no graces, and could not even dance. (With a fellow lonely-heart, who had the use of his family's car, he would drive out to remote lakes on week-end nights. They hung about the outside of open-air ballrooms, full of the prospects of audacious conquests and in their minds prepared to participate in all sorts of gay evils—but returned home alone, stopping on the way back for a lonely hamburger.)

It is probably the usual practice to look back on one's childhood as a time of innocence, and to regret the overlay of corruption which life has imposed. But I do not remember it that way. That eager little boy, longing to be liked and wanting to be good, had in him the corruptions appropriate to his age, could be sneaky and cowardly, was subject to lusts even if denied the temerity to gratify them, was capable of thievery and lying. A documentation of these charges would not be interesting enough to justify the pain of relating them; I am no Rousseau bent on spreading all my life on the counter as a prisoner must empty his pockets before the desk sergeant. Rousseau understood that what causes shame is harder to confess to than crime.

To a boy in his teens, the judgment of his peers means everything. Some boys are athletes and natural leaders; some bloom a little later, when charm and girls matter; others must wait for slower talents to prove their worth, and rarely get a chance to enjoy a triumph in the eyes of those they once most wanted to impress. The proper combination—a popularity with one's own age group that does not exclude a growth of more durable interests, incomprehensible to those around him—is hard to come by. I know I did not have it. Some whom I then thought favored by the gods became so dependent on first popularity that they in time denied anything individual in their personalities out of the need for continued approval. Since such a popularity was never within my own reach, and since I had no parents around to soften any blows I might receive, I early developed self-sufficiency, a quality much prized by those who do not have it, but one which I think shrinks the capacity for tenderness.

All of us boys, lying awake in the unfinished attic of the boarding-house after the lights were out, used to plot what we would do on our final day there: what grievances we would avenge, what awful truths we would deliver, once free of the threat of punishment. The ultimate vengeance usually involved some inventive form of pyromania. But when the final day came, though I left the boardinghouse with no regrets, I had no feelings of revenge either. I was simply glad to go. We were an unloved and unloving lot, we of the "broken homes" at Mrs. Leisen's. Years later, when I became a police reporter, I had to write a story about a young fellow caught holding up the cashier of an all-night movie. He had been the oldest boy at Mrs. Leisen's, and, though given to petty sneakiness, was not essentially different from the rest of us. I am well aware of how little separates us—the accident of escaping or being caught at some prank that draws the police—and of how often luck, or some instinct for virtue planted deep inside, beyond our reach, saves us from a wrong turning. Having the freedom of the streets, I luckily had little bent for joining the nights-under-the-street-lights idle company which, out of restlessness and bravado, demands more and more difficult proofs of the right to membership, in a sequence that descends from rowdiness to criminality.

We are condemned by our origins, but sometimes saved by a favorable wind.

I thought myself happy at the time, my head full of every popular song that came along, the future before me. I could be an artist, a great novelist, an architect, a senator, a singer: having no demonstrable capacity for any of these pursuits made them all appear equally possible to me. All that mattered, I felt, was my inclination; I saw life as a set of free choices. Only later did it occur to me that every road taken is another untaken, every choice a narrowing. A sadder maturity convinces me that, as in a chess game, every move helps commit one to the next, and each person's situation at a given moment is the sum of the moves he has made before. But in those merciful days I thought every door open, and when it rained I did not ask sunshine. I was attuned to my expectations. Foreshortened by memory, it seems a mumbling, insecure boyhood. Yet it wasn't like that, it must not have been like that, for it all seemed so natural then and I feel unharmed by it now. I did without, but in no spectacular way; I took my lacks for granted, and often exulted in the solitary pleasures of my paper route—the glisten of rain on the grass, the dew-fresh assault of ferns, the craftsman's satisfaction in rolling and twisting the paper and tossing it so that it scudded along the porch and came to rest banging at the base of the front door, announcing its arrival. Walking along delighting in self, lost in my own identity, planning brilliant artistic triumphs, or imagining my-self the devoted and pleasing servant of Miss Constance Bennett, the movie actress, while all those husbands of hers were showing themselves unworthy of her; humming tawdry current tunes that in my head were fully orchestrated but aloud must have sounded like a droning *vox humana* played on a comb, I went contentedly on my way. Solitude has its own arts.

Besides, my brother and I were not entirely forgotten. One day after school two strangers timidly introduced themselves to us. They were my mother's brother and sister, our Catholic aunt and uncle, Mary and James O'Reilly. What did they want of us? We were a little frightened of them. Were they trying to lure us into the hated Catholic Church (our minds were well prepared by then). No, it seemed that they only wished to befriend us. Gradually our suspicion decreased. They gave us spending money; they asked what clothes we needed. And they never mentioned the Catholic Church, or talked against my father. When I ask myself now why we were not at once properly appreciative of them, I realize that it was because our relationship began in bribery. What we asked for, they gave us, though they scrimped to provide for us.

Soon my brother and I were often hitchhiking the forty miles to Tacoma, where they lived. My aunt was not a good cook, but she tried; and she fixed us all the things we most prized—candied sweet potatoes, fried chicken, corn on the cob, chocolate ice cream. To think that anyone would plan a meal to *our* tastes! Ah, but there was nothing they would not do for us: take us on rides, listen to our chatter, buy us frivolities, spoil us thoroughly. Perhaps they felt sorry for us; but mostly we were all they had. They were that familiar Irish phenomenon, a brother and sister neither of whom ever married (still another sister became a nun). Brother and sister, living together with no one to lavish affection upon but their niece and nephews. With the awful awareness of youth, we detected that they needed us, and, I am afraid, often took advantage of them. They treasured every note we ever scribbled, and years later turned them over to us as souvenirs of our childhood which they thought would amuse us, but instead make me burn with shame:

How are you? I am fine. Say there's a keen pair of shoes I could get for $3.50 if you can spare the money. . . .

My father gradually became aware that he had been relieved of providing us with all our clothes, soon determined the source of the generosity and said nothing. We were happier that he knew: his silence was in effect a tolerance, and we no longer needed to feel like conspirators. The day came when my uncle wrote my father and asked if he might take us to the World's Fair in Chicago. My father did not answer him, but on one of our Monday night visits showed us my uncle's letter, and said that if the fellow wanted to spend (his tone suggested "waste") his money that way, he had no objection. Of that memorable trip—the first long train ride, the day coach smelling of dust and orange rinds, the meals in the white-tableclothed splendor of the dining car, the exciting fatigue of sitting up all night in the green plush seats, the hustle and immensity of Chicago, the festive tawdriness of the World's Fair—I remember best the side trip to St. Louis to visit some Irish relatives. We rode the city bus and were absorbed by the discovery that if there were only Negroes at a stop, the bus would pass them by. Once my uncle stopped to get his shoes shined by a Negro who had a little wooden box for his sidewalk customers to put a foot upon. My uncle was soon in friendly conversation with the Negro; my brother and I, ashamed of so flagrant a violation of southern customs, edged away from my uncle as if we did not know him. He even shook the fellow's hand on parting! We were aghast, and tried to explain to my uncle afterward what a terrible thing he had done. "There's nothing wrong with shaking hands with a colored fellow," he replied equably. "The black won't come off on you." I am not sure that these words would impress me as much now as they did then (we have all come such a long way) but the naturalness of his conduct was a hard lesson to me: instead of being ashamed of him, I was ashamed of myself.

My aunt was gray-haired, and somewhat sickly at times, but had that Irish trait of believing it her duty to make herself cheerful always. Any admission that she might not be feeling well had to be wrung from her. She thought always of others, and when alone, of her religion. There wasn't a petty thought in her, and I was so unperceptive as not to realize this; I took her selflessness for granted. She was not very adept at sewing or typing or spelling (I don't know how she held down her jobs, unless her employers saw in her the merits I slighted—her honesty, good nature and dedication). She sometimes spoke in malapropisms, and did not realize what she had said wrong even when her friends laughed; they laughed liking her and that was enough for her.

Not many years ago I returned to the West Coast on a visit. There was a family reunion, and a long drive to bring everyone together. Mary O'Reilly, her usual cheerful self, came along. But I had been back East only a week or two when she called up a friend and said simply, having thought about it a long while: "Take me to the hospital. I am going to die." She had not sent for a doctor earlier, having had a presentiment that she was already far gone with the disease that had taken away her sister, who was my mother.

While we were with her she had evidently concealed great pain so as not to spoil our visit. She died trusting in the hereafter, and deserving well of it. I had just time to write her all that she had meant to us, which I had never said before. I was told that the letter was read to her on her last day and that she smiled her pleasure, but I do not know whether she really heard. I only know that in my intellectual pride I had not realized how much there was to learn, and how much I did learn, from her. The wrangle that was religion in my upbringing, the smarty agnosticism of my college days had left me little room for faith. Religion seemed remote from me, something that happened to peasant girls on Italian hillsides. I could not imagine blinding flashes of light or the sound of heavenly trumpets over the billboards, apartment houses and gasworks of Tacoma, Washington. But from my Aunt Mary I have learned that no spectacular and conspicuous deeds are necessary, but much honor and courage, to live that most simple and difficult of existences, a good Christian life. If I myself did not have her faith I could admire qualities in it greater than any I lived by.

3. The Tug of the Times

A generation is whatever regards itself as one. As I advance in years, no longer—alas—able to invoke the mitigating defense of youth, and perceiving at my heels a new generation that is quite unlike my own, I realize that I am part of an era that historians can already codify: the Depression generation. It is a contemporary failing to want to pin labels on ourselves too soon; to speak of ours as the atomic age, the age of plastics or the age of anxiety, and we are apt to forget that the Holy Roman Empire was already 400 years old before someone thought to use the phrase, that the word "feudal" is a later coinage pinned backward in time by the historians, and that several centuries passed before someone thought of a name for the Renaissance.

But in the shorter span of here and now, we are tempted to tag and classify even when we may not permanently define. Before my own generation, in the years between the Armistice and the stock market crash, came the period we used to call, for the phrase served as well in condemning as it did in praising, the Jazz Age. Knowing it only by its novels and headlines, we saw it as a time of speakeasies, gangsters, short skirts and broken marriages, unthinking optimism and Yale boys frenetically becoming rich on the stock market. We knew it mostly through its critics: Sinclair Lewis' morose disapproval, Scott Fitzgerald's bedazzled disenchantment, H. L. Mencken's scorn. Priggishly surveying this preceding age, I can remember writing in my college newspaper that we of the Depression had been invited to share the hangover without having enjoyed the drink. I now see a younger generation than mine asking with the same uncomprehending disapproval what the 1930s were about. They, this younger generation, strike me as being without doubts and without curiosity about the workings of their society, and concerned only with finding their own secure place in it. How can they understand that we saw the collapse of all the certainties that our elders set store by, saw their confidence in themselves give way, saw them abdicate? Or so we were told. We were encouraged to try anything —just do something—and were warned that all the old yardsticks, calipers and compasses no longer worked. The laws of supply and demand had been invalidated by an unseen hand; gold was no longer money and banks were no longer safe. We felt heady with responsibility. We were a serious lot, and convinced that politics mattered.

Many were out of jobs in Seattle in 1932, when I entered the University of Washington, but the stonecutters and masons who knew how to apply a few Gothic collars and cuffs to squat campus buildings had plenty of work. The university was bursting at its bogus Tudor-Gothic seams; what had been a lovely evergreen campus drifting gently down to a quiet lake was now become an overcrowded educational factory for 10,000 students. Faculty salaries were being severely cut, but, by some devious triumph of the lawyers, there was money available which could only be spent on building still more buildings to take in still more students. Nobody who had anything to do with the situation was happy about it, but everybody who had nothing to do with it insisted that it be that way. To suggest that not every boy or girl who escaped out the front door of a high school had a constitutional right to go to college was to speak the unthinkable, and to show oneself undemocratic. What's the matter, don't you think people are equal? Just who do you think you are? So everybody went to college, and the instruction sank to the capacity of the laggards, but it called itself a college education and conferred degrees to prove it. I can think now of all kinds of objections to this reasoning, but it made my education possible, and who am I to complain?

What it lacked as an education, it made up for as an experience. Here we were in all our thousands, plain or pretty, fresh, eager and

curious: we enjoyed the discovery of one another, talking sentimentally with the girls along moonstruck paths, or disputing wildly
with other fellows under street lamps or over beer mugs. In pairs
we crowded into cars, with our dates in our laps, driving the evening
away, singing college songs or the latest tunes, enjoying the darkened
intimacy. Classrooms interested us less, though there were times
when the chance phrase of an instructor lit up a corridor of the
mind, as if it had been a wick awaiting just this flame. Full of confidence we were in those days, sure that our opinions mattered,
though they changed often. And we insisted over and over to each
other on the purity of our intentions in a world which we could
see was going to be quite impure.

I had elected to study journalism, which is neither science nor art,
and therefore made sure of getting a smattering instead of a schooling. The choice was deliberate: had someone urged the humanities
on me, I would have answered, "What good will that do me?" and
have been impervious to argument; college cost hard-won money
and I had no right to store my mind with vintage wines instead of
laying in essential provisions for a future paying job. And so I
learned the tricks of a trade, was taught some useful things about
courtroom procedures and the law of libel, and much else that was
only makework used to puff journalism into a full-time curriculum.
I was instructed at length in that perversion of English which is
called a news story, whose peculiarities are based on a lively fear of
the inattention of the reader. Our news stories, we were taught, must
overwhelm him at every moment; everything should be short and
snappy. We twisted our sentences about in order to begin with
prancing verbs, afraid that if we ever heedlessly opened a news story
with so plain a word as "the," readers would flee to the next column.
(Much of this I have since had to unlearn.) We called our journalism professors by their first names; they were friends, and still are.
If we were never introduced to much that matters, in those job-
hungry days what I got was what I asked for. When the choice of
diet is left to mice, they will invariably choose cheese.

Sir Richard Livingstone has defined the goal of education as the
ability to distinguish the first-rate. By this deceptively simple
measurement, I learned little in college. I came out of a state university ignorant of all science, of architecture and art and music;

dimly aware of certain Greek and Roman thinkers but not having read them; knowing no language but my own and that imperfectly; indifferent to poetry, asea in philosophy, hostile to economics, susceptible to history but untrained in it; possessor of good grades, a rented cap and gown, a bachelor's degree but not much education.

There were many of us in the same fix. The economic distress of that era undoubtedly exaggerated what is apt to be wrong at the best of times in a state university. An atmosphere of the main chance hangs over them. They are not places designed to spread culture or teach manners; students have saved their money, or their parents have sacrificed to provide tuition, with a practical purpose in mind— to prepare for the competition of the market place. Many of my classmates, intending to go into politics or business, asked of college only what they called "contacts." For others, conscious that they had been deputized by their families to seek a better living than their parents had known, college was a methodical exploration of technological mysteries. To be sure, a university was expected to be something more than a trade school; it should give students a passing acquaintance with the classics, suitable for surviving a dinner conversation or answering a quiz program, but in the main the criterion of any subject was "What good it will do me," and not our later selves but our immature minds were allowed to be the judges. One had to be able to earn a living, and culture could come later: the liberal arts were chiefly valuable for the patina they gave you of being an educated man. It was not all like this: sometimes a professor was able to show his students a delight in style or beauty or perception for its own sake, or was not embarrassed, despite the listless response of his class, to talk of enduring values. Such teachers were a minority. I remember the English course in which I was introduced to Keats, Shelley and Byron. A favorite professor of mine, whose method was Socratic, would read out these familiar lines:

> Hail to thee, blithe spirit!
> Bird thou never wert.

Then he would snort: what kind of stuff was that? Poets had a duty to talk sense, and we must not be seduced by their music from making them toe the mark. (If there is in fact any magic in these lines, I am afraid I shall never hear it.) Keats died early, still a romantic, and got off lightly; Shelley and Byron were good radicals of their day—but Wordsworth! The professor could hardly be brought to discuss his poetry, for Wordsworth had gone conservative after the French Revolution, and in the light of such a betrayal, what could be learned from him that would be of any use to us now?

A bleak utilitarianism was the salt-free diet of our times. We ranged hurriedly over the feast of mankind as if it were a vegetarian's *smörgåsbord*, sampled it in snippets, learned of it in "surveys" which became barren outlines memorized by rote, and related everything to the immediate and applicable.

Years later, on a Nieman Fellowship at Harvard, I got some intimation of what else a college education might be. I went expecting to find a deer park of the well-to-do, for like many Americans I thought that if Harvard men subsequently did well it must be because they enjoyed a monopoly of privilege and favored one another's careers throughout the rest of their lives. It might have been too unsettling to believe that if Harvard—and that too-small band of colleges in its class—enjoyed a superior reputation it might be because they provided a better education. How better? The classes were smaller; the equipment not markedly superior; the professors were often, but not always, of higher caliber. It was not through a monopoly of brains but through a different notion of its purpose that Harvard prospered. The excitement in the air is intellectual. This is Harvard's golden gift; in its standards lies its strength. Not to have to bend the knee to the state legislature might incline some of its professors to pomposity, but released the best in others, and where knowledge can be pursued disinterestedly, where standards of instruction are rigorous and students cannot expect to be sheltered from their own inadequacies, something like a community of scholars exists.

Harvard's crimson banner is a red flag to everyone else, for no one likes to concede superiority. But it is not necessary to like Harvard men as a breed to acknowledge the merit of Harvard's schooling, and I am even optimist enough to believe that its best can be approached by any university whose president and regents make the simple, radical resolve to seek quality, and who resist all efforts from any quarter to debase it.

For it is in providing college education that is less than it might be and poorer than it need be that the indulgent curse of mediocrity in American life begins. In education, as in so much else, we Americans settle for less and give it the grander name. We have made the democratic decision to give as many children as much schooling as possible. The old notion that what was to be promised was only equality of *opportunity* (which then must be seized if one is to enjoy its privileges) now seems too austere a doctrine. But is it really sound democratic dogma that everyone shall have a higher education, even if quality suffers and in the process the most gifted are stunted because their best is not required of them? We deceive ourselves if we think we do not diminish what we provide. Never in the history of the world have so many people had a college education, and never perhaps has there been such a proliferation of the second-rate. The trouble in education was once that too few could enjoy it; but such a hardship may in time prove less disastrous to society than to have a people educated to the belief that they are not ignorant, and too complacent to know—as the ignorant once knew—that they are missing something.

If we were honest with ourselves perhaps we might be driven to admit that we do prefer a little laxity of standards, that it is part of the great American code of abundance to believe that we do not, like the unfortunates of Europe, have to grub quite so hard to prepare ourselves, and that college should be a pleasant and not too demanding interlude before we enter the real world. Is that the American assumption? Accept it, and one might even concede that there is much to be said for the coming together, on those large state campuses, of people of such diverse origins; something, even, to be said for the distracting commingling of the sexes in our great coeducational universities. This may not be scholarship, but is its own kind of education. Such fruitful associations are, at any rate, about all that most students take away from American state universities—those vast, endearingly inadequate academic ball parks. As for myself, though I cooperated contentedly in the pleasures and concurred in the avoidances of my four years in college, I came in time to feel somewhat swindled.

That first winter of my college education coincided, in the wider history of our times, with the last months of Prohibition. Free from the restraints of our parents, eager to pursue the forbidden, we were ardent customers of a man who lived on a houseboat on the lake and sold rum or gin, indistinguishable in taste, for $1.80 a bottle. More exhilarated by our daring than by our drinking, we got ourselves known as a gay crowd. When summer came and I needed a job to tide me over, I called on an affectionate grump known throughout the journalism department as "Pa" Kennedy, a man respected for his canniness by the editors in the state. Yes, he allowed, he might be able to find me a summer job on a country weekly. It was only later that the meaning of his secret smile became clear: he had apprenticed me to a publisher strong in his Methodism and firm in the right, who had until recently been director of prohibition enforcement for the eleven western states. I did not drink so much as a glass of beer all summer.

South Bend, Washington, was a quiet fishing and lumbering town of perhaps 3,000 people. It was surrounded by timbered hillsides through which cut river valleys farmed by frugal Scandinavians extracting a marginal living. Only four miles away lay the town of Raymond, and it was a measure of Publisher Hazeltine's pervasive righteousness that there were 22 bars and taverns down one street in Raymond to slake the thirst of hardy Swedes in from the woods, but not a single bar in South Bend. This was the summer the banks all closed and reopened slowly one by one; Franklin Roosevelt had come to power and assured us all that the only thing we had to fear was fear itself. (This had so fine a lilt about it that it came to be believed even by those who had no job and could see no future.) So short was cash that some communities in our state were issuing and honoring wooden money. I was therefore to be paid no money, but given room and board, a meal ticket at the Chink's, and a $15 due bill at the local clothier who owed the paper for his advertising. The arrangement suited me fine; I reported for work eagerly. I met my fellow employees—the back shop foreman, the printer's devil, the lady reporter. They were cordial, but I detected a slight constraint. I was as poor as any of them, but I was that "fellow down from the university."

Awkward and suspicious when confronted by anything mechanical, I nonetheless found music in the clanking of the linotype machine and gloried in the lumbering rhythm of the flat-bed press; useless with my hands, I nonetheless found satisfaction in hand-setting headlines. These were first signs of a passion for journalism which began early and persists still—though I have become more prudent in concealing the emotion. (Employers should never know how much one *enjoys* his work.) My job was not to be in the print shop, or even, as I had hoped, the reporting of Fourth of July parades, Rotary meetings and the preparation of the "world's largest oyster stew" for the annual oyster festival. Instead I was introduced to an antiquated Chevrolet roadster known in the family as the Pea Green Peril, and told that I was to make the circulation rounds of the back country with the old man. He knew every inch of it, and directed me to doors, while he sat outside in the car.

We stayed in ramshackle hotels for the bills they owed us. We wandered down corduroy roads, dared crude plank trestles (I had not admitted that I was just learning to drive) and scraped the bottom of the car over rutted trails. Generally we found our prey at work in the fields, where they could not escape us. All, that is, except the Finns, who, occupying small pockets among the other Scandinavians, were so shy of strangers that you could pound five minutes on the door and, though you heard movement inside and saw smoke rising from the chimney, no one would answer the door. Perhaps they were the wisest, at that. For it was no pleasure to arrive at a slab-sided, unpainted farmhouse, identify yourself as from the South Bend *Journal* ("Largest Circulation in Pacific County of Any Newspaper on Earth"), look about at the torn oilcloth on the table, the Sears, Roebuck catalogue, the oil lamp, the broken victrola with its big horn, the gaunt woman with a dirty and tattered child peering out shyly at her side, the reticent man of the house in overalls—and announce that you wanted to collect a back bill. How much? They owed since 1929: that would be $7. You might as well have asked a million. Sometimes a farmer would answer surlily that he had only subscribed for one year, and it wasn't his fault if the dang paper had kept coming. At this point it was my duty to produce a small orange card on which was quoted a section of the postal law to the effect that anyone who continued to accept something in his mailbox owed for it. (I was later told, though I do not know the truth of it, that the very next sentence said that no one could, however, be compelled to pay.) These were honest but desperate people: they would swallow hard and say with hopeful finality that they simply had no money. And now, hating my glibness, I would reply confidently that this didn't matter: on the way up to their door I had seen chickens in the yard. We would accept them as payment at the rate of 50 cents a chicken, and would credit a sack of potatoes at $1. We would also accept old tires (and in fact we accepted and used such old husks that in one three-week stretch I fixed 19 flat tires on the Pea Green Peril). The chickens, put in crates in the rear end of the roadster, were often asphyxiated by the time we got back to South Bend, but Mr. Hazeltine did not seem to mind: we had cleaned up a lot of bad debts, and I believe he also sincerely thought he was doing the souls of his delinquent subscribers good.

A hulking, nearsighted, tightfisted man with a gentle wife, he had the courage of stern convictions. In the upcountry, identifying myself as from the South Bend *Journal,* I would sometimes be confronted by someone whose father, brother or son had gone to jail because the revenooers—at the instance of Mr. Hazeltine—had raided their stills. "If that old man ever shows his face around here, I'll fill him full of buckshot," I was often assured. The old man never seemed to mind being told of such pockets of resistance. It was not in that forthright old editor to pander to an audience.

Sometimes in the years since, caught up in the lunacy of the expense-account economy, mindful of the waste we wallow in, aware of a decline in the standards of workmanship and discipline, I am tempted to sigh for that past day of plainer values, lower prices and more honest work. There was a salutary rigor and a fellowship in sympathy during the Depression that is gone now. But then I think of the ill-nourished and hollow-eyed people in the shacks, willing to work but finding no market for their crops or jobs for their hands, and I would not have it back.

Only 16 when I entered college, I was so impressionable in politics that I leaped from attending campus rallies for Herbert Hoover (though years from being able to vote, I was useful for swelling a crowd) to Socialist meetings for Norman Thomas, passing entirely over Franklin Roosevelt and the Democrats. Had I been asked I would by then have said in my new-found wisdom—for I fell easily into the patter—that Roosevelt was merely offering palliatives when severe surgery was needed, and perhaps would have echoed Walter Lippmann that Franklin Roosevelt was simply an amiable aristocrat with an odd wish to be President. But I soon enough became so enamored of F.D.R. and everything about him—cigarette holder, jaunty press-conference wit, the courage of his handicaps, the boldness of his vision—as to make me forever indulgent of anyone on the other side who found Wendell Willkie's tousled hair part of his appeal, or thought it further proof of Dwight Eisenhower's sincerity that he had difficulty in finding his way out of sentences once he got into them.

Each of us is apt later to wince at the gullibility of his youthful beliefs, though it would be a terrible world if each generation set forth in full weary knowledge of the world's unchangeability. Idealism is the madness of the season when one is young, as selfishness is the madness of maturity. And so we called ourselves New Dealers, gloried in our anonymity, and took no offense at hearing ourselves addressed as the common man. We treasured the solidarity of being underprivileged, and because we had little, regarded ourselves as being of proven unselfishness. We thought youth made our honesty plain, and that the purity of our intent excused any lack of experience. We wondered that the old did not immediately abdicate to us, and put it down to meanness. We confused outspokenness with fearlessness, and believed that any kind of caution was only a cloak for dishonesty. We felt superior to our elders of the debauched twenties, and in fact fitted Yeats' description of the Whigs:

> A levelling, rancorous, rational sort of mind
> That never looked out of the eye of a saint
> Or out of drunkard's eye.

The puritanical streak in New Dealism has, I think, been slighted by the historians. Roosevelt scorned the wealth and waste of the princes of privilege, though he never made very clear the kind of world he meant to set up in its place. But one vision of it might be seen in an outriding fringe of New Dealism known as Technocracy, a movement dear to engineers and other systematic minds, which proposed to measure the social value of all labor and to pay everyone in units of work done, known as ergs or ughs (I forget which). Technocrats sternly believed that idle fripperies of taste and color were keeping people from getting enough clothing, a conviction which led them to limit themselves—as they presumably hoped to limit everyone else—to one style in dress. Technocrats wore gray suits. For men, this drabness might be relieved by a necktie of either solid red or solid blue; for women, by blouses in either of the same colors. Even their cars were uniform gray, and numbered.

"Utopian" was an epithet much used in those days, meaning too visionary, but in fact Technocracy resembled Utopia most not in vision but in humorless monotony. The 54 alike towns on Thomas More's dream island, each 24 miles separated, had nothing in their houses private and every tenth year people changed houses by lot. There were no alehouses, "no lurking corners, no places of wicked councils or unlawful assemblies," no occasions for vice and opportunities only for "laudable pastimes." Of course, for most of us, the leveling spirit of Technocracy or of Utopia was going too far, but a planner's severe notion of "laudable pastimes" and community enterprise was not completely alien to the trend of our thought. We were full of the parables of Socialism: where was the sense in having six competing delivery wagons to bring milk to the same block when one could do so more efficiently? We talked much of redistributing the wealth, convinced that poverty in a land of plenty was primarily a problem in distribution.

If the New Deal itself did not accept, neither did it loudly condemn Technocracy: Roosevelt was too sophisticated to be attracted by that kind of humdrum paradise, but too practical to spurn support from any quarter. Washington was then a GHQ of nostrums, borrowing, from the many amateur political movements that had sprung up, whatever it found useful or appealing, stealing from others—such as Huey Long's Every Man a King or pathetic Dr. Townsend's old-age-pension crusade—in order to diminish them as political rivals. Roosevelt was often accused of introducing Planning (as if the opposite were preferable!), but I think the contrary was true. He, and the "brain trusters" he recruited from the universities, played by ear; they did not in fact plan well; in their minds everything doctrinaire was suspect and they gloried in experiment. Some shudder at what might have happened had Franklin Roosevelt, with his popularity and eloquence, been less supple and restive of mind: What if he had used his immense power to socialize or communize the country? But perhaps the question answers itself: Had Roosevelt been of the mentality to organize squads of militants, he might have lacked the gay arrogance and acute sensitivity to popular feeling that made him the enthusiastic choice of his times.

What is hardest now to recapture of that era is its feeling that all the tested old ways had failed. Confidence—so essential to that swelling of the economy that we call credit—was gone. Along the deserted wartime shipyards on Seattle's waterfront spread a tin-can-and-gunny-sack village which, with its counterparts across the nation, gave a bitter new word to the language, Hooverville. The facts of shutdowns and poverty were bad enough, but when newspapers, with the highest as well as the lowest of motives, began to radiate a false optimism, minimizing or concealing bad news, people took to believing anything they heard, and many were convinced that National Guardsmen had been stationed on the roofs overlooking Seattle's main square to fire upon the surly unemployed should their demonstrating get out of hand.

It was a most inauspicious moment for a young student to be convinced of the verities of economics. Youth is always inclined to question the best of systems, but what were we to think when our questions (and a fool can ask ten questions while a wise man is answering one) were thought to be unanswerable? Our parents had lost their simple faith in homilies—a penny saved was *not* a penny earned, and it was not only the shiftless, but people eager to work, who could find no jobs. Our conservative professors of economics, no longer fully persuaded by what for a lifetime they had believed and taught, still talked about the ebb and flow of the market and about the natural compensatory mechanisms by which a multitude of individual transactions somehow resulted in an invisible equilibrium. But they knew something was wrong. Later, with improving times, conservatives generally forgot their own sense of helpless inadequacy, and, getting up from their sickbeds, denounced the doctor. Subsequently much was also made of the number of Communists corrupting the youthful minds of the thirties. But though there were in fact some Communists on the University of Washington faculty, I think the most shattering impact on college students was made by the times themselves, and the confusion of conservative minds that had lost their bearings and their certainty.

Amid these doubts and hesitations the campus Communists had a strength out of all proportion to their numbers, gained by their servitude to a fixed dogma and by their raucous support of one another. They clustered, and their mocking, assured questions reduced some of our professors to timidity. In that day professors were apt to feel their studies rarefied and to be anxious to enlist in the deeds of their times. They craved an identity with the common man, celebrated his plain folk song (unwilling to believe that most working men really preferred Tin Pan Alley) and sought what they called solidarity, a state of mind later to be denounced by them as conformity. Sometimes Communist sympathy in the faculty merely expressed itself as sentimentality toward the Soviet Union: I remember a well-cooked dinner at a professor's home where the wife seemed to get a special pleasure simply from wearing a Russian peasant-style apron. But the Communist ascendancy took harsher forms. As one of a handful of undergraduates at a professor's home one evening, flattered at being in such company, I was enjoying the conversation, the beer and the big crock of cheddar cheese, until my economics professor took his leave early, at which point my host (and until that moment my favorite professor) turned to the remaining group and said, "Well, we can talk freely now that the *Fascist* has left." The professor who said this was himself no Communist, but expressed his own views indirectly and feared to show himself less militant than the Marxists.

I cannot submerge the feeling that some among the campus Communists of that day were men of good heart aroused by the disaster of the times; a few were shortly to die for their beliefs in Spain. But their arrogance as a group when they had intellectual dominance, their readiness to crush the personal or professional reputations of those faculty men who resisted them, has remained in my mind, and has made it hard for me, in the turn of the tide that followed two decades later, to have much sympathy for their later attempts to picture themselves as humble devotees of freedom of thought. I also admit to the view that one must be prepared to expect unpopularity when taking unpopular views, and that neither the Bill of

Rights nor the statute of limitations can save anyone from that.

At the time I felt an implied self-reproach in the Communists' greater dedication to a cause, but when I tried to satisfy my misgivings about their system I would be scornfully answered: "Have you read *all* of Marx? Then how can you possibly discuss these things?" I was also put off by their unattractiveness: the men usually vain, soiled and humorless; the women apt to be knotty-haired, plain and aggressive. I wish I could say I withstood the appeal of Communism on impeccable intellectual grounds, but confess I was too lazy and ignorant to do so; I could see only the tactical deceits and was not persuaded that the end justified such means. I was prone then to judge beliefs by the characteristics they seemed to produce in their advocates, and did not like what I saw in the campus Communists. So I did not join what was widely billed as the ascetic academic elite of my times.

At about this time, when I was much caught up in the dynamism of politics, the dean of my journalism school, a shrewd and reserved man, jolted me greatly by saying, "You are a conservative who thinks it the duty of his generation to be liberal." To this day I am not sure how I should have answered this Delphic remark. I only know that I then wore my liberalism as a badge, was positive about Spain and anxious about the Negro question (though avoiding the Coon Hollow of my own city). I had never committed the heresy of believing that whatever is, is right (how could we, in 1932?) but was guilty of the deeper heresy of believing that whatever will be, will be right. This was known as a belief in progress, and whoever resisted change was, in the phrase of the day, "standing in the way of progress."

We thought of ourselves as sensible gradualists, and of legislation as a clean, white cure—people would lose their ill-gotten gains but there would be no unpleasantness as they would simply obey the law; I might not have the nerve to stand up to my boss individually but the law would make him accountable and the union would be my surrogate. We had high opinions about the improvability of man and believed that his lapses were only the fault of the selfish competitive system he was enmeshed in. Maybe I too talked of the necessity of breaking eggs to make an omelet, but this was only tough talk; we were in the right and we were in the majority, so there would be no trouble. I felt a vicarious triumph in distant victories over landlords, bankers, employers, mortgage holders, racial bigots; I had a feeling of belonging to a body of generous-hearted, tough-minded, forward-looking young people.

What I felt was largely an unearned satisfaction. Yet it is too easy now to mock the excess of those past efforts. The struggle was real then, and the opposition persistent. If unions later became sedentary and flabby, they were lean once, and in bloodshed, against the narrowness of industry and the malice of the press, they earned their triumphs. They had much good will on their side. In America at that time there was an atmosphere, not confined to New Dealers, of working together, as in a coal-pit disaster or after a flood. Nor do I minimize the ideals of those of my age who hurried to Washington from the campuses; if in an earlier day the ambition of every young man had been to enter the stock market, in my time courses called Public Administration proliferated and the ambition of many young men was to make government their life's work, content to earn a modest and steady income while performing useful service. (It was not only considered selfish to want to, but impossible to get rich.)

Much foolishness, envy and credulity resided in the beliefs I held in my college days and in my twenties, and some of the idealism with which I credited myself and fellow sword-bearers in the anonymous army either got lost or was never really there. The kind of world I would have built—the forced equality, the state overseeing, the pro-fusion of agencies—I would not like now; and yet many of the things that got done under that spirit—such as TVA and bank-deposit guarantees, stock-market reform and public works, mortgage relief and unemployment insurance—were essential measures that were blindly resisted.

It was left to the stubbornness of the opposition to keep all of our wishes, mercifully, from being realized, and often their objections resulted in legislation less haphazardly drawn. But this opposition, by its unwillingness to ease the hardships of the day, to display either compassion or vision, can hardly claim a superior wisdom. "Those who resist improvements as innovations," warned Canning, "will soon have to accept innovations that are not improvements."

The struggles of that day have had a curious ending: by some paradox of historical growth, what liberals have won, conservatives have inherited the credit for. (That barren thing, conservatism, said Disraeli, "an unhappy cross-breed, the mule of politics that engenders nothing.") Having absorbed what they could not prevent, conservatives later sound as if these were measures all sensible men had all along been agreed upon and any strife had been the result of an excess of militancy in the reformers. By thus swallowing their medicine unobserved, conservatives appear to have a settled solidity to their beliefs even while changing them, while those who want change seem to have a restless instability about them. But if a later conservative defends the equilibrium of his own times, he owes a large, and usually unacknowledged, debt to those past strugglers who made his present tranquillity possible.

Looking back, it now seems that if somehow we survived the Depression intact and even recovered from it, something was owed both to the audacity of the reformers and to the tenacity of those who resisted them—the reformers in control, but required to be mindful of the resisters. This tug of the times formed a lively tension, which was modified by the peaceful temper of the people, and the fortunate American inheritance of political safeguards. But so dispassionate a view of so arduous a time does not mean that yesterday's anxieties were unreal, that the end victory over the Depression was inevitable, or that the contest to establish government responsibility for national misfortunes was unnecessary. Even a belief in determinism presumes that a set of conditions will produce a protest against them—and in similar circumstances I would be on the same side again. For it is possible to recognize that equilibriums are achieved by a balancing, as on a teeter-totter, while knowing that all of one's own weight belongs at one end.

4. A Police Reporter's Lot

There are experiences in each person's life that he is grateful for but would not willingly repeat. Such were my days as a police reporter in Seattle. I can still call up at will, as others might summon up the recollected fragrance of thyme, the astringent smell that hit my face each morning at 6:30 as I opened the door of police headquarters: an amalgam of whiskey, sweat, vomit and the powerful antiseptic that the trusties mopped the floor with. And I do not long to go there again.

"I'm sending you down to police to take the college out of you," was the way it was put to me by the city editor. He was an immense Irishman with many children, great good humor and an occasional and dangerous flash of wrath which, because of his bulk, he knew he must subdue in himself, for he could smash chairs and crush us all if minded to. His father had been a cop. From Leo Sullivan, my first city editor, I learned many lessons in humanity. He had the poor man's scorn for the false respectability of "the better elements" in the community, but the working man's realism that some things had to be done their way or suffered in silence. As much as necessary, Sully distastefully gave Them what they asked for, and so long as it was a scrimmage involving people well able to handle themselves, he counted on circumstances to do their own redressing. But he had a wonderful way of blunting, disregarding or softening ill-considered attacks on the helpless. In doing so, he quietly resisted his superiors, but even more effectively moderated young reporters such as I, who out of ardor for a story and the misapprehension that one has a duty to report everything he learns, could be unthinkingly cruel in print. Sully was one to live and let live, that best kind of Catholic who knows what there is to know about sin and frailty but does not feel called upon to sit continually in judgment, who likes people but does not idealize them. He may have given in at times when he did not want to—he believed that one must always let the other fellow win a few—but he kept a part of himself that could not be reached and would not be invaded. From him I learned something of patience and proportion.

The brashness of youth wants merit immediately recognized, justice proclaimed and failure rooted out: I had to learn respect for seniority even when questioning its wisdom; to learn the steadfast values of routine; to recognize that a slow change made palatable to all is often better than a quick victory; to realize that men of settled opinions, though they may lack the invigorating candor and flash of youth, are often of solider judgment. In my itch to get ahead, I could be intolerant of the office drunks (one of whom kept his bottle concealed in a shopping bag in the cloakroom, with stalks of celery sticking up from the bag as decoys); I could be impatient of the old men of the copy desk, whose journalistic skill, whatever it once was, now seemed reduced to a pedantic fussiness over our copy as they excised all that we thought robust and original in it. Sully taught me the protective ways of our craft: their careers might be behind these men, but they had a right to their living, and we might be in the same fix one day. Out of an odd assortment of men, some much gifted and some not at all, Sully fashioned a reportorial squad that was agile when it had to be, steady under pressure and proud of its own performance, with a spirit unknown to those in the front office, who thought that counting their money and airing the opinions of their clubby group was what newspapering was about. It was part of Sully's instruction in humanity to send me to police, and what he meant by taking the college out of me.

The police station (they have much the same atmosphere everywhere, I have since discovered) is a place where moral judgments are left to those who write the laws. It is for people who have been left behind, and the pursuers and pursued often have more in common with each other than they do with the rest of society. The invader from outside must learn its demands and adjust to its tempo.

I learned not to burst out of a detective captain's office the moment I had my story, but to linger and talk a minute longer: the captain might have an obligation to give every reporter the facts, but would go out of his way only for the ones he liked. The conversation of cops is largely confined to three kinds of possessions: new cars, small arms and women. The first two they discuss in intricate detail, the latter they consider useful for only one thing, and every picture they see of a movie starlet involves a meticulous conjecture as to her suitability. Though the subject of women can also be widened to include speculation on national divergences, it is essentially repetitious. Beyond these subjects, cops tend to be a taciturn lot, with that impassivity of expression that is meant to hint at deeper knowledge but can as easily cover an artful stupidity. A natural cunning keeps them from getting too chummy with reporters.

Our editors and owners felt very superior to the police, and yet were never too eager in public criticism of them: there might be parking tickets to be winked at, and it was recognized that an assiduous and hectoring law enforcement might uncover niggling violations in our plant, or slow our delivery trucks as they sped our latest editions. Most big organizations, I suppose, tend to have ambiguous connections with authority: the world revolves around such practical lubrications, but it makes most editorializing on the subject somewhat hypocritical.

As police reporters we were thrust into an odd dual relationship with cops. The police liked us when we gave credit or withheld blame, but we were always poking around, sometimes into corners that someone did not want looked into. At best we were tolerated with wary, gruff cordiality as people who had to be lived with but might prove dangerous, and until we had been there long enough to have shown ourselves "reliable" we were often the butts of that favorite police pastime, the practical joke.

Cops never begin by suspecting the best in anyone; after all, a vivid knowledge of the low range of motives to be found in mankind is essential to the discovery of suspects to any crime. Yet though I saw a number of cops prepared to be brutal I never saw one who wanted to be regarded as without sympathy. Cops who walked in pairs through the tough precincts of the Skid Road were known to spend half their pay in handouts to the hard-up. If I had to choose among cops, I preferred those whose easy morals might make them petty racketeers but also made them indulgent of weaknesses in others, to that self-righteous kind who might be honest but could be unfeelingly cruel, and employed their uprightness to justify a streak of sadism.

Most cops develop a shell against life such as ambulance drivers and nurses must have: a refusal of sympathy, a stilling of observed pain, so as not to interfere with their proficiency at their own tasks. I tried to school myself in the same fashion, and could at least talk the lingo. "Come on over," the deputy coroner would say on the phone. "We've got one that's been floating in the bay for two months, and it's really high. Whew!" Or after a gruesome auto crash: "Boy, that was some wreck. We had to bring the old lady back with a shovel." Having steeled myself by sitting in on autopsies, I would reply in kind. Besides, I had seen these same coroner's deputies, so coarse to us, offer mute and kind support to those who came to the morgue to claim their kin.

Murder, fire, accident; death, destruction, dismemberment—this was the daily raw material of the police reporter. We were buzzards of disaster, quick to hover over trouble. We may have been unfeeling about it, but grief in quantity dulls the senses. In addition, much of what we reported came to us secondhand, over the telephone or from a policeman or fire chief who had been at the scene: it was already one remove from reality when we tried to impart synthetic drama to it. I exulted in headlines, and could be cast down if I did not make the front page. What newspapers loosely call tragedy (to the horror of all pedants) was the police reporter's business, and the more victims the bigger headlines. Every newspaperman knows this irrational appetite for numbers of wounded in battles, wrecks or blasts, and mocks it in himself. In the same way, newspapermen in the long hours of a "death watch" over a celebrity, or someone gravely injured, are apt to express—though not intend—the impatient wish that the fellow would get it over with, so that they can get the story into print.

An odor of corruption hangs over a police station, but though the
scent is pervasive it is hard to isolate. So many opportunities exist
for petty understandings with businessmen, or sleazy alliances with
lawbreakers. Every forbidden whorehouse and bookie joint in any
city must operate with the knowledge of the man on the beat, and
usually with the connivance of headquarters. We all knew that
among the honest cops were others who shared in the take, but
the essence of graft is that it does not take place before the eyes of
curious police reporters, and those who take bribes do not issue
receipts. A falling-out among thieves or an occasional slipup gave
us our rare opportunity to hint sagely of wider disclosures that
might be made. Over our blackjack games in the pressroom we too
affected the taciturn wisdom of being "in the know" and were
cynically superior to the uninformed uptown moralizing about the
sins of our city. We prided ourselves on a superficial hardness and
felt important in our jobs: the right to be inside a police line confers
some of the same pleasure others get in being shown a favored table
by a maître d'.

We came to live in the limits of the policeman's world, and made
our peace with it. If we sometimes saw cruelties or abuses,
much of what we shuddered at did not fit neatly into those little
spitballs of fact which become news stories, or if used had to be
weighed against the possibility of rendering ourselves *personae non
gratae.*

I have seen wretched rumdum drunks cuffed about and their heads
banged against the wall because the booking sergeant, in searching
them, had cut his hand on a razor blade in a back pocket. And I
have been in police court next day when the judge, asking why this
prisoner was all bandaged up, was told the old refrain: "He slipped
and fell in the elevator, Y'Honor." The judge would grunt and say
no more: he too weighed his silences. A detective lieutenant once
excused himself a minute while he shut his office door to listen to a
Filipino merchant reporting that someone had stolen a pair of shoes
from his sidewalk display table. A scuffling and cries of pain could
be heard inside, and then the detective rejoined me with the remark,
"I'll teach that goo-goo to think I'm going to look for his damn tennis
shoes."

If we did not write stories of such incidents, there were also occasions when we felt a sympathy with cops that we dared not express. On newspapers, there are certain "human interest" situations that, in a spare way, can permissibly be sentimentalized. Readers accept, for example, the fiction of the goodhearted whore. But it would not do to write too sympathetic a story about a corrupt policeman: in most newspaper writing, what one *ought* to feel is given precedence over what one does feel. And so, captive of our own formulas and slaves to respectability, we would write a hard story about a crooked cop and then say to one another, "The poor bastard."

Our preoccupation with "human interest" was hard for cops to understand. They had their own notions about what constituted criminality and deserved writing up, and were often reluctant to cooperate with us in reporting what they considered trivial offenses. Thus when a young girl slit her wrists, a homicide detective assumed automatically that she did not seriously intend to kill herself but was only trying to frighten her lover: had she really wanted to do away with herself, there were surer and quicker methods. (As for women who swallowed too many sleeping pills, they were subjected to the stomach pump and unsympathetic handling by the city nurses, who had enough work to do on bloody accidents and begrudged time to those who had willed their own misery.)

When some ingredient of human interest made news out of a shoplifter with a baby to feed, or out of a young punk who had stolen a car to joyride his girl in, the police were often protective of them, and then our roles were reversed: we, the press, and not the cops, were the unfeeling ones. Policemen might feel a duty to arrest these unfortunates but had no urge to add to their woes, and I could never be as angry as my city desk expected me to be when a cop frustrated us from taking a picture of these victims.*

We were apt, as police reporters, to be slightly indifferent to what a policeman regarded as one of the major achievements in his craft,

---

* The sure sign of police "cooperation" in taking a picture (usually of someone they are proud to have captured) is a startled look on the victim's face, and a door closing behind him. The procedure works this way: a detective is sent upstairs to the jail to bring down a prisoner, ostensibly for questioning. Having noted what the detective was wearing, I would station myself beside the jail elevator; as soon as I could see the detective's trousers and shoes in the descend-

the capture of a gang of safecrackers. These, and not murderers, are the true enemies of the police, and there is a heightening of tension at headquarters when a gang is brought in. People who kill in passion are generally angry only at their victims, and their courage is often spent before their capture, but safecrackers practice a craft learned only after a long apprenticeship in crime, and after a long time in prison, where the best instruction is; they have graduated from car thefts to burglaries to armed robbery to safecracking (the usual progression in crime) and they have planned their big move carefully. They have the tools of their trade on them, which is enough for a conviction; they are often two-time losers and, knowing they will be put away for a long stretch if caught, are prepared to shoot it out. Every cop regards safecrackers as men prepared to kill police, and perhaps has had a friend on the force who was killed by one. The safecracker expects no mercy at the hands of the police, and gets none; but the peaceful capture of yeggs is not considered big news by city editors, because a reader cannot easily identify himself with such hardened criminals.

There were other stories which made news but were not quite what they seemed. Police reporters well knew the practice of "cleaning up the blotter," whereby a young burglar, in return for facing only a second degree rap, will confess to more burglaries than he has actually committed, so that the captain of the burglary detail may proclaim an end to the "crime wave" that was beginning to embarrass him. We played along, for how could we challenge a signed confession, or resist a headline: ADMITS 30 NORTH END BURGLARIES? We were similarly content to write of coroner's "blue ribbon juries" though we knew he had recruited a handful of scruffy courthouse hangers-on, so as to avoid any mulish outbursts of independence among those selected by lot. We accepted the fact that friendship with elected officials, though on our part somewhat tinged with contempt and on theirs with distrust, might be mutually useful and

---

ing elevator I would rush through a door, letting it slam behind me, to alert our photographer that the next one through the door would be his quarry. As they got off the elevator, the detective would say to the prisoner "Go ahead and open the door." Then, as the prisoner stepped through, flash went the camera. This is known as stealing a picture: a tolerated form of theft which involves no punishment, except to the victim.

was usually harmless, an exchange of small favors that involved no commitments. We would not have remained silent about anything we regarded as substantial injustice.

And so, in this practical school, I had the "college taken out of me." If police reporting was often grubby, it was sometimes exhilarating. One of its pleasures was in scooping one's competition, for our paper did not encourage collaboration, or news-hunting in packs. We were placed in friendly pressroom association with our poker-playing rivals but did not hesitate to throw them off a scent, while staying within a loosely defined code of not being completely false to one another. We did not lie, but need not volunteer everything we knew. A cop might say, "Give this to the other fellow, too," and we would keep the promise—but only after we knew that his next edition had gone to press. It was a cordial rivalry, and in those days when newspapermen were joining unions and talking common fronts against publishers (who made common fronts against us) we would not have let anyone get hurt too badly too often. My rival, on the city's weakest paper, was raising a family on $15 a week.

When there was a pause in the city's mischief, when the fire alarms were still and the booking office silent, we police reporters would forage for news in that unique American institution of rough justice, the police court. Solomon presumably had time to consider his cases one by one; police court is justice on the assembly line. Aside from the judge's high oak bench, the most conspicuous object in the room was an immense cash register whose sharp ring was a coda to each case.

The day's routine of drunks sentenced and motorists fined was relieved for us by the appearance of hip-swinging, overperfumed women being fined $25 for prostitution (the madam stepping to the cash register with the money ready). Occasionally, in the midst of the singsong of sentencing and paying, drama formed itself— more often we had to give it a harmless little push. After a holiday, the city attorney would wander into the pressroom (for he liked seeing his name in the paper) to concoct with us what might, for instance, be a good line for an Irishman to say after being arrested for drunkenness on St. Patrick's Day. From among the shuffling rummies in the tank, he would then single out one with an appropriate

Irish name and coach him in his lines. The Irishman was probably a wino far gone in a two-week stupor from drinking bay rum or canned heat, and his arrest on St. Patrick's Day only a happenstance; in court, he would be able to mumble only an approximation of his assigned speech, but the judge would set him free, and we would have the kind of bright "item" so beloved by announcers from coast to coast in signing off newscasts.

Justice was not a word heard often in police court, though presumably its outward forms were honored. Sometimes an ambulance chaser would make a great show of invoking legal principles and procedures to impress a client; at such times, the processes of justice would slow down and become warier, but in the end the fine was usually the same. I used to try to reconcile what I heard in police court with what I had been taught of jurisprudence at college. I wondered why, in any conflict of testimony between arresting officer and speeding motorist, it was assumed that the cop alone had no motive for lying and therefore his word was to be preferred: wasn't he interested in making his arrest stick? In other cases, it would take a theologian to distinguish between guilt and provocation: I remember a policewoman who confided to me her off-duty hobby. She would go to an all-night movie and rub her legs against the man in the seat next to hers; if he made a pass at her, she would arrest him.

What was hardest to understand, for anyone who believed that there should be crime before there was punishment, was the catch-all offense known as being "disorderly." A cop would raise his fat right hand, solemnly agree to tell-the-trut-an-nothin'-but-the-trut, and then testify of some miserable down and outer: "I've seen him hangin' around. He was doin' no good for himself, Y'Honor." This was the entire accusation. Thirty days, the judge would mumble, as he thumped a rubber stamp down after the name on the docket:

SENTENCE SUSPENDED ON CONDITION DEFENDANT
AGREES TO LEAVE TOWN AND REMAIN AWAY

This was known as "floating 'em out of town," and was defended by the police as necessary to flush out the bums from the lower end of town, so that any newcomer would be conspicuous there who had money to spend (as reported by prostitutes anxious to stay in good with the police) and would be hauled in for questioning about the latest burglaries or robberies. In time, though I never accepted the theory of convicting someone as "disorderly" who had done nothing, I came to accept the fact. Except for traffic violations, that "gentleman's crime," police court cases rarely involve anyone but the misfits of life, who, if not guilty as accused, perhaps feel guilty of something else, and in any case are resigned to the breaks.

This may seem a hard saying, but these men did not seem cast down by their fate. I had to learn that well-intentioned people err in transferring to others the same degree of emotional response they would have felt in like circumstances. How can they stand this filth? a lady will say as she inspects a slum. They often stand it very well, lady, and don't want to do all that scrubbing and fussing you do. Visitors to police headquarters, seeing criminals for the first time and aware how shamed they themselves would be, cannot understand how unmoved a felon can be by the disapproval of a society he does not accept, a society he believes himself at war with. He does not want its pity, or theirs.

Still, for all the phlegmatic resilience that people are armed with, the part of my job as police reporter that was most distasteful to me was to be the bearer of bad tidings to a family whose son had been lost in a shipwreck, or whose daughter had jumped from a bridge. Some reporters, on such assignments, made it a practice never to tell the extent of the bad news but merely said that something had happened and that no further details were known. I thought it unfair to leave a family with false hopes; if someone was dead he was dead, and as gently as I could I would generally tell whatever I knew. I discovered that nature throws a protective shock over people at such moments: it is only several days later, in the homely task of putting away a person's clothes or in straightening out a drawer, that one realizes with finality that he will never see that someone again.

But this scruple of mine to tell the worst only made my next task harder. At the best of times, it was not easy—especially when scandal was involved—to switch the subject around to the fact that the city desk wanted a picture of the victim and of her family. (I hated this assignment most in the early morning, for a woman sobbing, dressed in a soiled bathrobe and with her hair uncombed, will almost never agree to be photographed.) What police reporter, in such circumstances, can swear on oath that he has never stolen a photograph from a bedroom dresser—or persuaded a cop to take it along for him, as "evidence"?

The ultimate degradation in police reporting is not what one sees but what one consents to do. It was my apprenticeship, and I did not argue large questions, for I was satisfied then—as I am satisfied now—that it is in the public interest to report the crimes, the arrests and the mishaps of a city. And without a prying and impertinent press, there would be less honesty and less solicitude for human rights around a police station. But this function of the press is used to justify too many intrusions into private griefs, intrusions which deserve no highfalutin rationalizations about public service, since they are practiced only to sell papers, and to satisfy what is called curiosity but is largely morbidness. Here's a woman shown as she hears the news that her husband has hanged himself—read all about it!

I remember with no satisfaction going into cells when the last person a prisoner wanted to see was a young reporter anxious to spread wide the details of his or her misdeeds. "Look," I would say, trying to pierce the shell of guilt, torpor and resentment, "I know you don't want anything in the paper. But there's going to be a story anyway, and you might as well get used to it. The only question is whether you're going to leave it to the cops to do all the telling, or whether you're going to give me your side of the story." And as this sank in, I would add, "You're going to have to face a jury one of these days. And juries—even when they say they don't —read the papers." We all had our standards about how far we would go in this sort of thing, and fastidiously disapproved of one reporter, known among us as Liver Lips, who would even get down on his knees in supplication and tell a murderess that he would lose his job if he didn't come back with her picture and story. Why people who were in this extremity should have been moved by concern that a reporter might lose his job if they did not help him out at their own cost eludes me, but Liver Lips excelled us all at such moments. He had a dogged conviction that, since he was a newspaperman and only doing his job, no one had the right to keep from him anything he wanted to know, and generally they didn't.

I was lucky not to have stayed too long on the police beat, for though it is a part of reality that the rest of the world wants to deny, it does not encompass all the range of motives in the order its inhabitants think it does. One lesson I learned there I did not take to heart until many years afterward. Had I done so earlier, I might not have been so zealous in believing that a world can be changed simply by passing new laws, for this is to ignore the old Adam in us all.

5. Go East, Young Man

Long aware that an American boyhood was different from a Dane's, from an Italian's or from a Hottentot's, I naturally assumed that it was they who must be odd. Only gradually did it dawn on me that though a public-school upbringing in a medium-sized American city was an experience shared with hundreds of thousands, it was not every American's lot, and that there were inevitable disparities between my own outlook and that of boys raised on an Iowa farm, in a small Vermont town, on the crowded sidewalks before a New York tenement or in the atmosphere peculiar to the South. I was a Westerner, a species of patriotism which if not loudly asserted is strongly felt.

In the old days when most living rooms were done in heavy furniture and dark curtains, thousands of Western homes had framed on the wall a picture of a cottage with smoke curling romantically from its chimney around this poem:

> Out where the handclasp's a little stronger,
> Out where the smile dwells a little longer,
>   That's where the West begins. . . .
>
> Out where the skies are a trifle bluer,
> Out where friendship's a little truer . . .
>
> Where there's more of singing and less of sighing,
> Where there's more of giving and less of buying,

And a man makes friends without half trying—
That's where the West begins.*

We sensed that this might not be classical poetry, but it exactly expressed our sentiments as Westerners. We thought that something in our surroundings and in our inheritance made us more open and generous than the rest of the country. "Welcome, *Stranger*," was a friendly greeting in the West: a newcomer must be made to feel at home. After that he was on his own, but the assumption was that he was as goodhearted as we, until proven otherwise, and would do as much for us. This was so instinctive with us that I remember the shock of first experiencing another kind of behavior in those business-like pit musicians who came to Seattle with road-show musicals. Recruited from New York City or Chicago, they were Jewish or Italian, had sallow complexions and long black hair and obviously felt superior to their present surroundings. But what really set them apart was that on seeing someone unknown to them *they did not smile*. Years of living in the East have not yet completely erased from my face an expression of indiscriminate amiability, of smiling whenever I catch someone's eye, though I am well aware that in the East, and even more so in Europe, this is regarded as forwardness, an uninvited attempt to establish acquaintanceship. I had to learn the impassive subway stare, neither hostile nor friendly, and to recognize the right to make an unapproachable island of oneself in the midst of a crowd. Rudeness is the privacy of New Yorkers. It saves them from intrusions; it reflects their consciousness—so alien to a Westerner—of economic and social distinctions, and their refusal to be involved with one another.

We in the West detected that people elsewhere spoke our language a little differently—through the nose if from Indiana, having trouble with a's and r's if from Boston, slowly and with marshmallow softness if from the South; and from having seen haughty butlers on the screen we could all mock the way Englishmen talked. We were convinced that only our own speech was natural, and anything else a variant. For all I know, this may be everyone's experience, just as our pride in salmon and oversized apples is matched by the New

* From *Out Where the West Begins* by Arthur Chapman, published by Houghton Mifflin.

Englander's pride in his chowder and his Indian pudding, the Southerner's in those odd leavings he eats.

As Westerners, we felt ahead of the times, having already discovered a place and a way of life that others would in time find, for we knew it to be a certainty, and considered it progress, that our countryside would fill up (it was only when it did so with an onrush, during and after World War II, that misgivings began to be heard over whether fast growth was improvement and larger population a gain). We lived stretched out, with room for lawns between our houses, and within easy driving of quiet, green places. Beyond us, when the days were sharp and clear enough to see them, loomed white mountains, cold and noble. Lakes and bays surrounded us, edged by forests of evergreens broken only by occasional clearings and modest cottages. No walls of estates locked us from the best views. Fishermen had the meandering rights to any stream; nearby were lakes to sail on and mountains to ski down. I was as proud of these advantages as anyone else, though inclined as a city boy to consider the countryside an empty space between two towns. To fortify our complacency in what we had, our newspapers spread eight-column headlines to report every heat wave in the Midwest or blizzard in the East. (Patriotism in weather, fed by local newspapers, is perhaps an American trait.) We were happy in our temperate climate, and objected only occasionally to the frequent not-too-insistent rain. This was God's country.

It was also man's country, and somewhat abused by him. The timber companies no longer plundered the forests, leaving ugly patches of stumps and debris: they were learning to replenish what they took, but their past greed still disfigured the land. Highways slashed through hills, leaving naked scars; the second growth of trees spread in thin monotony, and the roadsides were cluttered with gas stations, hamburger joints, and roadhouses shaped like chickens, derbies or lemons, competing in garishness for attention. Faded campaign posters were left on trees, billboards obscured the views and stray signs littered the fields. Cottages beside the road were often unpainted, and innocent of any proportion or style; old bedsprings and abandoned automobiles had come to rest in the weeds in the back yard. We either did not see all of this, our eyes on the hills beyond and editing the view in our minds, or made allowances. There was a squatter mentality about those times; we recognized that the people in these ugly shacks had little, and we admired them for making a new start here; in time, as they prospered, they might feel like sprucing up. We would not have thought of indicting them for defacing the land, yet that is what they were doing, along with those who had less excuse—the billboard industry and the proprietors of ramshackle roadhouses and used-car graveyards. Western man made little demand on himself to match the grandeur about him. When I later discovered the tilled New England countryside, with its white houses, black shutters and red barns, its relative immunity from signs, its neat stone fences and its respect for trees, I realized (as I was to come to realize in France) the pleasure and pride of a country settled for centuries, and the serenity to be found in homogeneity of structure and color. Not all the newness of the West, nor its easygoing license, deserved celebrating: they spoke rightly who talked of its *natural* beauty.

But I can be severe only out of an exacting love of what is my home country, and, even in deploring, understand. When one enthuses on his home town to someone unfamiliar with it, he stresses what is distinctive about it (in Seattle's case, the hillside streets coming down on one side to fresh lakes and on the other to salt water, and the view of distant peaks), yet the appeal of a home town is what is ordinary about it, not the grand panorama but the familiar street corner. Even the shop fronts, hideously universal as they may be, are a litany of remembered names.

Nor can I be neutral about the people. In a French village one sees people so plainly themselves and *making no effort*, as an American would say, to be otherwise. This making an effort has its wrong side, but it also accounts for that good-tempered American hospitality, which is a matter not of manners (and sometimes lacking in them) but of a genuine desire that everyone feel included, at home. There was not one world, in Seattle, of doormen and elevator operators and taxi-drivers, and another of those served. We sought an equality with them all, and would have thought ourselves snobs had we not. We made a point of seeing something in everyone, and usually found something to see: The milkman might not have read Chaucer but might have a better knowledge of flowers, or be wiser in rivers, than you, and perhaps had gone to the same school. We were not taught to regard him politely but to keep a distance: we naturally accepted him as a human being like ourselves. A few people in Seattle might be recognizably distinct—an occasional Greek or Pole with an odd name—but they did not clot in communities and accent their separateness.* Occasionally someone would be so unregeneratively unattractive that we had to concede that his unattractiveness reflected not a quirk of personality but a defect in his origins: we would concede a little guiltily—and still affirming our belief in equality—that he *hadn't had all the advantages* we'd had. This charitable Western assumption of equality may have no justification in reality; it is not universally felt even there, and may disappear as the West fills up, but it is nonetheless a heart-warming trait, whose absence throughout much of the world accounts for many of the world's needless hatreds.

But this Western attitude of considering no man better than you, and yourself no better than anyone else, has its drawbacks too. It generates much worthy community activity and some that is only pleasant and harmless, but it inclines to a suspicion of those who would set themselves apart in any way. It is all right to have odd interests, so long as you are careful to depreciate them. But if your separate pursuit demands privacy and concentration it is apt to be regarded as an attempt to set yourself off from, and therefore above, your fellow man; one becomes defiant or apologetic, but in either case unnatural, or abandons his private disciplines and settles into

* There were, of course, Negroes, Chinese, Japanese and Filipinos, who lived apart from us because of their lower income and seemingly of their own volition, as I thought at the time. The Japanese labored in truck gardens on the outskirts of town, had the cleanest stalls in the public market, and their bright children—as American of speech and thought as any of us—often became our high school valedictorians and salutatorians. The Chinese ran the laundries and chop suey joints; in the eyes of the police they got in trouble as the Japanese never did—mixing in narcotics, gambling and secretive tong behavior. The Filipinos made sunny houseboys for the well-to-do, but the rest of us too often knew them only through the headlines: since only Filipino boys were imported, they would often figure in the news as attempting to rape a white woman, or running amok, knife in hand. Proper white girls did not go out with Filipinos, and once a year our paper ran without explanation a picture of a crowded pier as a cannery ship came in from Alaska. The swarm of women who greeted the Filipino cannery workers would have all their season's wages within a few days, and after that no further interest in them.

Pearl Harbor, among its other effects, compelled a hasty revaluation of which among Asian peoples we were supposed to admire most.

the general ease. Skills which are spontaneous and communal are much appreciated: the ability to dash off a parody, but not the exacting solitude required to write a good poem; the capacity to entertain at the piano but not to play well, which compels too silent and respectful a hearing; and a talent for home decorating and a dabbling in paint will get you acclaimed as artistic—so long as you paint recognizable likenesses. There is, of course, a substantial minority whose standards of appreciation are considerably higher, but in the West one is apt to live not only among them but among everyone else—which may be why so many visitors from the outside world return cheering the Western setting, acclaiming its generous hospitality and casserole informality, but muttering about its intellectual sterility.

So deep in myself lies the Western attitude that a monitor inside my head wants to moderate the indictment, but it cannot be done. If a Westerner wants to pride himself on the generosity of his attitude, commending the good intentions that went into fashioning a pot, a painting or a piano solo, instead of risking the unpleasantness of judging by severe enough standards, he runs the risk of getting second-rateness in what is done. Asked to choose between what Yeats called perfection in the work or perfection in the life, the Westerner will usually settle for what makes him more sociable as a man. This elasticity of standards has the effect in a Westerner's personality of giving him an unforced assurance, even when his achievements are few. It gives him a serenity of countenance that is not blighted by a discovery of any inferiority of station or of worth; his self-confidence (that most precious intangible) is not destroyed too soon, as it might be in a more fixed and demanding society. He lives a combination of work and play and is perhaps not even conscious that this, too, was to have made a choice.

Sometimes, sitting with friends beside a campfire on the beach, enjoying the night stillness, the salt air, the lapping of the water, the sweet fragrance of the cedars, and hearing the odd cry of a loon far off, we would ask each other contentedly why anyone would ever want to leave the West. I did not think that I would be the one ever to do so; and yet it was I who left, feeling the cramp of a limited future there in my chosen trade of newspapering, forced by something inside myself not to be content with what did not engage my whole heart, and prepared to work wherever my imagination would be compelled to stretch itself, even if it meant living in surroundings less amiable and agreeable.

We Americans have developed an odd passion for crisscrossing our country at great speed, taking in sweeping views, finding a pleasure in sheer movement, reckoning up proudly how many miles we drive in one day, seeing everything to be seen but little of it intensely, absorbing impressions but palavering idly all the while, enjoying a family intimacy, seeing of other people only those who man the gas pumps or fellow motorists at roadside motels. The hours we spend on such motoring trips may account for the size of our cars: at these times we live in them. In this way many see quite a bit of the United States, taken as panorama, and enjoy a soporific realization of its expanse, while indirectly acknowledging that only an occasional national park, colorful cities like New Orleans and San Francisco, or historic ones like Philadelphia and Boston, are worth slowing down for, to study by foot. Americans feel at home wherever they see an A & P store or a Coca-Cola sign, and develop the sensation that they understand each other perhaps better than they do.

I have often been part of this aimless caravan, going everywhere in vast loops of motoring, and coming to have a feel for many American places if intimate knowledge of few. First came a great circle of the West's geographic splendors—the waterfalls, the deserts, the mountains—then a discovery of the flat inland horizons of the Middle West. Later there were forays into the Deep South—but since most of what was different about it I found myself unsympathetic to, I am quite prepared to accept the Southerner's insistence that only he is entitled to discuss the subject.

To be fair, only after putting down roots into a place (as I have not, in the South) does one come to know its soil, its rocks and its winds, and the rub of disasters on its character. I have come to know only one other American region well: a year in New England, with repeated visits since, and 14 years in New York City, have made me sharply aware of American qualities there that either disappear or become diluted before reaching the Pacific Coast—and I also became aware that other qualities I had thought universally American were unique to the West.

I came from a land where Indians abandoned their Sears, Roebuck denims and old Fords whenever they saw a dollar to be made by putting on war paint, getting on a horse and coughing over a peace pipe; suspicious of tourist-conscious local atmosphere, I suspected the storied New England character, cranky and frugal, to be an attitude preserved in aspic, like colonial Williamsburg. New Englanders themselves are fond of telling nasal Calvin Coolidge stories that either delight in, or burlesque, their reputation. But I learned that New England thrift was stinginess only when set against the voluptuous waste that prevails in much of the rest of the country, and discovered that New England's political conservatism —though I did not share it—could be conservative of the best in the classic American attitudes of dissent and independence. The New Englander takes knowing, and will not be taken by storm, has a dignity in his plainness that is immovable by that artful gregariousness which is the false excess of the open American nature. His dislike of all that New York stands for is no peevish regionalism: he would hew to an older set of values even at his own expense. I found his character a welcome tributary to the American mainstream.

This was my first discovery. The second was, to a Westerner naïve in his mid-twenties, more shattering: I discovered the Eastern world of privilege, and what must accompany it, the world of those without privilege. In the East were barriers that set off a world all its own, to a degree that was inconceivable in the West. In its extremer manifestations, in Virginia, in the orbits around Philadelphia and around Boston, lived those staunch old families so pleased by their heritage and regarding themselves as so favored by nature that admittance could only be by birth. Even in the outer rings of this circle, where the credentials were hardly of long standing, there was a tendency to prefer an insider's outlandishness to an outsider's merit. If this were all, it would be no bad thing, for it was easy to be content to be excluded from what one regarded as effete, stagnant and undemocratic.

But there was a wider area of Eastern exclusivity where the outsider could recognize, and reluctantly concede, criteria he respected.

These are people with a quietness in dress that amounts to a uniform, who would sooner be out at the elbows in what they deem acceptable than all dressed up in something they would not be caught dead in. At home and at school they have been taught values that do not depend on the approval of the crowd but only of their own set; they get a good education and rub up against art and music as a matter of course; they learn restraint of taste and considerateness in manners, without undue damage to their virility. They have an enviable ease and sureness about them; the best of them—like the best in England—are very good indeed. The poorest of them have an unassailable conviction of their superiority. In their way of life is much that I could wish for everybody; it is a pity that its benefits are unequally conferred.

These people were hospitable to those with the same interests, but the outsider soon learned the disadvantage of being late to class: the pattern was set in childhood, in the segregation—but also the discipline—of good private schools. Higher income may first have set this group apart, but was not its chief characteristic, for many who no longer had the income made do with less but still lived by the values: the touchstone is not money but upbringing.

The chief defect of these people was that their preoccupation with the canons of agreed good taste isolated them from some of the spontaneity as well as from the vulgarity of American life. They found it hard to separate the good from the rough in those who were not like them in upbringing. They did not so much dismiss the rest of Americans as fail to understand them.

When Westerners and Midwesterners gravitate to New York City, their first shocked reaction is to deplore the Eastern compounds of privilege, and to vow that their own children will go to a public school. In time, this noble resolution fades as they discover that Eastern public schools do not represent a full spectrum of the community as their own public schools did. It is only necessary to watch twelve-year-old toughs bursting out of New York City schools, cigarettes already lit, to know what these parents are being fastidious about. To send one's own child among them is not to immerse him in the diversity of American life but to confine him in something unrepresentative. How much easier it was to be democratic out West!

If national and racial prejudices are unevenly spread in America, it may be because groups which are well assimilated minorities in one area of the country dominate another, and where unchallenged exhibit a quite different personality. I came to realize this in Boston, the first Eastern city I lived in. I was prepared for the cold, gray Eastern mill towns inhabited by Poles, Croats, Hungarians, and the big-city pockets of Jews and Italians, but nothing in my lifetime of romanticizing my Irish ancestors as a gay and fey people had prepared me for the dour and resentful qualities to be found in that singular cluster known as the Boston Irish. Anyone who has read into the history of 19th Century immigration knows the frightful poverty the Irish left behind; concedes the depths of a justified hatred of the English and a scorn for those of their people who during the Famine "took the soup" in submission to the Protestants; realizes the shabby welcome the Irish got in the New World, what hovels in the back alleys of Boston they were cramped into, and how defeating were the NO IRISH NEED APPLY signs; yet, knowing all this, can be saddened to see a people so victimized by intolerance become so intolerant themselves, so ready to vote for those of shoddy charm who stir their spite and flatter their grievances, so ready to give houseroom to McCarthyism, anti-Semitism, or any other ill wind of hate. Their resentments I understood, but not their persistence in them, which was marking their own characters but achieving little else.

A Westerner's simple solution was that the Boston Irish should drop their old antagonisms and become "like the rest of us." But on second thought, did we want the American melting pot replaced by a bland bouillon cube, ready made, edges squared off, slickly packaged—wasn't it better for us as a nation to be a simmering *pot au feu* tasting sharply of contesting savors? Here we were, only half a century after the widespread alarm over the unassimilable millions debarking at Ellis Island, and already worried that Americans were becoming too much alike, and on guard against homogenized Americanism! Very well, let us have a society for the preservation of Old World ingredients, but not in cellophane: it must come to more than getting oneself up in *Lederhosen*, singing "Santa Lucia" or dancing the Highland Fling once a year. But if each group was to contribute to America something out of its own heritage, was there nothing better than hatred in their legacy to inspire the Irish?

After Boston, almost unwillingly I settled down in what called itself the greatest city in the world. Not the city, but the work to be found there, drew me. The jagged towers forming an asymmetrical harmony out of a thousand individual decisions had their celebrated postcard beauty, but the streets below needed a new Dante to bring hell up to date. New York is a city where millions are forced to work in the center, piled high in skyscrapers, borne up and down in crowded elevators in close body contact ("Make room for one more"). They must be taken there and removed each night through underground tunnels of lurching subway cars, where they stand packed, dull-eyed with fatigue and noise, self-concentrated and hostile, hurrying home to steel shelves where on unpaid furniture they spend their evenings watching the gray glare of the television screen. It is a city whose towers house businessmen who hire psychologists to study human fears which can be exploited to sell deodorants or tooth paste, and where glamor is set by synthetic personalities trained to appear relaxed and natural before hot lights and stop watches, so that they can create the right air of conviction about products they themselves never use. It is a city where people do not do, but watch: crowd stadiums to see others play baseball or football, go to galleries to see what others paint or concerts to hear others play, and pay comedians to bring them laughter.

Wipe the soot from your eyes and examine the city about you. Travel the trains, out to the shining suburbs which are neither city nor country, where rows of empty automobiles beside the railroad platform reproachfully, wastefully await their owners, away in the city until dark making a living. Those who live in these bedroom towns—people with sufficient salaries to command a place with clean air and a plot of green, along with the patience to make a long journey to enjoy it—realize the artificiality of any community where people do not work among those they live with, but what else can they do? As the commuter train makes its slow, dull, interrupted passage, peer out at the platforms where people lean resignedly against pillars as they wait for their trains: their eyes buried in newspapers or staring out and seeing nothing, their numbness apparent not only in their faces but in their elbows, their slouching hips, the way their feet are flatly planted in the concrete, and in the way they barely hear, and seem not to resent, the racket and roar of the express train hurtling by on the center tracks. Or come back to the city itself, past the abandoned brick buildings with windows empty, across the industrial river hedged by oil stations and warehouses and gravel pits—the only life stirring in the river below the slow shunting of barges. Now come the large housing projects all alike, geometrically sterile, with apartment buildings scientifically placed to catch the light yet somehow designed to keep out the life that agitated the slums they replaced. And beyond are the older places: fire escapes with laundry hanging out; grimy brick façades with upper windows open and fat women, leaning elbows on dirty pillows, looking torpidly out, or calling petulantly down to their children in the streets below—black, Puerto Rican or white—who play among ash cans and parked cars, or sometimes flee to a concrete playground beside the river. Where is the equality of opportunity here?

Not from them, but from among the ambitious all over the country must the big city draw constantly to replenish its talent and vitality, for the big city is not, as those who dream of it imagine it to be, a creator, but only an assembly point and consumer of talent. Ignore the multitudes about you, those Italians and Puerto Ricans with the look in their eyes of expecting a hurt; ignore too the well-to-do ladies for whom the city is the place where everything can be done for those who can pay; look instead at the city's most virile people—the successes. And what do you see? Too often it is marriage without communication; insatiable search for what, if found, will not satisfy; people who read detective stories or lending-library romances to pass the time; who otherwise read reviews, not books; who do not express thoughts but repeat remarks; who read magazines, hear music and tour museums not so much in pleasure as out of a felt need to keep up; who judge by dress and not by character; who shun the unexpected encounters of living for fear other human beings will make demands on them; who even spend vacations in places where they know the other guests will have been screened to be like them—polite, decent and facile in talk that says nothing and will not disturb. These are the kind that fill the apartment buildings on the desirable streets, who crowd the proper cafés and fill the bars. Those who come from outside the city have to learn to draw on their accumulated capital of tolerance, for something in the city dries one up, killing instinctive sympathy, and substituting a conscious and detached politeness which is not at all the same.

But as the seasons turn, as the static heat of summer, lodged oppressively between the tall buildings, turns to wind-swept autumn days when people walk head down against the wind, each with his mind only on his own purposes, self-centered and melancholy, oblivious of the gutter sight of collapsed ribs of abandoned umbrellas blown inside out by the storm, indifferent to the frail city trees shivering and shedding their gold leaves—on these days, one discovers a community of shared frustrations with his fellow New Yorkers, a common pride in resistance to the harassments about one: noise, dirt, crowds, hurry, rain, the slam of brakes, fume of buses and chatter of riveting. It must be easy to be well-behaved in heaven, we think to ourselves; but we have learned adaptability and even a mutual forbearance on the cliffsides of hell. Civility breaks but rarely through the prevailing rudeness of New York. When it does, it makes no profession of sympathy, fears to be identified as softness, and does its good deed gruffly as if half-expecting to be rebuffed. And then one comes to contrast his own lot—his advantage in having been brought up in the confident open spaces; having a job that stimulates, and the opportunity to get away from it; having the price of good restaurants and theaters to escape the turmoil of the city streets—and marvels at any good nature at all in people whose whole lives have been spent here, condemned to work at tedious jobs and live in squalid quarters.

Out of the congested streets of New York comes a toughness and resilience of character that knows what it wants and is unsentimental in demanding it. Its most familiar product is that pushing, fast-talking, ruthless fellow who will step on faces to get where he wants. The quality manifests itself also in that mordant, unsparing wit that is the style of those big-time comedians who honed themselves on hecklers on the borscht circuit in the Catskills; it is also to be heard among thousands of New Yorkers, cab drivers and delivery boys, who pass off their daily complaints in the same rhythm of caustic wisecrack and deadpan response, as if wit would be spoiled if given too good a reception. Economy of words, and those slurred, is the New York speech; courtesy, consideration and sympathy are carefully rationed: "So what? We all got problems."

The unsentimental, demanding metropolitan quality that is New York's gift to the rest of the country has its origins in harsh circumstances and European beginnings. Here there is none of the West's sunny benevolence conferred on all but on none deeply: Old World families, a unit to themselves, are capable of strong feeling within it, but against everyone else are armored like armadillos. Among these people—the Italians, the Poles, the Russians, but above all the Jews—humor is never far from melancholy. They seem to have been born generations ago, and never to have passed through naïveté. They know the price of things, and think you a fool if you do not. They demand value. They know that they must work to get ahead, and are not indulgent of those who plead their charm to escape being judged on their merit. It is not only the poor who have this severity of judgment; among Jewish intellectuals, among wealthy Jews, among other European groups in New York are inherited standards in music, in art, in medicine, in science: if you would claim a special distinction, then deserve it. I do not mean that all Jews, all Europeans, have good taste (any more than all Negroes have rhythm) and if it is tawdriness they want, they can be just as demanding of value. But there is in New York City a sophisticated nucleus centering around them that makes for exacting critics and appreciative audiences. This is not the world of the Western United States, pleased to have heard an evening of chamber music at all: New Yorkers insist that the performance must measure up, and from their ruthlessness come the big city's standards of quality, the seeming heartlessness that sets it off from the rest of the country.

I came to like even New York.

II. Man at Work
Journalism, Politics and Foreign Affairs

6. The Pursuit of Journalism

By now I listed myself on my passport as a journalist. I did so sheepishly at first, because on my old paper we thought a journalist was a newspaperman who wore spats and took on airs. But I now worked on a magazine, and the plain and honored name of newspaperman no longer seemed to fit my circumstances. I also gradually became aware that, whether I called myself newspaperman or journalist, not everyone esteemed my trade with the fervor I did.

Max Beerbohm once said that for literature he felt reverence, but for journalism merely a kind regard. A natural remark, I suppose, to come from a man with his feet in two camps and his heart in one. Journalism has always had a hard time of it among the literary, particularly among those who had to grub in it to enable them to afford writing what they wanted to write, which society treated as a luxury when for them it was a necessity. Literature, said Ezra Pound, is news that stays news. An English dictionary has, at least until lately, defined journalistic as a style "characterized by evidences of haste, superficiality of thought, inaccuracies of detail, colloquialisms, and sensationalism." Matthew Arnold thought journalism "literature in a hurry." The difficulty lies, I think, in regarding journalism as a kind of failed literature, whereas it aspires to be literature only insofar as it would like to be well written, and aspires to be history only insofar as it seeks to be accurate. André Gide was severer, but closer, when he wrote: "I call journalism everything that will be less interesting tomorrow than today." For the essence of journalism is its timeliness; it must be served hot.

Journalism is in fact history on the run. It is history written in time to be acted upon, thereby not only recording events but at times influencing them. This explains its temptation to passion and its besetting sin of partisanship. Journalism is also the recording of history while the facts are not all in. Yet any planner of battles knows the eternal conflict between needing to know enough to act and needing to act in time: a problem in journalism as in diplomacy and warfare. Adolescents and second-rate poets who specialize in large misstatements often tell us that life is chaos, but if life were only that there would be no such thing as monotony; life includes both the world we know (which, if we do not fully understand or appreciate, we are at least not surprised by) and the unwinding of the unpredictable. It is the function of journalism—daily, in the case of a newspaper, weekly in a magazine—to add up the latest unpredictable events and relate them to the familiar. Not a judgment for history, for too many facts emerge later, but an estimate for now, from the known; and it is a function essential in a democracy. If journalism is sometimes inaccurate and often inadequate, ignorance would not be preferable. Journalism's desire to reconstruct the world anew each day, to find a serviceable coherence and continuity in chaos, may be a losing game and is always an artificial one: it is circumscribed by the amount of information available, limited at times by the journalist's lack of imagination and weakened at other times by his excess of it. Yet it has its own uses, even when set against history.

The historian is often thought to be less scandal-minded than the journalist, but with an intimate diary in hand that has later come to light, and with a freedom from libel that a journalist never has, he may often be blunter. A historian is also thought to be more impartial, but must guard against imposing upon the past a pattern of interpretations he is fond of, while a journalist must write to people in the knowing present, suspicious of his flights of interpretation which do not match their own awareness of the times. At the very least the historian must be conscious of the occupational vice of retroactive superiority: he is like a privileged spectator at a horse race already run, who alone knows which horse went on to

BOOKS OF ALL PUBLISHERS

FOR A BETTER-READ
BETTER-INFORMED AMERICA
WAKE UP AND READ

PLEASE SEND:

BOOKS:_____

_____

_____

_____

_____

PHONOGRAPH RECORDS:_____

_____

_____

_____

_____

Name_____

Address_____

City_____

Zone_____State_____

☐ Charge account ☐ Gift wrapped (No charge)
☐ Remittance enclosed ☐ C.O.D.

WE INVITE NEW CHARGE ACCOUNTS

10-59

**A BOOKMARK
AND A GUARANTEE
OF SATISFACTION**

YOU have bought this book anticipating a satisfying reading experience. If the book does not upon closer examination appeal to you, bring it back to us and exchange it for another book.

OUR only requirement for an exchange in our shops is that the book be *currently salable* and in *new condition*.

THANK you for your patronage.

DOUBLEDAY BOOK SHOPS

BUSINESS REPLY MAIL

FIRST CLASS PERMIT No. 174 New York, N. Y.

Doubleday Book Shop

655 FIFTH AVENUE

NEW YORK 22, N. Y.

Open until Midnight
MU 8-5300

NEW YORK, N. Y.
655 Fifth Avenue
436 Fifth Avenue
Pennsylvania Terminal
Long Island Terminal
Grand Central Terminal
(412 Lexington Avenue)
Grand Central Terminal
(Vanderbilt Avenue Concourse)
526 Lexington Avenue
14 Wall Street
MANHASSET, N. Y.
1530 Northern Boulevard
GARDEN CITY, N. Y.
1144 Franklin Avenue
SCARSDALE, N. Y.
744 White Plains Road
WEST HARTFORD, CONN.
Bishop's Corner
BALA-CYNWYD, PA.
105 East City Line Avenue
HANOVER, PA.
4 York Street
BALTIMORE, MD.
6315 York Road
DETROIT, MICH.
18 Adams Avenue West
Fisher Building
Penobscot Building
19190 Livernois Avenue
GROSSE POINTE, MICH.
17116 Kercheval Avenue
BIRMINGHAM, MICH.
239 Pierce Street
TOLEDO, OHIO
3301 West Central Avenue
ST. LOUIS, MO.
310 North Eighth Street
48 Maryland Plaza
CLAYTON, MO.
8131 Forsythe Boulevard
MINNEAPOLIS, MINN.
921 Nicollet Avenue
MIAMI BEACH, FLA.
934 Lincoln Road
PALM BEACH, FLA.
228 Worth Avenue
NEW ORLEANS, LA.
633 Canal Street
BOSTON, MASS.
Associated with the
Old Corner Book Store
50 Bromfield Street

win, and, looking about him, wonders why men of seeming intelligence are making such bad bets or getting so worked up over
what will not turn out as they expect. A reader of history must make
the effort of imagination to realize that though he knows the out-
come, the participants did not; what has become a finality (and
may even have been, as a later era sees, inevitable) was not so
regarded at the time, or if anticipated, may have been considered
as still in doubt, and as something to be resisted, delayed or fore-
stalled. Viewed forward, as decisions that had to be confronted,
history can be as exciting as the best journalism; viewed backward,
as mechanically determined, history becomes dull, and its actors
mere marionettes who did not have the wisdom (really only the
information) of the historian who sits in later judgment. These are
some of the difficulties of history, to be set against its advantages of
greater information, knowledge of "how it turned out" and leisure
to reflect. I do not intend to demean history to exalt journalism, or
to make them of equal worth where they are not, but only to elbow
a proper place for journalism as a trade not alone in its disabilities
or in its value.

As long ago as my first course in journalism at college, my professor set as a theme for us to write whether we thought journalism
to be a game, a racket or a profession. With that instinctive cunning
which settles quickly on students at examination time, I could see
that to defend journalism as a profession (which one part of me
wanted to believe, and still does) was to invite mockery; of course,
it was not exclusively a racket, so I wrote of it as a game. But I
would have been happy then, and content now, to describe it as a
craft. A newspaper editor friend of mine once told me that he
thought most people fell into their occupations by chance, but
that men *choose* to join the circus, work on a railroad or enter
newspapering. Fresh out of journalism school and full of exalted
notions that I could see had to be unlearned, I liked his comparison
for being down to earth.

Journalism may be as much in need of principles as medicine or
law (I believe this to be true), but without anything comparable
to bar associations or medical societies with effective power to
censure or expel, its principles are not enforceable. The individual

journalist may have the duty, but often does not have the opportunity, to tell the truth as he sees it. He is a hired man, and because he is, his is not a profession. Nor are publishers under any professional restraint. Newspapers enjoy postal subsidies on the assumption that the existence of newspapers is in the public interest, but publishers as a class do not consider themselves to be operating public utilities—and it is perhaps as well that they do not, for to make newspapers into public utilities would be to invite evils greater than the present haphazard irresponsibility. We are left then, if we would have trustworthy newspapers, with the conscience of the individual publisher, which can be a very wee, pea-sized thing; his fear that rival organs of communication will achieve greater creditability by their being seen to be fairer (an increasingly effective brake on him); or he may have to take into account the standards insisted upon by the journalists who work for him.

As a group, newspapermen are much better than their papers. They too are faced with temptations: the hope of advantage if they give the boss what he wants to hear, and the quite opposite temptation of wishing to indulge their own prejudices. There are hacks among them, as well as cynics and panderers, quite often in high places, but there is a community of undeceived newspapermen who know who among them is cheating on the facts, and they do not always award their good marks—as those who are scorned by them imply—only to those who hold similar political views.

A good journalist is a rewarding sight. He enters a trade where the pay is low—low at least for the qualities of intelligence, energy, experience, judgment and talent he must bring to it. He must have a zest for events, as accountants must love figures, and carpenters wood. He must have a dedication to facts and a scent for humbug. He is probably by temperament an observer, not a doer, standing outside of events, often in distaste, and must beware of becoming, like a baseball fan, a heckler of plays that he himself could not have equaled. He must cultivate skepticism while avoiding cynicism. He must learn to cover people, meetings and causes for which he can have sympathy but to which he must not display loyalty: he must learn to feel but not engage. He must be incorruptible; the temptation to be otherwise comes not from bribery, which is rare, but from a reluctance to pursue that kind of news which will go against the grain of his paper's views or his own convictions (it takes courage to give unpopular causes their due). He must be swift while also deliberate. He must go where he is not wanted, and be resistant to those who are too welcoming. And for all of this, his hours will be long, his pay inadequate and his standing in the community not particularly high. Newspapermen must warm themselves by their own fires.

Those newspapermen who have "crossed over" into publicity and advertising, where the pay is better, would like it understood that they are still in the "same game." It is true that newspapermen often have to do menial and even venal jobs, such as furthering their paper's promotional stunts, and it is true that public relations men are often newspapermen who can write stories that appear to be news and are run as such, but the end is different: the publicity man's intent must always be to serve a master that is not the newspaperman's. The appearance may be similar, but the difference is everything. Sometimes when we who remain journalists come across an advertising copy writer or a publicity man in a bar—confident and leisurely on a fat expense account—we have a hard time deciding whether the resentment we feel comes from scorn or envy. In the end we are what we are because there are satisfactions in our business that the others lack: a delight in craft, a stimulus in variety, an occasional compensation in wrongs righted, a somewhat adolescent urge to be where things are going on and "in the know." That man is lucky who is content in his work, finds it stretches his powers and rewards his time: so many Americans seem to be working at jobs that do not gratify them, living only for their hours away from work. A good newspaperman may be displeased by his circumstances, but need not be ashamed of the calling he has chosen.

It is not all cakes and ale. Journalism is a fitful trade. Newspapermen like variety in their assignments, which is another way of saying that they may be deficient in concentration. They pursue a subject only about as far as, and rarely much further than, the passing public interest. They are servants to a fickle public; they must seize its attention by novelty, hold it by new injections of interest, and then move on to something else. A newspaper can risk boring its public at its own peril. And so (newspapermen hate to admit this) journalism is in some respects not a serious business. Its role is at times similar to education, requiring simplicity of instruction without falsifying the subject matter, requiring diversions, distractions and recesses, though sometimes demanding concentration; adapting its material to the absorptive capacity of the audience, and even, alas, having to compete for attention with less worthy amusements. But it cannot compel compulsory attendance.

Newspapermen might also not like to acknowledge that for many readers the daily newspaper is simply an entertainment. Such readers may take a half-interested look at the headlines, but they then hurry to the comics or the sport pages; they look to their newspaper for instruction, but in cooking more than in public affairs; they may seek information, but it is about television programs and not foreign events; they may want guidance, but about house furnishings and fashions more than what is offered them on the editorial page. In awareness of this, publishers are apt to be shrewder than their employees, ready to pay fat prices for a syndicated comic strip or a canned gossip column, knowing that they can exploit their monopoly of either, while slighting the news budget—for after all, they reason, everybody has access to the same news and what reader really appreciates a consistent edge in news coverage? In this I think publishers wrong, but not as wrong as I wish they were: a newspaper's coverage will be good only if its editor and publisher have a passion for making it so, and find excellence its own reward. Increasingly, as newspapers pass from the hands of those who founded them into the possession of their uninterested sons, their lawyers or their business managers, they become only vehicles for making money, and perhaps not as efficiently profitable as a garage or a hardware store. These merchants fill their papers with merchandise, and ask of their editors only that they stay out of trouble, out of libel suits, and play it safe. The proportion of mediocrity in the American press thus far outweighs the good. A good newspaperman, though he need not be ashamed of his calling, can rightly be outraged at its practice.

Finley Peter Dunne thought it the duty of a newspaper "to afflict the comfortable and comfort the afflicted." It is a rare newspaper today that feels any mission to afflict the comfortable. If reporters seem jaundiced, it is because they have to cover so many windy luncheons, and solemnly record the pompous hypocrisy of the respectable. Sometimes they are included in the counsels of small groups where the others, feeling safe because they know the newspaper's publisher is one of them, talk the cant of the well-to-do, forgetting that the reporter himself does not share the same economic stake in their prejudices. Newspapermen are apt to be against the successful and the affluent. In politics, they are usually Democrats— except when the Democrats, after too long in power, became too affluent themselves. No role satisfies the newspaperman more than that of redressor; the chance to be angry, to rout out the rotten; but newspapers being what they are, angers are grooved—confined principally to what can be found out, or if not found out suspected, to be wrong with government. Many, though not all, reporters willingly accepted this role against the Democrats, only to be disillusioned when publishers proved not such ardent pursuers of error in a Republican administration. But a captious, searching attitude towards any administration (Republican or Democratic) must be the demeanor of all journalists, for by an accident of historical growth the role of watchdog of government in American society falls to the press, replacing the question period which British ministers must undergo in the House of Commons.

Jack the Giant Killer is a pleasing assignment to a newspaperman —but less so when only some giants are marked for the kill. What if big businessmen had the same careful inquiry as government: had to answer why this relative was in unmerited high position, why that expensive entertainment was allowed, whose head rolled for that bad investment; had to say who consented to this scheming in black markets or that shoddy legalism to thwart a competitor; had to explain why they tolerated an inferiority in the product, had to justify this connivance with an unsavory politician or union racketeer, or that use of company funds to promote selfish ends? In theory, companies have their own machinery for checking such practices, but in reality so long as profits are high very little else is asked of a boss. A publisher, asked why he did not concern himself with this kind of investigation, would say that these things are the domain of *private* business. But are they not touched with public interest?

Unjustified waste in business, as much as a government's taxation, grabs at the public's pocketbook—but it is not generally considered fair game for newspapermen.

Business is a privileged sanctuary, even when its institutional ads are picturing it as just a collection of open-faced "folks" like you and me, interested in nothing but the American way, the improvement of product and the remembrance of millions of fond little shareholders. Public relations men who in government perform a useful enough service for lazy newspapermen by gathering up facts for them—while discouraging independent inquiry—are even more sleekly successful in business at putting out what they would like known about a company and diverting newspapermen from what they do not want known. It remains for an occasional outburst of grudge by a disappointed contender, a stockholder's fight, or—long after the event—a congressional committee investigation, for anything adverse to be heard.

Executives, those unexamined pillars of the community, have such press immunity, and such scorn for the fumblers in public office (any fumbling of their own passing unrecorded) that when one of them is persuaded to go to Washington as a public duty, is subjected to brash reportorial questions, and is no longer safe behind an imposing walnut desk and the stillness of wall-to-wall carpeting, he often seems somewhat less spectacular. It then becomes harder and harder to recruit them for public service, these businessmen who at directors' meetings like to say how uplifted they are by challenges.

A journalist too energetic in seeking out the malpractices of business risks condemnation as being against business itself, yet the same logic should apply that applies to government—that it operates best in the public interest when made to operate in a spotlight. But this is a radical thought, and lest any man think the press timid, there are angry writers to point to, whose splenetic outbursts are read by millions. Note, however, what they are mostly mad at: there is a good living to be made in a shrewd grooving of acceptable grievances.

"Truth always prevails in the end," wrote Lord Acton, "but only when it has ceased to be in someone's interest to prevent it from doing so."

If a newspaperman finds that his itch to investigate is encouraged only in some directions, if he finds himself asked to work within the known political prejudices of his publisher, purity of motive is not all to be found on one side. The development of reporters' craft unions (particularly at the outset, when Communists played too big a role) suggested that they, if they had their way, would be as biased, as ready to favor their own, as publishers. The contest of wills between newspapermen and publishers, such as it is, is apt to be muted; in many places the publisher has such clear ascendancy that no struggle goes on. Many reporters are without pronounced political opinions; others get it established early that they wish to stay clear of the "dirty" stories; still others find no disharmony between their politics and the paper's. For the rest, there are those who say, "I only work here"; there are others who are inwardly restive, and those who find some rationalization such as Ambrose Bierce's: "If asked to justify my long service to journals with whose policies I was not in agreement and whose character I loathed . . . O, well, I persuaded myself that I could do more good by addressing those who had the greatest need of me—the millions of readers for whom Mr. Hearst was a misleading light."

Some of the sting went out of the struggle when reporters, in themselves reflecting the feelings of the country, passed from militant enthusiasm for the New Deal to at most a sentimental predisposition toward the later Democrats. This change of mood was matched by the rise of practical-minded publishers who had decided to make a necessity out of virtue. This new breed of publisher made it a policy to give no unnecessary offense to any powerful group within the community, even unions. They found themselves up against radio and television, whose dependence on government regulation made them early in the game decide to play the news fairly straight. (For all the pseudo-philosophizing about the impossibility of being objective, I have never met a newspaperman who did not know how to follow the injunction to "play it straight.") So there has been a trend toward less flagrant outbursts of violent feeling on the editorial page, and less apparent partisanship in the news columns: on many papers the good deeds of the other side simply get small space, and lengthy treatment is accorded anybody whose views coincide with the publisher's. This is considered subtler, but I am not sure who is being fooled: if readers do not recognize every shenanigan inflicted upon them they are at least aware of a stale predictability in a paper's coverage. Tedium is a dangerous feeling to develop in readers. Sometimes one is tempted to sigh for the old days of honest wrongheadedness boldly proclaiming itself.

There are some who suggest that the way to make newspapers more responsible is to put their ownership into public trusts. But trusts can only preserve; they cannot create; and either the papers become the responsibility of dynamic managers (at which point all the old problems return) or they risk lapsing into staid sterility. Given our prejudice for an independent press, the only answer, if not a completely satisfactory one, is self-responsibility. There are some American newspapers—all too few, but to be honored all the more—whose publishers ignore the prejudices of their fellow businessmen and even defy the passions and whims of their public. A similar kind of dedication is felt by many newspapermen, even though this is to ask a great deal of low-paid men in a society which puts a premium on other values; it requires an austerity of mind to accompany a vividness of imagination. But what is so heartening about journalism is how widely this notion of responsibility is felt. And it is ready to have more asked of it.

7. Scout to the Outer World

In making a living as a journalist, I have worked twenty years for publications whose policies I have often not fully agreed with. The relationship has not been, as a Marxist might think, all master and slave, for one puts his own stamp on what he does, and if this stamp is sometimes blurred by where he works, it can still be his own. I have not been able to say in print all that I might have wanted to say, but I have known frequent occasions when the publisher, too, let be said what he did not agree with. There are journalists who give in easily, who become more royalist than the king, and spend their days trying to anticipate his verdicts: a publisher should fear these far more than the dissenters, for they can do greater harm while seeming to cause less trouble. And there are other journalists who feel a constant need to prove their integrity by asserting their contrariness, and become tiresome washroom heroes. I have, looking back, seen many occasions when I am glad my own views were challenged; I could not say with Metternich that "error has never approached my mind." I would not like to work at a place where my own prejudices fully coincided with the owner's: it would be intellectually stultifying; abrasion is necessary to fashion our pearls. I prefer a give and take—so long as the gives don't far outnumber the takes; when they do the time has come to move along.

After five years as a reporter and then assistant city editor of a Seattle newspaper, and a year's happy interlude on a journalistic fellowship, I went to work in New York City for *Time* magazine*, that pert and agile news magazine which, like a nuclear reactor, is astir with millions of atoms of opinion assaulting each other with great force. *Time*'s peculiar problem is the handling of judgments and convictions on an anonymous magazine, where the need for brevity prevents that easy solution of the daily newspaper: giving each side the space to have its say. Before each issue of *Time* goes to press, men of intelligence, and sometimes of passionate opinions, must somehow resolve their differences. The winner tends to be, but is not always, the man of higher rank; at other times, when debate is joined, the answer may have to be a "weasel," the phrasing that avoids or begs the question. No vigorous journalist is satisfied by a weasel: his political sense may be gratified in having avoided the saying of something abhorrent, from his point of view, but the journalist in him loathes a straddling evasion. Perhaps too many weasels also dissatisfy the reader: perceiving dullness, he detects an avoidance; whatever *Time*'s other failings, this is not usually one: forthrightness is its style. The difficulties are accentuated when journalists have to be, to get their jobs, quick of mind, skillful at dispute, and forceful writers. Even if there were no editor-owner above, with convictions and crotchets of his own, there would be an editor's problem in creating a recognizable consistency of viewpoint out of the clash of so many conflicting and articulate personalities.

The contemporary American newspaper is much different from the way it was in 1923, when *Time* was founded, for not only magazine imitators but newspapers themselves have been influenced by the organizing, summarizing and condensing of news; of telling the news through people; of exploring fields most newspapers slighted, such as art, music, science and medicine; of pursuing brightness and brevity of style (and sometimes, alas, borrowing some of *Time*'s less felicitous mannerisms of writing, which outlived the usefulness

---

* In the British House of Commons there is a mandatory practice known as "declaring one's interest" before discussing a topic in which one has something at stake. At this point, I must declare mine, for as I write I am still in *Time*'s employ. The reader may feel that he is about to be cheated of sensational indiscretions; but for my part I am just as eager to be on guard against self-interested praise.

of novelty). If newspapers borrowed from *Time,* it was only fair trade, for in the beginning *Time* borrowed greatly from them, before gradually developing a world-wide news service of its own, second in size only to the New York *Times'.*

One of the interior necessities of *Time's* new way of organizing the news was a division of labor: if any considerable event, such as a four-power conference, was to be reported compactly, there was no space for the windy and repetitive "reactions" from each capital: they were all packed into one terse story. And thus another simplicity of ordinary newspapering was done away with: the lengthy stories under separate datelines, which might gratify their writers' egos but were hardly a service to the reader. Instead, by a fragmenting process so common now throughout all American industry, two specialized jobs were created: a writer in New York in effect lost his legs; reporters abroad, furnishing factual information and guidance, lost their hands. Except in rare instances, such as the report of a battle or a street scene he had himself witnessed, this new-style foreign correspondent did not file stories intended for publication. He cabled raw material to be merged in New York with files from other correspondents, with what might be found by reading the daily papers, might be asked for in Washington, or searched out in libraries by industrious women researchers. This method had immense advantages: it enabled a correspondent in Iran to spend all of his time getting the story and bothering less about its literary presentation; it enabled a writer in New York at the same time to bone up on Iran's past, and to relate its doings to what was going on in the world around it, and to assemble in one story material from many sources.

At its best this kind of teamwork produced a compact and lively account that individual correspondents often despaired of matching. But it could be frustrating too: nobody—reporter, writer or editor—could consider such a story "all his." It was anonymous, it was bound to be impersonal, and with so many hands at work on it, kneading, shaping and flavoring this doughy lump of facts, background and hypotheses—and bent on attractively packaging it—it could easily go wrong without anyone's quite knowing why. And as each news story fought for space against others—a French political crisis versus a new archeological find in Sumeria; a Pennsylvania election versus a California murder—more and more emphasis was placed on the judgments, capricious or sound, of the editors. The process was always fascinating, and could be exhilarating, but it had its perils, and was sometimes lacking in safeguards.

The blending of information from many sources into one news story is no mere exercise in digesting. On news magazines, correspondents are encouraged to file, along with facts and color, their own often intense views on what they cover. These judgments are set against what a Washington reporter learns at the State Department, whose assessments usually add technical information and a note of caution (though the State Department, one soon learns, never confesses itself surprised by events, and when forced to change course can prove that it has always favored the course it has changed to). Downing Street and the Quai d'Orsay are also tapped for interpretations, and if they must be discounted, they do reflect experience and detachment. Finally, as a source of private information for the editors, there is the luncheon circuit. Most foreign governments arrange off-the-record luncheons in New York for visiting prime ministers, foreign secretaries and diplomats, inviting a fairly regular group of about 15 television and radio commentators, editorial writers and magazine editors. These sessions rarely produce information, but do enable one to size up a man at close and informal quarters. Big news organizations such as *Time* also hold weekly luncheons for generals, congressmen, architects, ambassadors or anyone else in the news, where they may speak freely, knowing nothing will be attributed to them in print. Any editor is therefore faced with a bewildering amassment of fact and opinion in every area. The final step by which all this material becomes a compact news story is thought.

It will be seen that in such a process the usual hue and cry about bias has little meaning. Everything about the operation requires conclusion-drawing, and it must be an innocent reader who can imagine that topics of great complexity can be reduced to a half-column of type without intruding the writer's or the editor's prejudice (his idea of what matters and what doesn't matter) into it. It is the soundness of his bias—his capacity to weigh conflicting claims of, say, Israeli and Arab, against the knowable truth; to qualify verdicts with sympathy when sympathy merits a claim and to resist it when it does not; to assess the strength of arguments and to recognize the claim of force; to respect the weight of legitimacy without being indifferent to the cry of justice—that makes his conclusion either sound or suspect. The result is a judgment, or a bias if you will, but this is not the same thing as partisanship.

Time was founded by two audacious men fresh out of Yale. They were full of young men's impatience with cant; they would end the prevailing pretense between editor and reader that both knew what they did not; they would blow away the fog of pomposity which equated soundness with dullness; they scorned the mealymouthed and would not be afraid to have opinions. Every newspaperman carries in the back of his head some favorite variation on the old saw, "Give me the scissors and let me write the headlines and I don't care who writes the editorials." Very well, said these young men from Yale, there will be no affectation of a nonexistent objectivity; whoever selects and discards the news is exercising judgment: he is no eunuch free of bias; it will be healthier to admit that he even has opinions. And, they went on, let us be rid of this humbug that equal space to one politician's sensible remark and the other's platitude makes an impartial balance. They could see that each time the President of the United States made a speech, the news services would solicit congressional "reaction," evenhandedly balancing three condemnations from the opposition with three predictable plaudits from his own party, and always therefore finding congressional reaction "mixed." Was this a useful truth? When these same congressmen knew they would not be directly quoted, they more candidly characterized the President's speech, and generally agreed, whatever their politics, on whether he had scored or not. The young men from Yale decided to be free of time-serving twaddle; they would say on their own that his hearers considered the President's message a flop; it was only a step further to saying on the editor's own authority that it was a flop. All of American journalism has been revolutionized by this practice: the trend is to interpretative analysis, as it is sometimes grandly called, or getting behind the story to tell what it means—and those who denounce the change should be condemned to living under what went before it; they would not be happier.

News is what an editor decides it is. If the right to select news is presumptuous, and in the abstract arrogant, the practice on most newspapers is quite modest and mechanical. There is surprising agreement among editors as to what is news; with these hard-working and plain-spoken men, the evaluation of stories—choosing which deserves bigger headlines and more space—is almost automatic, and responses from coast to coast are almost interchangeable. They labor hard, and have learned to give as much care, and as much regard for clarity, to the unimportant item as to the major news story. This disciplining, like a boxer's daily workouts before a fight, enables them at the crucial moment to handle a big story as instinctively as a little one, and the only difference is a heightening of tension in the city room: that thrill that differentiates newspapering from grocery clerking. It is a contained thrill, the satisfaction savored only when all the work is done and the first smudged copies of the paper are put before everyone. That thrill I was later to miss on a weekly magazine, but it is a thrill that sometimes presumes an absurd concentration on being up to the minute, instead of being either thorough or intelligible. On a weekly news magazine the equivalent thrill comes from having time to round up and weigh, and perhaps the wit to recognize, what others are too busy reporting to see or assess. And the frustration comes from a writer's having what he regards as sound insight dismissed in editing as an unacceptable opinion.

In the smoothing-out process that is necessary to put out an anonymous product that speaks with "one voice," a deadening uniformity sometimes comes creeping in. But there is never any lack of passion in the corridors of *Time*, among writers and editors, about what ought to be said: one man's objectivity is another's bias. Sometimes, I think, the worrying about prejudice in American journalism is greater than it need be, for constant slanting is self-defeating: it carries its own antitoxic remedy. And readers are hardy animals: in the end one is apt to be trusted as far as he deserves to be.

I came to realize that facts do not speak for themselves: facts are employed—and it is necessary to find out who is using them and why. If the need for making judgments was thus assumed, I preferred a vigorous expression of them to that studied dullness of writing which seeks to conceal its omissions, and often conceals them from the writer himself. The worst kind of suppression of news, because the hardest to remedy, is that dodging incapacity to see the hottest news because of the glare around it; there are those who think that timid conclusions are somehow righter ones, and blandly expressed the safest of all. In our business we come to spot those who get a reputation for objectivity by ducking or blurring all difficult judgments. I am ready to accept the need to make up one's mind about the meaning of news and, once determined, to speak out forthrightly, so long as (and this is the essential qualification) the judgments expressed, however unsettling they might be to any bloc of readers, serve no other motive than the desire to get at the truth. I have always defended *Time*'s opinions that far.

After a year and a half as a staff writer at *Time*, writing mostly of politics and American affairs, I was put to editing. At the age of 29, I found myself presiding over subjects I knew little about—art, music, sport, education and books. So efficiently is *Time* organized, with writers who know their specialty, and researchers to protect one from error or to seek out information wanted, that this was not as catastrophic to the magazine's good name as it appeared: in so tight a web, each holds the other up. But I was not satisfied to leave it at that, and on days off took to prowling the art galleries and going to concerts when I could, in an enforced self-education that had much lost ground to make up. My taste in music, at that time largely confined to popular music and symphonies, was widened to include chamber music and opera (but not oratorios!). In art, I progressed from the familiar position of "I don't know much about art, but I know what I like" to the discovery that I didn't really know what I liked, and a process begun twelve years ago has given me much satisfaction since.

Being hurtled into the unknown and expected to act as if it were familiar territory had its unsettling side. I remember being asked to lunch with the violinist Szigeti, and introduced as the music editor (actually, I edited the music writer, who was in fact our critic). I spent the entire lunch fearing that I might give away the fact that I did not really know the difference between adagio and andante. At that point I took stock: I could either grow a beard like a television commentator's and make a pretense of knowing what I did not; I could confess that I was in over my head and get out; or I could more closely define what it was I pretended to be. I finally concluded that editing was my business: I did not know music (at least in the sense of having the right to pontificate about it); what I could learn, if anything, was the *journalism* of music. Within limits, ignorance in an editor has its uses: he can ask the same innocent questions a reader would, and in time learns something. The worst position was not to know, while pretending to.

At that time, *Time* was being run by a remarkable and exacting editor, T. S. Matthews. He had all the Eastern caste marks—Episcopal bishop's son; St. Paul's; Princeton; Oxford; good tennis, good clubs, good taste. In addition, he was thin, trim, and of a cleft-chinned handsomeness. When he spoke, in short, vigorous outbursts as if unable to contain himself any longer, he spoke *in sentences,* not as most Americans do in hesitations and broken-off phrases. He was shy of manner, but from reserve, not timidity; he was growing hard of hearing; he seemed unapproachable. As if to offset these disadvantages, he instituted weekly teas for the staff, which I later learned were difficult for him: they certainly were for us. He had been a poet, had fallen into book reviewing, and without having intended to make journalism a career now found himself, after twenty years, managing editor and then editor of a weekly magazine with close to two million circulation. He brought unique gifts to it. It was he who changed *Time* from its first harried, curt manner to a style of good, conversational English, which at its best could be a pleasure to read. He was fussy about grammar, intolerant of genteelisms, impatient with sloth and adamant against journalese. He had a headmaster's severity about him, and could be merciless in neatly written marginal comments ("Sounds funny in Choctaw; try it in English"). He believed, in Sydney Smith's phrase, in the duty not to praise when praise was not due. He had that talent of a born editor for lifting the quality of a piece of writing without seeming to have changed it: with a deft insertion of a reverberating or bright phrase here, and the penciling-out of a banality there, he could make copy seem better than it was.

Not having risen methodically from cub reporter to editor, he was not trammeled by the quirks and rutted habits of journalism, and had a mind that roamed free, forever questioning why some settled newspaper practice compelled the printing of something that was really not of interest, and at other times awakening our vision to what the blinders of our trade had kept us from seeing. He had a leaping, curious, witty mind, at its best in matters of the imagination —art, theater and literature—but with a certain impatient innocence in the more prosaic fields of politics and economics. He sometimes acted as if the front page of the New York *Times* assembled itself each day, and was indifferent to how much footwork, labor and skill—how many tedious hours of checking, of condensing full texts, of prying out facts from those who wanted to withhold them—went into getting out the *Times*, and could not see why those who had spent the day marching through tedium had not at night written like angels. Facts were for others to find; insights were what he prized; and in bringing him facts we could be made to feel that we offered him lead pellets when he had asked for pearls. He was never pleased by his own work and not often pleased by others'; but his rare praise, like his friendship, was to be treasured. From Tom Matthews I learned to set myself higher standards and to be discontented with what was only good enough. He widened horizons for me. I served ten years under him before he parted company with *Time*.

He was succeeded as managing editor by Roy Alexander, who had been his chief deputy and whose personality and talents so complemented Matthews' that their long joint reign had been a wonderful school of journalism for us all. Alexander was a newspaperman to his finger tips. He had been a star reporter and desk man on the St. Louis *Post-Dispatch* in its great days, had been a young marine in the first World War and an eager flier between the wars (in fact, during the second World War he would often sneak away to test-pilot planes for Grumman, although he was by that time the father of seven children). Alexander was totally without side. I was often to be reminded of my first city editor, Sully, for both were Irish

Catholics with large families, were generously built, thoroughly professional, and deceptively relaxed in manner. They had a kind eye
for the weak and a natural preference for the underdog, and were
not given to moralizing about the frailties of others. These qualities
made neither soft. In Alexander's case, they were offset by a strict-
ness in raising a family, a soldierly attitude toward doing a job
thoroughly, and a monastic distaste for indulgent luxury. What he
called his peasant complex made him always a little uneasy in those
upholstered gathering places of celebrities, and no more than T. S.
Matthews did he have an ambition to be a public "personality."
Alexander's casual manner, his natural gift for being at home with
anyone, his readiness with a tension-breaking remark, his continual
thoughtfulness of what might ease the way for others, made him
easy to meet—so easy, in fact, that many never did discover that he
was also hard to know. He screened his depths and was content to
be regarded as he seemed. He placed his stamp most on the "bread
and butter" news in *Time*: politics, the military, business, science—
all fields in which he had many friends and was well-informed. But
those who, seeing his fondness for the company of soldiers and
fliers, his enthusiasm for sports and his familiarity with politicians,
mistook these traits for a lack of discrimination in other things were
in for a surprise. He had a passion for opera and much knowledge of
it; if his mind was quick it was also schooled in logic; as an executive
he knew how to make time his ally; he was thoroughly grounded in
theological disputation and religious history, was happy in Greek and
Latin, and I would sometimes come upon him escaping from the
tension of work by reading Aristotle.

There was a third man at *Time* by whom I was much influenced,
its cofounder and "boss," Henry Robinson Luce. Someday a proper
biography will be written about this man who changed the face of
American journalism more than anyone else in his time, but it will
not be written by me. If this were England, he would have been
Lord Luce of Rockefeller Plaza, but in America his name is less
familiar than that of the latest caterwauling guitar player or spoiled
deb. Consider the life of a man who at 24 (with a young friend,
Briton Hadden) borrowed the money to start *Time*, a radically different way of telling the news, which after anxious first years made
a great success; who at 31 (shortly after Hadden's early death)

launched *Fortune* at the unheard of magazine price of $1 a copy just as the stock market crashed, and risked the money to stay with it though industry seemed in no mood for a luxurious examination of its glories and troubles; and when he was 38 launched *Life*, whose circulation so exceeded the estimates that the company was nearly ruined by its good fortune in its first year, but which went on to reach and hold the largest circulation and largest advertising revenue in the history of American weekly journalism. He might have used his magazines to spread his own name, but chose not to. But he has left decisive thumbprints on all of them. As a publisher, he could be high in praise of stories that pleased him and blunt about those that did not; he worked hard and expected others to. He read widely, mostly in history and biography, and was shrewd enough to perceive that the desire for self-improvement was strong in the American character; where others thought it essential to talk down to the reader, he believed that any subject could be made interesting, and that anything important could not by definition be dull. His magazines had immense influence in a dozen fields—in photography, in storytelling, in spreading a knowledge of art, science, medicine, economics, religion and history, but perhaps less where he would have most liked to have been influential, in politics (the source of the most serious criticism of his magazines). A man of business acumen and considerable wealth, he could be almost indifferent to money and was willing to spend vast sums to explore the Congo by air or to photograph the Sistine Chapel in color: economy was never an excuse for not doing properly a story he was interested in. He was totally indifferent to advertisers' pressure: wouldn't hear of it.

He had a driving ambition to be first, and liked the company of others who excelled in their fields, and was apt to lose interest in losers and to dislike failures. He liked the elegance of grand salons, of evening gowns and candelabra, but when hard at work would just as soon eat at a drugstore counter. He was a man of wide acquaintance but held himself essentially aloof, as if fearing the dependence of friendship: he was thus one publisher who did not inflict on his editors a set of friends to be protected in print. A restless, preoccupied man, he could be demanding and brusque, but capable of many kindnesses. He surrounded himself with first-rate people, whose independence of mind he valued, though in areas that mattered most to him he wanted his own views to prevail: it was his magazine.

His method of work was to talk things over with his editors at small luncheons, or to summon them singly or in pairs to his two-story book-lined aerie atop the Time and Life Building. In his office, they would often find him in shirt sleeves, feet up; at other times, when he sat square to the desk they could tell by his curtness that the session was to be earnest. Sometimes he wanted to impart a nugget he had picked up the day before in Washington, which an editor should be aware of even if unable to print it. Frequently he wanted to talk about some facet of the biggest story of the day. The Russians, or India, or France—or perhaps even the Democrats— might have just brought off something that was from his point of view shattering; before considering how to combat it, he would muse on the enormity and fascination of the event, being first of all a journalist; at such times the devil would often be given more due than he later got in print. What *Life* was to say editorially might then be discussed, or a general attitude hammered out for a *Time* story, but these were not hard and fast instructions, nor binding if later facts, or more reflection, favored a different conclusion. When mutual trust existed, when it was understood that one would not try to sneak something past him and was prepared to defend a later change if asked to, much latitude was allowed. There was more free speech and greater informality at *Time* than the newspaper I had worked on, or on most newspapers I am aware of. Luce never, as old man Hearst did, instructed anyone to write to order: each point was discussed out, often impatiently; and at times, in sessions that were quite plain-spoken, he could be dissuaded. He was human enough to want to win, and the discussion favored those who bent to his will, but he did not really want a school of sycophants around him. On occasions when the news awakened differing passions, however, the effect of these sessions was more agonizing for editors than if they had simply accepted only the necessity of taking orders, for editors were assumed to assent without private reservations to what they agreed to carry out, and Luce would have been dismayed by a cynical obedience. Arguing with him was not simply a matter of overturning prejudices peculiar to his position and his class; he was knowledgeable, dogged of memory, quick-minded, able in dispute, and had a lively independence of thought.

A man with no small talk of his own, and not much sufferance for it in others, he could make serious dinner conversation stimulating, for his range of interest was wide. Sit him next to a painter or an archeologist and he would not be tongue-tied, as others might be, by a sense of how little he knew of the other's specialty. "I've always understood," he might begin, with the air of a man ready to be corrected but not likely to be, "that the high point of sculpture for all time was the Greek era. Why is it that no one has been able to do better since?" The artist beside him, instead of exchanging trivial pleasantries or trying to make technical complexities explicable to a layman, would soon find himself deep in a discussion that spoke to the universals of his craft. The question always uppermost on a journalist's tongue is "Why?"; in Luce's case, with his interest in successful people, the next question in each field was "Who's Number One?" and the recurrent instruction to his editors was "Find out."

Many ingredients have gone into the making of press lords such as Luce, Beaverbrook, Patterson and Hearst—flair, luck, application and, of course, a sound commercial instinct. They were men who knew the conventions of their craft, if only to ignore them. Surrounded by merchant-publishers, they had the audacity to be unpredictable (the quality most often neglected by heirs vowing to carry on in the same spirit). They usually had a seventh sense of timing: often I have seen Luce restrain editors who wanted to put a new face on the cover of *Time*; Luce's instinct told him how long to delay until a crest of public interest in the man was reached. These were useful traits, but if there is one single quality that sets apart a press lord from those who are only conscientious practitioners in the field, it is, I think, curiosity: a swollen, omnivorous, unceasing curiosity, the kind that made Captain Joseph Patterson dress in old clothes and roam the Bowery to see what kind of people his tabloid readers were. For at least 30 years, Harry Luce had inhabited the privileged world of the powerful, but he had never lost the delight, even the thrill, of dinner at 10 Downing Street, a picnic aboard a yacht with the Dutch royal family, or a sortie through the Philippines.

There is a special, almost compulsive quality to a press lord's curiosity. Most people gather knowledge by comparing, relating, discarding; what is left they pack into an ever-increasing snowball. What they once establish they put behind them; what they have not examined they take on authority. The press lord, being intelligent, does the same thing—but with a difference. He is essentially restless of mind. He may have deep convictions, and in fact is sure that he has—his patriotism, his religion, his politics—and is faithful to them in his fashion. But he is always doubting, always testing, sometimes to satisfy a nagging worry, sometimes with the intent of confirming and strengthening his beliefs. ("When we have arrived at faith," said Saint Anselm, "it is a piece of negligence to stop short of convincing ourselves, by the aid of thought, of that to which we have given credence.")

Of nothing is the press lord more suspicious than fashionable opinions, which he believes can be artificially made. Pursuing some grail of his own, he mistrusts certainty and rejects easy assurances and even sometimes the consistency demanded by his own beliefs. Lacking the pyramid of settled opinions that many others have, not satisfied with what is accepted and established, he is forever seeking new answers. These skeptical men long for certainties. And here what is essential to the man becomes valuable to the press lord. He is attracted by a new voice here, a novelty there, excited by the experimental, the paradoxical and the changing. At such times what was previously accepted in his mind must be measured against the new, with no advantage given to seniority. In the practice of journalism, this delight in the latest discovery puts him on the same footing as a mass audience, an audience that is forever changing, forever adding to it young people learning things for the first time, and containing the numbers of people who do not build their own pyramids, but clutch at jackstraws. In large-scale journalism, the well-informed curious and the uninformed credulous meet at the common level of novelty, both free of the rigid encumbrances of fashionable authority.

This excited curiosity, this restlessness of mind, this dissatisfaction with conventional explanations is, I think, the essential characteristic of the great press lords. It cannot be feigned, though it can be made use of, for these men are sophisticated enough to put their curse to good advantage. This is called trusting one's own instincts.

As the years passed at *Time*, I found myself brought back to American domestic affairs and politics, but this time as the national affairs editor. I was thrust into handling the Truman Administration's later troubles, the Korean war, the Hiss-Chambers case, Dean Acheson, the firing of MacArthur and the congressional hearings that followed: thorny issues, every one of them, and often difficult for me, though my own political views had moderated with the years. In 1951 I became foreign news editor of *Time,* a job I have come to regard as one of the prize perches in all journalism. Before me lay the whole world, defying me to make sense out of it: to distill in seven or eight magazine pages, with the help of half a dozen writers and 30 foreign correspondents, what was going on, and to seek coherency in it. Foreign news is a subject I felt happily at home in, full of diversity and complexity but susceptible to judgments that were independent of politics; a subject which had interested me for 20 years, and endless in what there was to learn.

Learning and telling: these are the twin necessities of journalism. Those who practice it must mediate between two worlds, must be able to talk to a specialist in his terms and then to explain to laymen in theirs. The art of journalism, I have come to believe, is first to survey a subject in all its roundness, then to seek in it a simplicity that does no violence to its complexity. For this, one can never know enough background, yet must never let the accumulation of details choke him into incoherence. Learning must be worn lightly, for though readers want everything made plain they resent baby talk. One develops an impersonality of voice which might be called Third Person Authoritative: a style that is informative but never preachy; able to imply by tone in the midst of a narrative whether this news should be considered disastrous or only distant and intriguing, because a reader, with his own cares, can hardly be expected to regard with the same degree of gravity the problems of every nation, big or small.

Third Person Authoritative is a necessary style in anonymous journalism, but it is an artificial manner and has its limitations: one

comes to reflect not his own passion, grief or anger but the right tone
of a public servant; to be compassionate about political refugees if
they are the right brand, but sightless to ordinary poverty and injustice if they do not make an appropriate point. One trains himself to stand off, never to be wrought up, to avoid personal pique
against a person or a people. By thus continually damping his emotions one risks becoming in time devoid of feeling. Yet journalism's
relationship to the controversial must be like the teapot handle's to
the teapot: able to transport the hot while keeping cool.

A million, two million, three million people may be reading one's
words—an audience whose attention must be captured, whose memories may have to be prodded, though never conspicuously, whose
diverse sensitivities must be taken into account. It is a lazy convenience to regard those millions as some kind of mass, but if there
is such a thing as a mass mind, I do not want to cater to it. The
maker of soap flakes might profit from so regarding his customers,
but it would be fatal to a journalist: a death to his imagination.

Those who cater to what they regard as a mass mind like to talk
about giving the public what it wants. But this implies that there is
one great public. "As a matter of fact," said the late Willis J. Abbot,
editor of the CHRISTIAN SCIENCE MONITOR, "there are many distinct
publics with sharply divergent tastes. It is for the editor, then, to
choose his public. If he believes that there are more morons in the
field than any other class and is indifferent to all save mass circulation, he will make a paper for morons and exult in the volume of
circulation thereby gained." I had an equal distaste for mechanical
"mass editing" when directed at a slightly higher level of readership,
and had no use for those magazine editors who took constant polls
of their readers, and gave them back, in the proper proportions,
what they seemed to want—so much sex, so much fashion, so much
sport, with the Pope on the cover to please the Catholics and fatuous
cheer from a double-breasted Fifth Avenue preacher to satisfy the
Protestants.

In the end, an editor edits primarily for himself. The only sound
criterion in editing is to say: this interests me; *ergo,* it should interest others. This does not mean that an editor's function is to be
merely a mirror of his readers, faithfully reflecting their tastes and
their ignorances because he shares them. If this were true, an editor

would have to restrict his curiosity to the lowest common denominator of his readers, so as to avoid unprofitable idiosyncrasies. What an appalling obligation that would be! I know of tabloid editors who deliberately avoid any recondite interests and who keep their minds empty for fear of losing the "common touch." This is an abuse of the human personality that I see no excuse for. An editor must be free to develop an interest in Roman coins, bird calling or curling—and his only duty, in returning to his job, is to keep an editor's scrutinizing eye on his own hobbies, and to know how much they can be inflicted on the reader, if at all.

Editing lends itself dangerously to inflation of the ego: it is easy to confuse the volume of one's voice with the quality of what it is saying, and to forget that opinions are made no sounder merely by being widely distributed. For myself, in editing, and in writing the anonymous journalistic style of Third Person Authoritative, I can only work on the assumption that the reader is every bit as intelligent as I (or if some are less so, others are more so) and my claim to the right to speak has to be that I have made myself more informed in detail, or have taken more time to reflect, on the topic I am discussing. Implicit in this view is a picturing of the reader as someone who was practicing law or baking a cake while I informed myself on what I was writing; he could tell me something that I didn't know about law, and she could tell me something about cooking—or the ways of the human heart. We go different ways, and if she or he is interested, I can tell him about the way I have gone and what I have found out.

As a journalist I did not think myself judge, prosecutor or lawgiver. I was a scout to the outer world, keeping a sharp eye out for untoward movements in the distant hills, and reporting back the lay of the land. To me, it was a good job and honest work.

8. The Gamy Game of Politics

In days past, if one really wanted to study the practice of politics, the best school was a presidential campaign train. Perhaps the last major expedition set forth in the wartime year of 1944. There were to be later short journeys in the dying tradition, such as Harry Truman's whistle-stop campaign of 1948, before the custom became a casualty of the air age and of television, to be replaced by nervous "prop-stop" flights around the countryside and the big set-piece television appearances. But the 1944 campaign train assembled for Tom Dewey was a coast-to-coast big swing, with ten sleeping cars full of newspapermen living together for thirty days in convivial confinement, hitched on ahead of two railroad cars for the candidate, his family, his advisers and mimeograph machines. At the very end of the train was the inevitable back platform where the candidate appeared at monotonously frequent intervals to wave at the townspeople gathered in apathetic curiosity, to shake hands each time with a different regional leader but always with the same pose and same smile, and to say a "few words" to the people he was so happy to be among again, finding at every occasion some remote reason for feeling particularly close to Nebraskans, or if in Oregon to Oregonians, and ending with a few homilies that we came to chant by heart, to the unchanging effect that it was now time for a change.

There was always something peculiarly synthetic about Tom

Dewey as a man of the people, and it might have been better for the neutralizing of my political beliefs had I been subjected to a similar experience with Franklin Roosevelt. Thirty days of back platform banalities, interrupted by the big occasions where in major speeches the candidate seeks to make a maximum of friends while incurring a minimum of enemies, is a devastating education in the hypocrisy and tawdriness of politics, and the essential narrowness of range and unfreshness of political ideas.

After ten days of it I had a loathing of the politician's insincerity; after twenty days of it I came instead to feel sorry for the candidate, that poor fellow imprisoned in his ambitions, making a manikin's gestures and grimaces as he moves along a tread, like a duck in a shooting gallery, while inside him some impulse to sincerity longs to peep out but fears it would be politically unwise. So he smiles at the political leaders who he knows were until recently against him, courts people he doesn't really care a fig about, repeats his speech writer's hyperbolic denunciation of the enemy though he knows better, meets with interested lobbyists—the beet growers, the veterans, the cattlemen—and contrives answers that will satisfy them as promises but not commit him as pledges; hears himself praised for attitudes he doesn't hold but dares not deny; makes speeches to the credulous who must be falsely comforted and the indifferent who must be synthetically roused; gives ear to the crackpots and tries to satisfy them with a smile while avoiding an endorsement of their nonsense; is handed from one group to another of smiling faces and outstretched hands, having been coached in advance who will be there whose name must not be forgotten ("Why, of course I remember you . . . My old friend"); is badgered by reporters, some of whom on instructions from their papers or out of their own prejudices are out to "get" him; faces an unending assembly line of lukewarm creamed chicken, canned peas and apple pie luncheons which must be eaten even if he has no appetite, while hundreds of people are craning to watch his every expression, hoping to catch him off guard; is everywhere encouraged by uninformed enthusiasts and privately discouraged by hard-eyed insiders who want some further commitment from him; and all the while he seeks to appear fresh when he is tired, interested when he is bored, and candid when he is not. He is caught up in falsity and comes to believe it, must swim in the sham and must doubt neither it nor himself. He has become a personage, not a person. Perhaps, when it is all over, he can wash it all off, as in a bath, and get down to his own skin again? But it never all comes off.

Up front in the campaign train, having drinks in one or another's bedroom compartment, playing cards at one end of the "work car" or writing cables to our editors as we sat facing our portable type-writers side by side at long wooden benches, were the eighty cor-respondents. They included the best of the Washington press corps, a tight-knit and sharp group, as well as a number of other reporters who apparently had made themselves agreeable to their publishers. Roaming from one state to another, through counties that were dry or counties that did not permit liquor by the drink, we declared our press car to be sovereign territory of the State of New York temporarily adrift, which in practice meant that we pulled the shades down at night and the bar was open whenever anyone wanted a drink. Before the trip was well along, the correspondents had generally divided, as dinner companions or in sharing taxis together, according to their political views. Little neutrality, though much honest effort at fair reporting, resided in that politically so-phisticated group; and the opportunities for bias existed not only in registering the enthusiasm or apathy of the crowds but even in estimating their numbers.

There was political apathy aplenty in that wartime year of 1944, with the aging and practiced Franklin Roosevelt lying back, busy with the war but also aware that this was the best politics, while Thomas E. Dewey roamed the countryside with a retired general at his side to be photographed with, hoping thereby to indicate that he too could discuss military and world affairs, an expedient which at best could not match Roosevelt's meetings with Churchill and the bustle of accompanying braid and brass. For days, though the Dewey strategists timed their morning arrival at each major city so that the caravan of cars to the hotel would pass through streets crowded at the going-to-work hour, the candi-date was met only by chilled knots of the faithful, and the sirens of the police escorts barely stirred onlookers long enough for them to turn their heads. At last, at Los Angeles, the candidate drew a crowd that filled the Coliseum, drawn perhaps as much by the promise of movie stars as by the threat of a speech. One by one, members of the Republican colony of Hollywood came forward to say a practiced line of spontaneous greeting to the crowd and to the nation-wide radio audience—the movie tough talking in character as one who wasn't fooled and knew a real man; the movie heroine playing her familiar engagingly helpless role, but sure of one thing this time. . . . Later, when another reporter and I got the script of this travesty, I found myself forever cured of interest in the political manifestations, on either side, of Hollywood actors and actresses.

Two days later, as we crossed the desert, the campaign at last came alive with Franklin Roosevelt's campaign-opening speech to the Teamsters in Indianapolis. Before those cynical friends of the poor he gave a masterly, swaggering political speech—that one which has already reached some anthologies with its climactic complaint about criticisms of his family: "They now include my little dog Fala." Before the speech, Dewey's press secretary (James Hagerty) had come to our work car to announce that something had gone wrong in all the wealth and weight of electronic apparatus in the back car of the train, and that Dewey would be unable to hear Roosevelt speak. To the correspondents aboard, who were able to hear the speech well enough on the dining steward's tiny portable, this announcement strained belief.

Next morning's stop in Belen, New Mexico, is the vignette of Candidate Dewey that lingers longest in my mind: of the man who slowly got off his elaborate campaign train and in a glass-cage telephone booth in front of an adobe rail station, surrounded by curious little Indian and Mexican children, and by equally curious but more discreet newspapermen, heard for twenty minutes, as the special train stood waiting, what must have been the universally discouraging reports of the impact of Franklin Roosevelt's initial speech. The campaign was already all over; and though Dewey drastically changed his fighting style in his next speech at Oklahoma City, switching from the confident young statesman to the slashing, angry district attorney, there was nothing more he could do.

A man of vigor and intelligence, a good administrator though unable to conceal an arrogance of manner, Thomas E. Dewey lacked that one intangible in a politician that is hard to define but impossible to be without: that which is loosely described as "heart."

(Others have suffered from this same chill inability to convey "heart"—men of such varying views as Robert Taft, Dean Acheson and John Foster Dulles; and it remains to be seen whether Richard Nixon, despite an increased grounding in public affairs and a gift for adapting his manner to a given jury, would overcome a similar deficiency when he sought office in his own name.) Tom Dewey may have the melancholy distinction of being the only presidential candidate of our age to have lost (in 1948) what would otherwise, except for the accident of his personality, have been the victory that rightfully belonged to his party.

Looking back on the era of the forties, it seems to me that a natural swing of political power in the United States was twice frustrated: by Truman's surprising triumph over Dewey, and at an earlier time by Franklin Roosevelt's use of the developing war situation to get himself reelected in 1940, prevailing over both Wendell Willkie and the two-term tradition. By 1940 the great impetus to reform had spent itself, but when a short time later, after Pearl Harbor, Roosevelt proclaimed his switch from Dr. New Deal to Dr. Win the War, he in effect gave himself a new mandate. By 1944 he was a used-up man. But the war was still on, and he had visions of the peace to be made: for him to renounce office would have been harder than it was for Churchill unwillingly to abdicate after victory in 1945. He has to suffer before history for his decision, and not alone for being a tired, credulous and dying man who faced Stalin later at Yalta.

During the 1944 Dewey-Roosevelt campaign, the Republicans had done their best to create a "health issue," and, to meet it, Roosevelt had driven all day in an open car through the rainy streets of Brooklyn to prove his vitality. A photographer took a memorable picture that day of the gaunt, slack-jawed, soaked and agonized President; the Republican New York *Daily News* devoted its whole front page to it, and I remember my own distress and righteous argument when *Time* similarly featured it: but whatever the motives for publishing the picture, it was legitimate "news" and the real issue of the campaign. Why did Roosevelt run that fourth time? I no longer rush to impute motives as I once did, and recognize that Roosevelt in 1944 and Dwight Eisenhower in 1956 were importuned by advisers, some of them in good faith and some not

necessarily so, who pleaded that only men of such prestige and experience could cope with the crises before them, and if this advice
pleased some subterranean vanity of theirs, both Roosevelt and
Eisenhower consciously, I believe, regarded themselves as making
a personal sacrifice.* Unfortunately in each case, not only their
health was demanded in sacrifice, but also their reputations. Stanley
Baldwin, the British Prime Minister, once ruefully observed of his
own country: "Half the mistakes from 1918 on have been the work
of tired men." The same might be said of the United States of the
forties and fifties.

On each occasion, in 1940, 1944 and 1948, though destined to lose,
the Republicans had done what was historically demanded of them:
they had provided a presidential candidate committed to inter-
nationalism. How much this action pained them was evident to me
at the 1944 Republican convention as I watched a greater ovation
for the defeated contender, a handsome, white-haired mediocrity
from Ohio, than that given the party's choice, Thomas E. Dewey.
John Bricker, who heartily disliked the New Deal and plainly dis-
trusted foreigners, was the man in the hearts of the Republican
delegates, but their heads told them that if they hoped to win votes
from the Democrats they had better pick a nominee sufficiently international, sufficiently moderate in hating. When even this sacrifice
did not win them the prize, the reasonable men in the party lost
ground to a new generation of wild men, many of whom won off-
year elections in 1946 with demagoguery that was the first warning
of an ugly hatred and pinched spirit. These were small, vindictive
men, convinced that their kind of "fighting Republicanism" was
what was needed. When they were defeated again inside their own
party in 1948, when Thomas E. Dewey was preferred to Robert
Taft, and when Dewey, acting as if office were already his, did not
even win when he was supposed to, the Republicans were doomed
to desperate measures. The agitators demanded blood; the best of

* It is noteworthy that the crisis which Eisenhower decided needed his
continuance in office despite ill health was not the world situation, or even
the unfitness of the opposition party, but what he implied was the incomplete
transformation of his own party. It was not a reason that appealed to his party
managers, who ignored it. Once reelected, Eisenhower seemed to have no clear
idea of what it was, or who it was, he objected to in his own party, and
turned aside all questions on the subject.

the moderates were not only discredited but had lost faith in their own advice: they were willing to try a little of what the agitators demanded.

The freak election of 1948 owed something, but not as much as Harry Truman thought, to his chirpy and crude campaign (as a campaigner, he was a demagogue of the old-fashioned school, accusing his opponents of unspecified rascality but not of treason). The result owed more to a lingering public mistrust of Republicans, and the accident of a candidate who was no one's choice, put forward unenthusiastically by politicians who did not themselves like Dewey. That no issue really separated the two parties could be judged by the domestic stalemate that prevailed for the next four years. Harry Truman had raised a shrill cry about a "do-nothing" Republican congress, but his own did little more, and this suited the times.

But it was in international matters that this cocky little man left his mark, and earned a higher place in history than anyone who knew how casual was Truman's selection as running mate by Roosevelt in 1944 had a right to expect. From the atom bomb decision to the launching of the imaginative Marshall Plan, from the building up of a remarkable European alliance to the hard decision to fight in Korea, Harry Truman and his Secretary of State, Dean Acheson, acted with the vigor and sweep required of them. Having behaved so well in high matters, Harry Truman did not think it mattered how he acted in low ones, and by his choice of court jesters, by his own petty spitefulness and an occasional coarseness of expression, demeaned his office. If personally honest, he had shown an ability to accommodate himself to practical politics ever since his days in the Pendergast machine. The cry of corruption that helped drive the Democrats from office may have made too much of one mink coat, several influence peddlers and the crookedness of several tax collectors—but it had leverage out of proportion to its importance because the public could see that the Democrats had been in office too long and would become thoroughly corrupt if they prolonged their stay. At the end of Truman's term, Democratic politicians did what they could to preserve themselves in office by choosing in Adlai Stevenson a high-minded outsider, but the end of the 20-year Democratic era was long overdue. After Stevenson's defeat, critics as perceptive as Elmer Davis regarded the election results as bitter evidence that Stevenson was too intelligent and too good for the American people. But I think that Stevenson, as any other Democratic candidate in 1952 would have been, was defeated before he was nominated. The public acted as the times required.

The New Deal need not, I think, fear for its secure place in history. Great achievements belong to it. But from its earliest days it was marred by Franklin Roosevelt's blithe disregard of tradition, and from his attempt to pack the Supreme Court to his defiance of the two-term limit in office he was too free and casual about inherited customs. He was not a man of deep principles, and when confronted once by two quite contrary drafts of a speech he was to deliver, his characteristic instruction to his speech writer was to "mix 'em together." Distressed by his highhanded ways, many were sincerely fearful that Roosevelt, by his aggrandizement of the federal payroll, might be able to perpetuate himself in office. Franklin Roosevelt had many cynical actions to answer for. ("You know the first thing a President has to do in order to put through good legislation?" he asked Rex Tugwell early in their Brain Trust relationship. "He has to get elected.") On occasion he deceived and double-crossed. No doubt men of his temperament inspire themselves with the conviction that their higher aims justify such methods, and sometimes history agrees with them. Roosevelt perhaps expected history to remember TVAs and Atlantic Charters, and to forgive much else in their name; Harry Truman probably counted on a similar selectivity in history. But if clear-eyed history so decides, in its own good time, a contemporary public may not always be as ready to be reminded of only one half of a politician's nature. It is an iron law of political behavior that if regimes escape chastisement for their lapses at the time of the event, they will be punished later, and often for seemingly irrelevant reasons.

After twenty years of one party in power, years of convulsive changes at home and abroad—a depression, a great war and a smaller, undeclared one—the times were askew. It took a strong cry to bring down a strong regime: that is, perhaps, the only rationalization there can be for that unhappy period of our lives, the only time in which I have felt ashamed of my own country, the age of McCarthy. That era is still too close to us and, like the bitter Age of Reconstruction that followed another war a century earlier, too painful to dwell on. But a few things must be said about it. The tinder had been long agathering. At a time when the entire nation was sick to death of the frustrating inconclusiveness of the Korean War, and so used to considering itself the most powerful nation in the world that it could not understand how it could be challenged by the likes of poor ancient China, the devil theory of betrayal—that someone had "sold the pass"—was easy to spread and tempting to believe.

From the early thirties, and the popular fronts of that decade, the New Deal had shown an undiscriminating hospitality toward the left and a sympathy toward what was known as the Russian Experiment. When Communist espionage cells were discovered in our government, the public had a legitimate suspicion that others might be found, and the right to be satisfied by a thorough exploration. But so placidly entrenched was the Democratic administration, and so exasperated were its critics, that the one could cry "red herring" and the other be ready to render verdicts of guilty before the evidence was heard. The press that took a truth about Alger Hiss and made it a lie about Dean Acheson was in no moral stance later to reprove Joe McCarthy for going too far in his talk of "twenty years of treason."

For it had only remained for someone sufficiently unscrupulous, though arriving a little late on the scene, to heighten an atmosphere that was much like that of the days of the informers in Nero's Rome or Titus Oates's England. The last final lie said over Joe McCarthy's grave by political associates who knew better was that he was a dedicated fighter against Communism; he was no such thing, only an unprincipled adventurer who got a pleasure out of roughhousing and couldn't see why the victims too did not enjoy the scuffle (the amiability with which he cuffed them about was what most bewildered and terrified his victims, while the public at large, until awakened by the television hearings, thought him a fearless crusader). Over his grave should be written the simple epitaph: THE TRUTH WASN'T IN HIM.

That McCarthy's greatest hour of influence should have come after and not before the 1952 Republican victory must be charged, I think, against Dwight Eisenhower, whose aloofness from the battle, whose odd notion of a weak Executive, whose distaste for brawling and wish to be liked by everybody was to culminate in his standing aside from defending even one of his own top officials, his Secretary of the Army, a man chiefly guilty of an unadmirable playing-along with McCarthy's soldier-boy staff because the "White House team" had indicated he should. The headless White House of this period is what gave the country its helpless feeling. A public that wanted reassurance about the loyalty of its civil servants, but also expected any investigation to be fair, might have been in the majority, but it found no leadership where it had a right to ask leadership to be. And this must, I think, be held against Eisenhower's performance in his first term.

A soldier without politics, and in fact one who had leaped to prominence under two Democratic presidents, Eisenhower had practically been dragged into office by acclaim, so that a man unidentified with the carping futility of the Republican past might take the Grand Old Party into the bad new age. For though the Republicans had approved of entering World War II, and had given a grudging budgetary sanction to the Korean War after it was begun, they had had in effect no full responsibility in world affairs since the last Hoover days of 1932.

It was thus Eisenhower's assigned historical role to induce his party to accept the necessities of a new age, an age of large budgets and big government, and to accept an active involvement in world affairs through alliances and interventions. The demand of his first term was that he take over a going policy from its discredited agents, that he moderate its excesses and persuade the entire nation to accept it. This, despite subdued murmurings from the holdbacks, he effectively achieved. The man so uniquely qualified by the warmth of his personality for this first assignment was persuaded to run for a second term, ignoring the natural promptings of his age and health, because the party managers had no one else who could win. The sting had gone from the times, and a grateful nation cheerfully re-elected the molder of its tranquillity. But the demand of Eisenhower's second term was that he formulate new political, economic and diplomatic policies to confront a changed situation, and neither the state of his health nor the experiences of a life-time in other pursuits fitted him for his task.

Will history's verdict on Eisenhower be that he was a good man but a weak president? If so, something has to be said about the processes that brought to power a man so popular, but with such in-determinate political views that he was actively sought as a candi-date by both parties. Some who idolized Franklin Roosevelt scorned a later public for hero-worshiping Dwight Eisenhower, but only so politically neutral a popular figure as this successful soldier and likable man could have ended the country's deep divisions. Those divisions were the result of an administration too long in office and of an opposition too long out of power—for, to rephrase Lord Acton, lack of power also tends to corrupt. Along with its achievements, the Democratic party had an accumulation of blunders persisted in, had fallen back on dishonest appeals and big-city machines, and had become sleek and arrogant: all of this was enough to set up in its opponents a "get-even" spirit. But as a result, many were so ap-palled by the alternative often offered by the opposition that they continued to vote Democratic long after the party's first purity was gone and their own enthusiasm was spent. Everyone was caught in the circle; the emergence of a new breed of mean-spirited op-ponents was itself the result of the continuing failure and despair of better Republicans. When at last this new breed came to power in an abnormal period, its vengeance in the age of McCarthy was hot and unselective; many who were marked for its retribution were not guilty, or at least not guilty as charged.

But, to bring my own political views up to a later date, I had, in the midst of the shame so many Americans felt for the ascendance of base men and the weaklings in high places who gave in to them, the feeling that these men too were the product of an unnatural time; and if those who wielded the bludgeon in wrath were guilty of the crime, there was a sense in which the victim had a complicity in his own death.

A continuous preoccupation with politics had left me neither Republican nor Democrat, though perhaps with a lingering in-dulgence of Democrats, for I think that a better national balance is kept when big government and big business are in tension rather than in cahoots. I do not think either party has a monopoly on knavery or virtue, but cannot share the moral satisfaction of many who style themselves "independents" and consider themselves above the chicanery and vulgar striving of party. They are generally people who refuse to involve themselves, and then feel cheated by the interior choices others have put before them. It is very easy to call tolerance what is only indifference, and I think it was G. K. Chesterton who pointed out that turnips are singularly broad-minded.

If I were a cartoonist I would add a third animal to my political zoo, to accompany the elephant and the donkey: it would be a spotted cow, to represent the independent voter. It would be neither black nor white, though pleased by its own random mixture; it would be sitting down most of the time because it was unused to taking stands, and it would have a bemused expression on its face, which might be taken for confusion but might also be vapidity.

If politics is so often the arena of the hardy second-rate, it is because the field has been left to them. If a public feels contempt for politicians, I think it has only itself to blame; it may not want crooks in office but does not trouble to discriminate, and frequently throws out good men who do not bow to it. By temperament a politician is thoroughly adjustable. If he is blatant, he thinks it required of him; if less stirring and prodding were sufficient to make people take the trouble to vote, politicians would gladly modulate their vulgar pleading to the amount that pleased the public. An acquaintanceship with politicians, at least of the caliber of those elected to Congress, reveals them to be better than they are generally thought to be. If none can be unreservedly admired, few can be thoroughly despised. Their collective wisdom can be doubted, but I believe that their technical competence is often greater than critics allow. One of the pleasanter shocks of newspapering is the discovery that someone whose opinion one abhors frequently turns out in person to be quite appealing. In part this is because a politician instinctively knows how to make himself agreeable, but it is also because, as John O'Leary, the Fenian, observed, "Never has there been a cause so bad that it has not been defended by good men for good reasons."

We all know the baseness of politics but disregard how often a politician votes a certain way, when all the pressure is against him, not out of hope that a well-informed public will appreciate his decision, but out of some inner prompting. Politicians are often meagerly endowed intellectually, but their encyclopedias are the faces and characteristics of other men, in which they are well read. For this they are often scorned by the intellectuals, but as an Englishman, F. S. Oliver, once put it: "An artist starving in a garret because he has ventured to outrage popular taste, may yet paint masterpieces, but political masterpieces can only be made by a politician working in energetic partnership with a prevalent opinion."

Though held in low esteem, politicians are asked to pass judgment on quite complicated matters of finance, taxation, defense and foreign policy—skills for which they earn little thanks. They are judged instead by the simplicities of their views, and by how well they oblige their constituents in small favors. That great inert public which is so scornful of them is rarely at their side in the crucial moments, when they hear only from the interested. Politicians are in a rough game, required to have at the same time a sensitive antenna and a thick hide; they are abused unfairly and must give as well as get, while preserving some corner of equanimity. "If you can't stand the heat," asked Harry Truman, "why don't you get out of the kitchen?" And in fact all politicians come to have a realistic tolerance of the wild poses or petty deceits their fellow politicians must engage in. Amateurs are prone to forget that a Democratic politician probably has more in common with the Republican opponent he is traducing than with the Democratic garage mechanic whose support he solicits.

Our constitutional forefathers, in all their wisdom, saw no need for political parties and made no provision for them, but parties are as natural a development as anything else in society which springs up unbidden but, serving a purpose, survives. It is only when taken at their own seriousness that parties appear so absurd. As citadels of contending dogma they are a farce, but as a device for alternate government (which is, after all, what distinguishes democracy from dictatorship) they have their use.

American political parties are commonly likened to big tents, broad enough to cover everyone; they are, in fact, increasingly like circuses, with as few roots among the generality of people; like circuses they come to town infrequently and, with superb organizing skill, put down pegs and set up their attractions. Their big finale in the center ring, the quadrennial political convention, is, like a circus, designed to overwhelm, to succeed not by a perfection of details but by the assault of the total, to dazzle by noise and light and timing; but it has become a clumsy circus act, lacking in speed and pace.

Parties must talk two languages, one for all to hear, the other for the committed. For while they need to attract the widest support, they must also justify the militancy of those groups with private expectations. The place where these conflicting interests come together, and are dissolved into one lumpy mass, is the party platform. To judge parties by their proclaimed platforms would be to put one's trust in a collection of ridiculous accusations, studied evasions and dishonest promises, assembled by men who know that any candidate worth his salt will feel no need to follow them, though he must be tactful in his disregard of them.

In the British definition of political responsibility, American political parties are irresponsible. A congressman adheres to a party, but feels an obligation only to his electorate. He does not accept responsibility for the conduct of an administration even when his own party is in power, and will disown it rather than go down with it. He may at all times by his votes safely oppose the administration without dislodging it or himself in so doing. What the British find hardest to understand about American politics is the opposition of a powerful Southern committee chairman to a Democratic president, or the resistance of a Republican majority leader to a basic recommendation of his own president. But the British system, if more logical, has great disabilities too: an M.P. will think twice about voting against his party if it will bring down the government, or will subject him to party expulsion; even the Opposition, with its "shadow cabinet" assembled on the front bench in expectation of office, must be mindful of the need for discretion and discipline. Independence of vote is becoming rarer in British parliamentary life: the proportions of each majority are set at election time, and remain relatively fixed except for by-elections; abstention is almost the only form of protest left. I cannot believe such an inflation of party regularity would be good for us.

Partisanship in a euphoric period is a special branch of the politician's art. In good times, when there is no dramatic division of society, with one side wishing and the other resisting change, parties must woo the same audience, an audience that is widest in the middle. They must therefore make roughly the same appeal, though one makes it in Lincoln's name and the other in Jefferson's. I remember once trying to explain to Nye Bevan at lunch in London the difference between Adlai Stevenson and Dwight Eisenhower. That foxy politician merely observed, "When candidates matter, elections don't."

In such blurred times, when no great issues divide them our two political parties sound like two great ocean liners in a fog, unsure where they are but blatting their horns and pushing forward, knowing nothing else to do. When nothing really separates the two parties except rivalry for office, it becomes the business of campaign oratory (that special outer province of truth) to maximize their differences, and while the incumbent can wear a relaxed air to suit the relaxed public mood, the opposing candidate—as in 1956—must labor twice as hard to show that there is something to be worried about, and to the contented public is apt to appear agitated only by ambition. When the middle of the road is so wide as to take up all the paving, the politician who has captured that middle has all the advantage: it is his rival who must disturb the calm, accent differences and raise his voice. Eisenhower, though presumably an amateur in politics, had a flair for occupying the middle, making himself likable and pledging earnestly to do the decent (but never defined) thing. He was so gifted at avoiding factionalism that he would not even let himself be ranged against those who were ranged against him; and even when challenged over the failure of one of his programs would not so much defend the policy as defend his own probity. This talent for shifting the argument from the inadequacy of a program to the purity of his motives was the envy of his rivals—and sometimes the despair of those of his admirers who wanted something done.

Though seemingly much different, I think both Eisenhower and

Stevenson owed much of their popularity to their lack of resemblance to orthodox politicians, for after twenty years of disagreeable contention the public was dissatisfied with both the sleek in office and the angry out of it. A new style politician had emerged, better at talking comfortably before the television camera's unblinking eye than shouting from a stump, and able to succeed as a politician by convincing the voters that he too had no use for conventional politicians. In fact, increasingly as government has become more complex, the decisions which must be taken admit of less and less polarity of the kind that make for dramatic party stands. A Republican will proclaim his undying opposition to "government giveaways" but will find himself unabashedly supporting agricultural subsidies; a Democrat may proclaim his desire to soak the rich, but will then cooperate in the preparation of an equitably distributed income tax, and seek campaign contributions from businessmen.

We have come a long way since the days when Lord Melbourne thought it the whole duty of government to prevent crime and preserve contracts. The big decisions have been made, though the oratory lingers on: we are committed under either party to a vastness in government, to a continuing regulation of money, to a protection of the entire economy from severe pains; we have been thrust into the world, and cannot escape having both allies and enemies. At times it seems as if the only issue left to politics is whether programs will be administered by their advocates, or by those who may be trusted to be halfhearted about them.

If the conflicting claims of party argument have long ceased to have any recognizable validity, is there then nothing that really divides the two great political parties? Are their differences as meaningless as those of the Blue Faction and the Green Faction in ancient Byzantium? Many people are sure that something does divide the two parties. If both Republicans and Democrats make the same sounds, the knowing are convinced that they can intuitively distinguish a difference in intended emphasis. It cannot be the platforms, for they are designed to be read ambiguously. The candidates? Here we get our first clue, though a misleading one. For it is possible to lay the spectrums of elected Democrats and Republicans over one another, and to find each, at either extreme, extend-

ing as far as the other. The greatest conservatives are often Democrats (though most of them come from the South, where party has
no meaning because it has only one meaning). Critics often make
great play with this oddity, but I think they make too much of it.

Anyone who attends the conventions of both political parties, one
after the other, recognizes immediately their differing atmosphere.
Republican delegates are apt to be respectable and guarded; most
of them do not seem to be politicians but to be businessmen or
housewives with a militant interest in politics; they do not express
themselves freely but seem to be eying the state chairman, as if
they feared to state an irregular opinion. They take up banners and
march with a Cromwellian righteousness, as if every wave of the
standard represented a solemn act of faith. The Democrats, on the
other hand, seem to have an exuberant delight in politicking, and
an indulgent tolerance for the gaudy scene. Democratic delegates—
except for a few labor-union militants who can also be Cromwellian
—are usually courthouse politicians sweatily enjoying the show.
They talk freely to newspapermen, acknowledging their quarrels.
From all of this it is easy to conclude that the Republicans are
the party of the respectable, of the "people on the hill," and that
the Democrats are the party of the masses. In important respects this
is true, but if it were completely true there would be no need of
elections: the Republicans would be outnumbered and never win.

In the end, I think the true difference between the parties lies
fundamentally in the kind of voter (not candidate) that each attracts. Many voters, of course, have simply inherited their political
loyalties, or found themselves Republican or Democratic at an early
age, but if this were a universal explanation of voting preferences
every election would turn out roughly the same. I believe that
the margin of victory in any election comes not from any substantial
body of voters scurrying from one side to the other, but from the
degree in which either party stirs the latent impulses of its marginal
followers, and I suspect that even among those who style themselves
independent and profess a disdain for politics, most people have
either Republican or Democratic leanings. We now enter a more
mysterious area—what each voter believes he stands for when he
declares himself Republican or Democrat. For example, a workingman who voted Republican used to find it best not to confess his

preference to his fellow lunchbox-carriers, yet did not regard himself as betraying his class, but only as being steadfast to his principles. What principles? Voters are popularly said to vote agin', rather than for, but despite this folk wisdom I believe that most people regard their own political attitudes as affirmative. What then is the guiding affirmative quality of mind which a voter finds reflected in the party he chooses? I would name it to be, in a Republican voter, prudence; and in a Democrat, liberality.

By these terms I do not simply mean what each means by accusing the other of being tightfisted or spendthrift, or to suggest that each lacks the virtue of the other, but only to indicate where I think the emphasis in each lies. The Democrat's liberality has made him more adventuresome abroad, and more openhanded at home. The Republican's prudence is founded more on a sense of individual obligation, and of individual advantage. One party sees the unequal state of society as, by and large, the natural result of the individual's unequal merit and unequal effort; the other thinks it the duty of politics to redress an inequity of economics. It would not be fair to the Republicans to describe them as Disraeli described a politician, as "susceptible of deep emotions, but not for individuals." But they are the ones more inclined to remember that the piper must be paid, and that they will probably have to pay him.

When these attitudes are transmitted into programs, they result in a Republican foreign policy which is apt to demand recognizable and immediate results for its aid, in the shape of alliances, pledges or favored position, and to be insensitive to the feelings of other nations. As for the Democrats, their generosity, particularly in domestic matters, too easily becomes indulgence, and their sentimental favoring of minorities (racial groups, unions) often takes the form of alliance with the cynical and tough leaders who speak in the minority's name but not in its true interest.

9. Making Allies and Losing Friends

The big Cadillac leaves dun-colored Teheran, its streets vivid with sidewalk hawkers, the flow of filth in the jubes, and neon signs in Arabic scrawl. Effortlessly it heads northward to the pleasanter suburbs, in the shadow of brown hills and cold Mount Demavend. At the palace gates the car stops, and I am sent on alone, up the graveled garden path, where every few feet among the ordered flowers and reflection pools a steel-helmeted soldier bangs his feet together, swivels his head, and stands at watchful attention as I pass. Soon, inside the palace, the Shah of Iran is showing me to a settee and taking a chair beside it; no interpreter is present, for this serious young king has lately mastered English. Since I know his age and he does not know mine, I wonder as we talk during the next two hours whether he is measuring me as I am measuring him. We are of the same age, though he is palace-bred, in a poor country, and I am modestly raised in a rich country. The Shah has a quiet and earnest manner, and a confidence that has only lately won out over the nagging knowledge that in his insecure and ancient nation, his own dynasty is only as old as his father, a soldier who seized power. "Formerly I had to smile at people when I did not want to," he told me at one point. "But now—now I am in control."

To the Shah, this man facing him, this round-faced American with deforested hairline and rounding stomach (adding a new ring each year, as a tree does) is foreign editor of the news magazine the Shah carefully reads every Thursday night, after the bundle has been opened at the airport and the top copy rushed to the palace. I am thus a sort of unofficial representative of my country and can be asked questions that the Shah might not want to put so directly to the American ambassador. When we met, he was just back from Khrushchev's Moscow, where he withstood Soviet hospitality and conceded nothing. Now, after we had talked a while of Nasser and Nehru, he returned to an earlier question: Why does America treat its enemies better than its friends? My answer was spontaneous, and perhaps the State Department could say it better. I did not think we had treated Iran so badly: we were equipping its army and guiding its agriculture; we had helped to stabilize its regime after the palsied frenzy of Mossadegh; we were introducing honest administrative methods (where other modes of action had a two-thousand-year head start). Yes, the Shah conceded all this—but why do you do more for Nehru, who flouts you, than for Pakistan, who sides with you? Why let Nasser blackmail you? I had to acknowledge seeming imbalances in this numbers game we call foreign aid. So many considerations affect our decisions: measuring one nation's size, another's need; spending to reward one country's friendship and to diminish another's hostility; finding that at times a nation's stability justifies, and at other times its instability requires, help. Sometimes, knowing full well that someone was playing both sides, we matched a Russian offer, but in doing so were not being deceived: such aid was not given in the same spirit as that we gave to those we found trustworthy, and if trickery had its temporary successes, loyalty had more lasting claims on us. And finally, I argued, the amount of aid a country received was after all hardly the determinant of where its allegiance must lie: Iran belonged with the West because only the West wanted for Iran and could help it get what Iran must want for itself—independence, stability, progress. I think that the Shah agreed with most of this, but still wanted more aid.

A few weeks later I was sitting in Nasser's Cairo office and the scene was quite different: agitation outside his doors, the bank of eight black telephones beside his desk, the American desk gadgets, the American cigarette and Western-styled suit. Here in this trim and handsome young soldier with the too-quick smile were all the contradictions that made our task so hard: the zealot in khaki who overthrew his fat king, reduced the corrupt hold of the pashas, drove out the British occupiers and seized the Suez Canal; who was modest in his style of living and in money matters incorruptible; who wanted to restore pride to his miserable people and to give them economic chance. For so long he had seemed the kind of leader his people needed; and for a time even the not-easily-deceived Israelis thought so too. He was not yet, when I met him, the founding head of the United Arab Republic. The Anglo-French-Israeli invasion of his country was a month in the future; he was still interested in courting Western journalists. Having lately seized the Suez Canal he was cock-a-hoop over the Egyptian success at running it, and full of clever defenses of his action. It was all America's fault: "You can't slap me in the face." All that he had been criticized for, including his acceptance of Communist arms, was only response, he insisted: "I don't have a foreign policy. I only react," and he repeated this thought later as if it were something to be proud of.

Were Nasser's flaws an accident of personality, an ambition marred by vanity and trickiness, a conceit in evasions, and the flightiness of an impatient opportunist? Or were his weaknesses inevitable in his circumstances and the natural result of introducing Western methods to peoples who are destined to use them to expel the West? The simple Egyptian soldier learns leadership, cleanliness, patriotism and the use of modern weapons; he discovers the venality of his rulers and has the Western techniques to overthrow them. We think him Western because he knows about Buicks and padded shoulders, but he knows nothing of Jefferson or Thoreau. The Western gift of radios he uses to agitate against the West, and to cafés throughout the Middle East electronic devices, in his service, bring primitive appeals. Such is the disturbing, explosive power of our gifts.

The doubts of a friend, the maneuverings of an adventurer—these were the kinds of problems our foreign policy was caught up in. It is one of history's cruel tricks that when we Americans, in World War II, at last accepted the responsibility of great power it was

already too late to carry out with idealistic impartiality any intentions we might have had toward the world: the emergence of
Russia at the same hour blighted our mission and perverted our
plans. We had not aspired to world leadership and responsibility;
we had merely wanted to be rich and to be left alone, and we have
never quite recovered from the hurt discovery that the world did not
judge our intentions so innocently. Nations such as Britain and
Portugal and the Netherlands and Japan might need empires to
sustain their small homelands, but we felt self-sufficient in our
own wide territory and were only reluctantly persuaded that we
could not live in entire isolation from the rest of the world. We
thought of that world, in Asia and Africa, as picturesque and primitive; in Europe, as hopelessly quarrelsome and decadent. Our
mission, if one was required of us, was to be ourselves—honest and
well-meaning. We had not prepared for world leadership, and found
in this fact evidence of our virtue; so intent were we on our own
pursuits that we did not take the trouble to learn either the world's
languages or its ways. Having (we thought) been dragged into the
first World War, and betrayed into the second, we had no clear
ideas of what would be asked of us; we didn't want to run the
world, and were quite ready to delegate the task to a committee of
nations, large and small; we had no territorial ambitions and even
tried, after each victory, to limit the covetousness of our allies. Of
course, we ourselves might want to hang onto such bases as Oki-
nawa, but resented it when others accused us of not practicing what
we preached.

When we did sally forth into the world, clear of conscience and
empty of mind, we imagined ourselves a liberating force, eager to
see other nations win their independence, anxious to teach them
sanitation and production and democracy. We found ourselves regarded instead as the world's greatest conservative power, and we
were asked to defend our hogging of the world's goods. We thought
our economic doctrines would show the way to easing poverty in the
Middle East and Asia, but instead found these ideas welcomed
often only by those selfish elements in the community whom we
most despised. We know that capitalism, moderated in practice by
legislation and inspired by social ideals, could help an entire people,
but other nations thought they already knew all about capitalism,

basing their judgment of it on what they had observed of the greedy practices of those of their own people who saw only to themselves and not to the needs of the community. And they were encouraged in this belief by the Communists: for the first time in our history, another nation was going around the world spreading lies about us. We thus emerged as a great power at a moment when we could not enjoy the fruits but must be sobered by the responsibilities. There was no avoiding our destiny. Less than two centuries after declaring our independence we found it necessary to proclaim a declaration of interdependence. We might not like it, but the world needed us, and we it.

We set forth awkwardly, a clumsy giant. Yet considering our inexperience, our delusions, our naiveté, and the inadequate size of our diplomatic corps for its expanded tasks, we began well. No American need be ashamed of the generous impulse or the beneficial results of the Marshall Plan; and if we awakened late to the full perfidy of our wartime Russian ally, our mistaken trust may condemn us as unsophisticated but does not dishonor us. We have shortcomings to answer for, but not Hungarys. In the crucial year of 1948, the year of Czechoslovakia's fall and the Berlin blockade, we stopped the tide in Europe. In Asia, where China collapsed the following year, we were less awake—and had less to build on.

Hurrying to catch up to our difficulties, we made the mistakes of our enthusiasm. Sometimes it seemed as if we had decided to rephrase Theodore Roosevelt's maxim into "Speak loudly and carry a big wallet." We tended to preach, and if cynicism is not one of our failings in foreign affairs, self-righteousness is. Our actions were a curious amalgam of altruism and self-interest: we were enthusiastic in our altruism; others could see the play of self-interest below it; and if we tended to minimize one half of our nature, others tended to ignore the other half, and thought us hypocritical. Since under the democratic process it was necessary to convince the taxpayers of the practical benefits of humanitarianism, Europeans could overhear even our best instincts being meanly justified. In the end, cynical European politicians, asked to do something which their nations should have done anyway, and with reluctance would in time do, agreed to do it "for the Americans" and raised their price. We were more agitated about the danger than they; we huffed and we puffed; we badgered and rewarded; we cared, we exhorted. We tried to unite our allies, to win over the uncommitted and to roll back the enemy. We tried all means short of war, and failing (or at least, falling short of our high ambitions) we lost faith in strenuous exertions.

Old-fashioned diplomats had all along scorned such fervor; they believed in restraining our rhetoric and limiting our goals to what we might hope to achieve. But we all knew the inertia of such people; and some of the limited successes we did achieve could not have been won at their pace, so we felt right to ignore them. Yet, in the main, they were right. The crusaders were disappointed; disappointment brought disillusion, and we lost our taste for adventures.

Crusades, at the moment of opportunity, provide a wonderful impetus, and enthusiasm compensates for a lack of precision in aims. We felt a lift in the opportunity to rebuild Europe after the war; it was the homeland of many Americans and the cultural home of us all. But when that crisis was over, and the area resumed its hardened shapes, we found ourselves asked to do something about Asia, where we had no such cultural links and where the problems gave no promise of dramatic solutions. Asia was a morass, its leaders suspicious if not hostile. Proud new young nations felt an irritating need *not* to express gratitude for help; they wanted economic help and we gave them arms, which they might accept but did not cheer. And as we got caught up in claim and counterclaim of ancient feud, asked to side between Indian and Pakistani, between Jew and Arab, or between Arab and Arab, we learned that the proper weighting of aid to one side or the other was not for amateurs of passion: the public's feeling of participation went out of foreign aid.

Crusades are thus too fitful a method of conducting foreign policy, and when enthusiasm falters we find ourselves too loudly protesting the rightness of our beliefs to cover our decreasing willingness to fight for them; we tire of foreign exertions and lapse into passivity. But events do not wait until we care about them; with or without public enthusiasm behind it, foreign policy needs tending. At this point, I believe, professionals must prove their worth, making gains or averting disasters which the indifferent public will hardly be aware of, let alone grateful for. Foreign policy cannot be waged by a full people; the public's role is to agree on, and to insist upon, basic objectives.

In our first hasty improvising of barricades, at the outset of the cold war, we were dealing with European nations that were generally as concerned as we were. We insisted that they stand up and be counted, and made our aid conditional on their pledges. This worked fine in the obstinate reign of Stalin, but it was no answer in the fluid era that followed, or in the extension of our concern to those Asian areas whose peoples could not even be convinced that a danger existed from Communism. Our passion for making pacts, our desire to construct majorities in the United Nations, reflected a wish to erect imposing armadas, which in practice limited our pace to the slowest ships in the convoy. Much money was spent bribing nations into joining alliances with unlikely neighbors, and then trying to smooth out their feuds once they were partners. We made the mistake of thinking our loudest friends were our truest ones, or our most important. We made the military the touchstone of everything, and if the Pentagon was not full of what Lloyd George called "epauletted egoism impenetrable to ideas," it was often insensitive to nuances and cavalier to nations that did not share its singleness of mind.

It is always a mistake, I think, to let the Pentagon determine our foreign policy, allowing it to measure everything in terms of immediate military advantage, which must sometimes be at the expense of ultimate political advantage. Our basic military requirement may be simply put, though expensive to achieve: it is never to provide Russia with a *military* temptation. This requirement met, statecraft should be left free to move in other directions. In dealing with a world at peace, it is an error, I believe, to make the National Security Council—instead of the cabinet or the State Department— the most powerful foreign policy instrument of the Executive. The Pentagon is full of platoons of press agents bent on crying their own lacks and raising terrors (the Pentagon's own awareness of this peril not having taken the course of submerging its internal rivalries). They constantly ask: What if war were to come tomorrow? And they make of every transitory shift of forces or new invention a new threat. The Pentagon's rightful function is as a costly but negative necessity. If it is indeed the Pentagon's soldierly business to be alert to all dangers, it is not, and was never constitutionally intended to be, the source of sound political estimates in our foreign policy.

It is not because our danger is negligible but precisely because it is great that the arts of peaceful diplomacy must be given a chance to play a wide field, beyond the narrow military game of bargains and demands. Diplomacy must be able to operate on neutral ground, able even to reach into enemy-occupied territory, not with threats but with offers that are hard to refuse, so as to open these lands to our influence. We must not give the impression of fearing a peaceful future, for such an impression makes us cut a foolish figure.

Of all our multiple military alliances, only NATO has true meaning and a force in being: the rest I regard as largely paper triumphs, full of imposing proclamations to hide unspecific commitments, a device which may provide our newspapers with reassuring maps of our "friends" around the globe, but does not much deceive the enemy. NATO, which also has a standing army of press agents, forever seeks renewed proofs of our affection, though I believe there is no more need for it to be in the forefront of the public eye than the Pentagon or a fire department. A city conscious only of fire cannot get on with being a city, and a continual preoccupation with fire engines leaves the impression of a fondness for arson. Some people have wanted to graft extraneous political purposes onto NATO, hoping that these schemes would gain by NATO's reflected strength, while at the same time NATO would be made more lovable. But a 15-nation military alliance which loops from Canada to Iceland to Turkey is a natural grouping for few other purposes.

The Russians are free of some of the more vexatious problems that beset our alliances. Among their subordinate "partners," the Russians have the capacity to suppress disagreement. (Bulgarians not only cannot criticize Moscow but cannot even question whether Romania is contributing its proper share to the common cause.) This kind of advantage we may sigh for, but we do not seek it. With nations that they cannot order around, however, the Russians have shown a talent for asking minimal commitments—of the French, only that they not like the Germans; of the Indians, only that they favor a policy of "Asia for the Asians"—whereas our requests to young and sensitive nations, or to old and jealous powers, have too often been crowded with demands and pledges that have had significance only in domestic American politics, and caused needless refusals and resentments. We have been slow to scale our requests to the possibilities, making military pacts with like-minded nations, but not scolding or abandoning the others. In a world where rigid alliances exclude too many nations whose friendship we value, we must seek a relationship with these others that neither slights nor over-solicits them.

To argue against too great an entanglement in pacts is not to argue against the necessity of relations with other powers, but only to suggest that we beware of making clusters that add little to our strength and inhibit our flexibility. Rather than line up our friends in rows (often in waiting lines for money), casting the neutrals into limbo and the occupied Communist states into hell, I think we would do well to make precise bilateral agreements with other nations, inheriting neither their enmities nor their past errors. We need to be linked to our friends, but not strapped to them.

They, in turn, are entitled to be free of some of our demands on them. The congressional habit of requiring extraneous pledges from those we help is often galling to our most important allies, of no consequence to more cynical powers, and acceptable only to those who have most need of us.

We have sometimes heard Formosa and South Korea described by militants as our "truest" allies when in fact they are only our most jeopardized partners. Any listing of our most reliable friends is topsy-turvy that does not have at its head Britain and Canada. With these nations we have a community of traditions, language and political institutions, a past partnership in hazard, a common high development in technology, an established record for keeping one's pledges and fighting valiantly, an unforced compatibility of ideals and interests.

With Australia and New Zealand we share most of these same sentiments and purposes, but less immediacy of geography. With

France, a nation whose location is strategic, whose culture warms us all, and whose past is great, we have a similar mutuality of interest; but for many years we found its people weary of effort but insistent on grandeur, its politicians unwilling to take hard measures but ready to extract hard bargains, and its best brave men too often immobilized—at least until the advent of General Charles de Gaulle to power—by a national decision to decree helplessness in its rulers. With Germany, our admiration for its dynamism and technological genius is tempered by our lingering memory of what uses these resources have been put to in the past. And so the list of allies goes, not in any simple declining order of usefulness to us, but on many intersecting planes of consanguinity and peril. It is diplomacy's business to reckon the best relationships with each, rather than to try to force nations into handy aggregations that blur what is individual to their cases, or to require a pretense of equal enthusiasm for hard tasks. (I remember Sir Winston Churchill once privately warning an American at a time when the United States was trying to chivy Britain into a common European club: "I will not be dealt with as part of a blob!")

In our solicitation of allies, we have had to deal with nations which had the means but not the resolve, to resist the common enemy; those who had the resolve but not the means; and some who might be useful if issue were joined but would make no pledges in advance. Among our partners in our multiplicity of arrangements were degrees of technical experience, degrees of fighting skill, degrees of geographical importance. There were also degrees of trustworthiness: the ironclad pledge of a dictator might make him seem a stronger friend than democracies with hesitant and fickle publics, though he might in fact be a weaker one, unable or unwilling in an emergency to summon up the fighting spirit of his people. We were involved in shadings infinitely more varied than our oratory suggested or our haste to hustle everyone into compacts made allowance for.

And as we got deeper into such perplexities, we discovered the further difficulty of dealing with those adventurers (such as Tito and Nasser) who in a world divided sought to fish in troubled waters. They were big enough so that they could not be ignored, and had a nuisance value which they skillfully exploited. They would

not be our allies: they saw their destinies otherwise. How were
they to be dealt with? I think that, since we could not be sure
of trusting their word, it was foolish of us to press them so much for
pledges and reassurances. The best tactic was to consider their
temperamental bents and their countries' drives and, projecting
these, expect each to follow the logic of his ambitions, no matter
what he might at any moment say.

In Nasser's case we were also confronted by the dream of a
united Arab nation extending from Basra to Morocco, an ambition
that seems to stir in many Arab heads, but with varying degrees
of urgency. No one could blame Arabs for not feeling much
patriotism toward desert lands whose borders had been drawn
by previous occupants, but it still remains to be seen whether
what would unite them outweighs the factors of family, faction, and
sect that divide them. Perhaps a united Arab world does not ultimately have to be against the West, but I believe that any ambitious
Arab politician who wants to hurry the union in his own lifetime
will be.

Among the prejudices we could once afford when we did not
have to be accountable for them was a sentimental approach to
colonialism.

Before the Second World War, most Americans held the simple
view that the world was divided into two camps—the wealthy European powers fattening off the miseries of those they exploited, and
the rest of the world, in which we included ourselves, whose peoples
had either won their independence or were bound to. This attitude
affected the unabashed way we maneuvered to keep the Dutch
from getting back into Indonesia, or the French into Indo-China
after the war. It also explains that curious wartime performance of
Roosevelt's at Teheran, when he made common cause with Stalin
against Churchill, seeing in Russia a vast continental nation like
ourselves which did not lust for territory and might be enlisted
in an idealistic crusade against the British, French and Dutch to
end the injustice of one nation ruling over another. We cheered
Britain's "creative abdication" of India and Pakistan, and could
hardly wait until Britain parted with everything else. We sentimentalized the young patriots of each Asian nation as if they were

George Washingtons, and likened every revolutionary movement to our own. (In this, as some sophisticated Europeans have pointed out, we sometimes got our analogies mixed: we identified ourselves with the natives, who were like our Indians, instead of with the *colons* of Algeria or the white settlers of East Africa who were like our colonial forebears.) Not content to side with rebels, we romanticized them.

For years we took up with native peoples everywhere, and were full of curbstone wisdom about the rights and wrongs of distant contests. Seeing people underfed, raggedly clothed and illiterate, we too easily accepted the argument that their condition resulted from their being held down by others, and did not realize that the colonial powers had, besides extracting wealth from the land, often given these people what little they knew of stability and of those specifically European notions of impartial law, civil service, widespread education and the protection of minorities.

We acquired some strange companions. The Arabs, whom we would befriend, have a rich past, but in contemporary politics their only intelligible message to us sometimes seems to be: "You've got to understand us: we're hysterical." Were it not for our memories of Buchenwald and Belsen, we might think that no enlightened European could be guilty of the mutilations and blood lust of some of our friends in the lands ruled by the scimitar. We have been told much about the evils of foreign exploitations, but when local princes and merchants shared in the new wealth, we saw them spending it on jewels and limousines and concubines, with no feeling whatsoever of communal responsibility for the misery of their fellow Arabs.

And if we sought in every revolutionary struggle a parallel to our own past, we might have said to rebels, "We see your Thomas Paines and Nathan Hales, all right, but where are your Jeffersons, Madisons, Hamiltons and Franklins?" In lightheartedly lending our weight to every back-street plotter against the British or French we did not foresee the day when these rebels would not be content to condemn their foreign rulers but would also want to expel indiscriminately all foreign interests. We did not anticipate that the somnolent, hot and primitive Middle East might rouse itself, like China in the Boxer Rebellion, against everything foreign.

The cold war has since made us more conscious that in any world showdown we are on the side of, not against, Western Europe; together we are a small enough part of the world's peoples that share certain standards of behavior, attitudes of mind, technological skills and cultural heritage. And even if we have not consciously chosen Europe we have been lumped with it: the Russians have skillfully transferred the hatreds of the old colonial masters to us, and we are made to appear not only imperialist like Europe, but the biggest imperialists of them all. Europeans themselves are more and more insistent that we must choose, and that the choice must be in their favor.

Is it all so pat as that? Something deep-seated in Americans does not like the "feel" of colonial rule, and this instinct, I believe, goes deeper than mere historical idiosyncrasy. There is something distasteful about the white man's peremptoriness in the Far East— the cry of "Bearer" in India, of "Boy" in Hong Kong, or the way he claps his hands to summon servants in Japan.

Perhaps, as we have plunged into the world, we have come to understand, as we once did not, why the British, once they brought their wives to the Orient, isolated themselves in compounds. The original impulse was as simple as the need for privacy and assured sanitation; and it was the loneliness of the separation from a distant home that led them to create those clubs which were little tropical islands of transplanted Mayfair. The colonials also brought with them, as has often been said, law and order. But it was an order that sanctioned past misdeeds, and too often left no room for a peaceful alteration of conditions. The conquerors brought with them too their Bibles and works of political thought, whose noble messages proved a powerful subverting force: if these works inspired a respect for Western culture, they also raised the question: Do not the notions of universal brotherhood and equality also apply to subject peoples?

British colonials in particular had a Roman capacity for getting relationships understood; in the terrible expression of the American South, the local people *knew their place*, and so long as there was no hope of changing it, an understanding of status made for an easier living all around. But the peace was the tranquility of the upper hand. It became an increasingly expensive arrangement to sustain, and its cost can often be noted, I think, in colonial faces (particularly the women)—a certain tautness of expression required by privileges insisted upon, and intimacies guarded against. Nor could any system be defended when young men seeking to win the place and esteem in their own land that their talents entitled them to found their futures shut off at a certain level of advancement. We were repelled by this condition, not because the Communists preyed on such able and thwarted young men, but because we thought it wrong.

We have since found, as our oil companies and our armed forces have created colonies around the world, that we too are inclined to fashion little air-conditioned suburbias reminiscent of home, full of Coca-Cola bottles and toilet paper and juke boxes, not so much out of aloofness but out of loneliness. We find our intrusion in the Middle East not quite what we intended. Our techniques are quickly learned but our codes are not, partly because we do not always observe them so carefully when far away. Our goods overwhelm and corrupt. We surround ourselves with a retinue of people who minister to us, and who copy our worst traits but not our best; and though we are not to blame for their conduct, we share the stigma when they are envied or despised in their communities. In making our little islands of sanitation and education, in Saudi Arabia and Venezuela, we may not be as overbearing and "snooty" as the British, or as cruel as the French have sometimes been, but we too often create unintentional ill-will, and must not believe those flatterers who tell us otherwise.

Yet if there are similarities to colonialism in our presence around the world, similarities which can be misrepresented by our enemies, the difference is real, and we cannot leave the Communist interpretation of our motives unchallenged. Most of the awkward fixes we find ourselves in are the result of *not* trying to set up political dominion over other peoples. We seek to influence—but we also defer to—those rulers whose countries we would do business in, or in whose domains we would establish military bases.

Nor is our association with other peoples always unfriendly. If we sometimes find new nations proudly sensitive, we also find a refreshing and contagious enthusiasm in them. We recognize a spirit that was once our own. Not long ago, the young Philippine ambassador to Britain, Leon Guerrero, told a British audience: "To the traveler from Asia, Europe seems old and weary, tired of so much history, tired of making and enduring it, tired of having so many things happen to her. Europe just wants to be left alone. But young Asia has a lot of history before her; she wants to get so many things done that the past left undone. In terms of history it is the Asians who are the new Elizabethans, sure of honor and glory, reckless of the odds, enchanted by self-discovery, feverishly impatient of success."

But in sympathizing with these "feverishly impatient" nations we have often found ourselves responding to precipitate demands for self-government by peoples who live in countries where democratic institutions are unknown, who know how to ape Western constitutions but have not undergone the West's long and piecemeal transition from autocracy to the ballot box; peoples who are largely illiterate and without a stabilizing middle class, and if given independence may be doomed either to a dictatorship or chaos. Independence usually brings an increase in national self-respect but a decrease in administrative efficiency. Then the emergent national hero is discovered to be not as pure as his posters have represented him or as democratic as his own manifestos have proclaimed him.

It must be said of independence, as G. K. Chesterton said of democracy, that there are some things, like blowing one's own nose, that one can do better for himself than he can have done for him. Against this notion, those around the world who, to sustain their own pride of name, family or nation, would deny it to others, are on a losing course, even if what they take pride in may be more desirable than what it is replaced by. In seeming at crucial times in recent years to choose Arabs over French, Egyptians over British, the United States does not say that it prefers these people to Scots, English and French, who are more like ourselves, but only that we recognize the validity of certain claims they make in their own distant lands, however crudely and violently put forward. This may sometime involve seeming retreats on "our side"—but we did not always belong where we were, and could not hope to stay there in the future on those terms. Not all Englishmen and not all Frenchmen misunderstand this position: many of them need no prodding from us in their desire to transfer authority to emerging peoples as fast as it can safely be done, hoping to establish a mutually fruitful future with those they once ruled.

For this is the way the world is moving—borne sometimes by humanitarianism and Christian teaching, sometimes in response to the taunts of the Communists or the uproars of the discontented, but mostly by the currents of the time. We may not wish always to have to take into account the petulance and ignorance of young nations; we may at times not wish to be associated closely with people distasteful to us; but it is not necessary to like what we cannot avoid, and we must ask ourselves what we hope to gain by seeking to oppose these trends. We may hope to defend islands of quality, because our hearts are in it; we cannot hope to defend islands of privilege. In many respects we are faced internationally with the problems inherent in the expansion of the voting franchise in our own country in the 19th Century. "Are *these* people our equals?" some may ask. The answer, I think, has to be—in rights, yes.

If in colonial policy our hearts are in the right place, our heads are not always. Sometimes it seems as if all we propose to the deficient nations of Asia is the possibility of individuals getting rich, which is not the kind of doctrine to inspire a young guerrilla beside a flickering candle, prepared to dedicate himself to improving the living and health of his entire people. Right as we think the economic and political methods of the "American way" are for our own circumstances, responsive as they may be to the gradualism of our development and the homogeneity of our peoples, they are not necessarily universal specifics. We need not try to sell others socialism—but should at least accept, in view of their more straitened circumstances, the need for vaster planning than individual resources can often provide. If we go about it right, we may also hope to show them that enlightened business practices have much to offer, in initiative and originality, against the best of statist planning. Our firms abroad make a profit for themselves, and would not be interested otherwise, but they also add to another nation's "social capital" by employing and educating its people, teaching them skills, seeing to their health, providing them housing, and setting up transportation networks.

What we bring to other peoples should not only be weapons and a scolding message that they do not hate our enemies sufficiently; not millions in economic aid, with political conditions attached and capable of being systematically misrepresented by the Communists; and not Buicks for the few. What we have to offer is our belief in the worth of individuals, our pragmatic gift for imaginative solutions to immense problems, our talents in techniques and organization, our regard for their own independence. I do not think we should constantly beg favors of these new nations to win their participation in uncongenial and phantom alliances. It is a melancholy reality that if we force these people to "choose," they may well choose against us. We need not always flatter and patronize their leaders by supporting them when we think their causes wrongheaded. If they are asking to be accepted as mature nations in the name of justice, we owe support only when we think their claims just. We need not shower aid on them, but should let them ask for it, and let them, as George Kennan has suggested, show us how *they* propose to explain to their people that such aid is benefiting and not subverting them.

I am convinced that the best rampart we can erect in Asia and Africa is a line of stable, self-respecting and self-confident peoples, who are not necessarily our allies but are not our enemies. This will strike some as too modest and half-hearted an ambition, for they judge by dollars spent, noise made, and dubious promises extracted. They are the ones who also complain of the lack of "gratitude" of those we press our money upon, and proclaim our fears to.

10. Dig Shelters or Plant Trees?

Our present relations with other nations of the world have been set primarily by the cold war, but they are complicated—in ways both harmful and helpful—more than is generally recognized, by the fact of the United Nations. So many people applaud the ideal, and mean so well, that it is easy to sentimentalize the U.N. Even from their point of view, it is a dangerous habit.

The United Nations is officially described as the cornerstone of our foreign policy. It cannot be, and we might have liked it better had we from the beginning defined it more realistically. It is not a parliament of mankind but only a grouping of nations who *promise* to behave properly toward one another but who cannot be coerced into doing so. The U.N. is valuable for carrying out noncontroversial world tasks such as narcotics control, postal uniformity and the eradication of yaws. It is useful (though embarrassing when our position is awkward) as a world forum, with a readily assembled audience which can focus swift attention on emergencies. It provides us with a convenient means for retreating from bad positions: we can defer to the wishes of the U.N. when we cannot admit that in reality we are simply backing down.

As an assemblage of nations professing to care about one another's opinions, the U.N. can have a moderating effect on events, though not where we would most like it to, for its censure, as Hungary showed, does not much deter the Communists. The Krem-

lin does take adverse world opinion into account, but not as determined numerically by the votes of governments they seek to
overthrow.

The prestige of the U.N. is often jeopardized by the way its
friends demand of it more than it is empowered to provide. In the
beginning, we and the other big powers insisted on a privileged
position in the U.N., but when the Russians took such frequent
advantage of their veto, we labored to strengthen the role of the
General Assembly, where all nations, big and small, meet as equals.
This strengthening was a useful device during the Korean War,
but fictions have unforeseeable consequences, as when, during the
Suez crisis, Britain and France felt obliged to heed the General
Assembly, though, as the U.N. was originally constituted, they
might have interposed a Security Council veto.

The U.N. General Assembly operates under the fiction that the
world is a checkerboard on which everyone has the same power of
movement and the same limitations. In fact, the world is more like a
chessboard on which there are pawns and queens, unequal in their
rights and capabilities. As one of the giants, we have often looked
foolish, helping Lilliputians to tie bonds about us. We flatter ourselves by amassing huge majorities, sometimes crudely achieved,
on our side, but we must be careful not to exaggerate the virtue of
these mandates, because they may someday be turned against us or
may prevent us from doing what we think needs doing. We owe a
decent respect to the opinion of mankind for all of our actions, but
we must not make the easy mistake of measuring this opinion by the
votes of a body in which a nation as democratic as Canada and one
as feudal as Yemen have the same value; where the voice of European nations is registered by Communist occupiers who sit in their
seats, and where to win majorities we find ourselves pandering to
South American dictatorships who take our money and cynically
vote our line.

At the heart of the idealistic weakness of the United Nations is
the fact that it professes to be a parliament convened to insure
justice in the world, but must base its notion of justice on the *status
quo*. It declares itself against aggression, but, as of the time of its
founding in 1945, had to ratify as legitimate all existing aggressions,

including those in Eastern Europe. The natural impulse of the U.N. is to freeze all problems inside existing borders: being an assemblage of sovereign states, it hesitates to question whether these borders make sense. Many of the world's boundaries—such as those in the Middle East—are the outdated, careless work of distant landlords parceling out fiefs. Insofar as the United Nations prevents nature from taking its own course, such frontiers may be changed only by internal subversion and absorption, which are therefore encouraged.

Whenever a too-strict legality conflicts with man's notion of justice, explosions invariably occur. Throughout history nations have found their borders by taking what they could seize and hold: by this method, dynamic nations waxed great and waned. This was a process full of evils, but can it be stopped by freezing the world at its present borders and arguing that these are the only *just* ones? We are then forced to clothe the weak, and sometimes the undeserving, in the mantle of legality, though we know from the past that weakness can be as much a threat to the peace as strength.

On balance, I believe the United Nations to be useful, and like all growing institutions it may be able to adapt itself to its circumstances. Whenever I stroll its corridors by the East River, I find myself gratified by the sight of so many intermingled nationalities, even though I realize that their voting usually follows the hard lines of national interest. I think we must not be deceived by the weaknesses of the U.N., and must beware of confusing its majorities of convenience and faction with ultimate wisdom and justice.

The heart of our difficulties with the United Nations, of our need to bargain for votes, to traffic in causes we do not believe in, to abstain in matters we really care about—so that the ringing voice of our own beliefs is no longer clearly heard in the world—is, of course, the existence of the cold war.

I have left talking about Russia until last, because if it is discussed first, there seems nothing left to talk about: we are quickly asea in imponderables of such magnitude that everything else seems inconsequential. Our foreign policy is often paralyzed, I believe, by an overconcentration on trying to defeat Russia in every area of the world; it is a paradox of the present situation that we may best fight the cold war by not seeming to be forever waging it. When we make aid dependent on cold-war conditions which are less real to another nation than they are to us, that nation feels it is doing us a favor in taking our money and wants to bargain for more. When we extract too many pledges from it we often diminish what we should in fact encourage—a nation's sense of its own independence. When we choose up allies, we often get the weaker ones and inherit their disabilities, needlessly abandoning the more prideful (and more important) just because their attitudes are more prickly. To say that our foreign policy should be administered less in cold-war terms requires, in my view, not just a shift in propaganda tactics but a searching re-examination of its entire emphasis. The maximum danger of involvement in a war in, say, the Middle East will come when the Russians have first achieved a *political* success in putting us on the wrong side of events there.

We have too often been put in the position of defending privilege, as if that were what capitalism is about, and too often made to defend racial injustice on the grounds of standing by our allies. We must offer the oppressed somewhere else to go but Moscow. If our commitments require us to defend the autocratic rulers of backward nations, we should at all times be *seen* encouraging the people of those nations to come forward. In our alliances with European powers, unless mutual self-interest is the cement of our alliance there is no alliance: we need not be tongue-tied by the need to "stick by our friends" when we think their policies are wrong. Our purposes are in fact not always identical, and the pretense that they are involves us in needless hypocrisy. All foreign secretaries naturally operate in the circumstances they must work with, and if they are aware that our support of their more dubious measures is not so automatic, that fact will modify their decisions. Eventually, I think, the success of our foreign policy depends not on little tactical triumphs of the moment but on our sponsoring everywhere what we believe in—those ideals which were for so long our appeal to the world. What we must do may sometimes seem to run contrary to the superficial demands of the cold war, but only in honoring our own convictions can we in the long run operate most effectively against the Soviet Union—not, as we often seem to operate, by erecting ineffectual pacts, promising to liberate peoples we cannot liberate, boasting of our riches, or lecturing the world on our moral superiority when others can plainly see our moral failures.

There is a familiar Confucian saying:

> If your plan is for one year, plant rice;
> For ten years, plant trees;
> For a hundred years, educate men.

We sometimes act as if, in this era of Communist threat, we can only plant rice and dig shelters. Our continual preoccupation with ultimate weapons has led us into deep-end speculations which presume as a likelihood what is only one possibility, thereby dulling our minds to the wide range of other avenues open to us. We hear ourselves urged to match Russia's lopsided military and scientific development, though surely we can still take wider views than Russia's of what kind of society we would like ours to be. We may be the first generation compelled to live under the threat of total destruction, but we must live as if other arrangements are more likely, since the earth's survival is of benefit to our enemy as well as to ourselves. We must not be so busy listening to the final bell that we do not hear the sounds either of termites nibbling or of opportunity knocking.

We have all been forced, unwillingly, into educating ourselves about Communism in these past few years. In my own job as a foreign news editor, I have been compelled to read much dreary dogma and interminable Marxist speeches, and constantly to analyze murky motives. I do not claim to be an expert, but only to have suffered much. There is much help to be had in this labor. So many Russian specialists in government agencies and in American universities now pore over every scrap of Communist material that an amazing number of facts and interpretations are readily available to an editor. But the most candid of these specialists will admit that the area he does not know about is of greater importance than the area he does know about. The combination of secrecy and chance in the Kremlin's behavior makes forecasting Russian policy a risky practice, but ignorance does not excuse us from making the effort. Even in my own news job, assessing each week's reports of which commissar is in the ascendancy and who is riding for a fall, or in trying to judge whether a threat issued by the Kremlin should be taken as real or as propaganda, one must construct a hypothesis about the Russians by which to measure the importance of passing events. Perhaps I should try to define mine.

I have no trouble in believing that the Kremlin leaders would like to do us in, if only they safely could—but it is only after one goes beyond this simple proposition that the subject becomes interesting. I think the Russian leaders are alert, unceasingly ruthless men, but also cautious. As for Communism itself, it has in effect two faces: that of its propaganda appeal and that of its own concealed reality, and it is useful to separate the qualities that belong to each. Communism's humanitarian pose is directed toward backward peoples; the other face, that of its power reality, is what is usually directed toward us. Communism alternates these appeals, at one point saying that Communism will in time prevail because it is right; at other times, it demands a simple tribute to its strength. But increasingly, I think, it stresses the fact of its strength. Let us look at the power reality first.

How Communist is present-day Russia? Those of our specialists who have invested much time in the thankless study of Marx and Lenin have a natural tendency to find all the answers to the Russian enigma in the ancient sacred books. To be sure, that peculiarly turgid style, inherited from the German, of laying down judgments as if they were blocks of granite and immutable laws of history persists. The concentration on dogma in a dictatorship is perhaps not so footless an exercise as an American is apt to consider it. Dogma is designed to serve at once as history, religion and news, with a loudspeaker pervasiveness that is truly an opiate of the people. Those long hours spent in factory indoctrinations, "agit prop" meetings and endless broadcasts of dogma at dictation speed—how lucky we are to be free of them. But they are a malevolent modern improvement on the controls of ancient tyranny, more efficient than the old Persian apparatus of King's Eyes and Ears. Much of the churning about what goes on is designed to accommodate rigid doctrine to changing practice. Practice without theory is "doomed to wander in the dark," Khrushchev has said, and this criticism sometimes applies to our own practice. But Khrushchev the pragmatist has all along been even more insistent that "theory must be tied to life. Theory, my friends, is gray, but the eternal tree of life is evergreen."

Each abandonment of unworkable Communist doctrine must be justified as paradise postponed, and a new coherence found that makes the deviation seem the true course. Communists honor the old faith every Sunday and twice on May Day, but, as I heard a British conservative, Lord Coleraine, remark after a trip to Russia, the church militant seems increasingly to be becoming the Established Church. Anyone who can rationalize the Byzantine splendor enjoyed by the Soviet elite with the barren demands of Marxist dogma can rationalize anything. Stalin's successors give the impression of wishing to be the masters of doctrine, though their actions often prove them the slaves of it. Doctrine saturates the thinking of Communist leaders because it is the only history and economics they have had, and accounts for so many of their misconceptions about the rest of the world. More than the others, Khrushchev, that shrewd and audacious plug-ugly, has given the appearance of a man willing to try any scheme and, if it works, to send it around to the Communist theologians to have it reconciled with dogma. Looking at the photographs of the well-fed technocrats and spent revolutionaries who rule Russia today, one senses that preservation in power, not perseverance in dogma, is their guiding motive.

But as Soviet Communism becomes less pure in theory, it may, I think, become more effective in fact. Marxism may not work, but modern tyranny does. Hitler and Stalin proved that a 20th-century police state can successfully render ineffectual any attempt of its own people to organize against it. Stalin's successors in Russia, and their partners in China, may have the sense to be less irrational in coercion of their peoples, but must still rule by force. Our propaganda argues that because a system is evil it will not last, but I do not believe the fall of Hitler and Tojo proof of this reassuring belief but only evidence that these particular dictators made war against too formidable a combination of powers. If one's only test of society is its deployable strength in the pursuit of national ambitions, then it must be admitted that dictatorships have advantages as well as disadvantages when set against democracies.

In any measurement of the two systems, we have the benefit of a century's head start. The Soviet rate of growth has been faster than that of the United States since 1950, but since we had already reached a high plateau of production, comparative statistics are misleading. We are at times, however, too inclined to take comfort from our leads in steel production and electric power, forgetting how much of our steel is diverted to automobiles and other multicolored pleasures. We exult in the greater creativity of the free man (which is a fact) but may forget that power dams and nuclear stations are morally neutral and do not judge the philosophies of those who use them. Until we are jolted out of our complacency by something like the orbiting of the Sputnik, we forget the advantage a dictatorship can have in focusing its resources on what it most wants to achieve. The Russians have run up their gains by subordinating other goals, by producing consumer goods of less variety and lower quality, by a high investment rate in industry, and by a willingness to tolerate lowered consumption and, if need be, famine. The wastage in the Russian system is immense—from the deadening blight of propaganda, the forbidden subjects, the loyalty proofs and required dishonesties. But we too—judged solely by the cold statistics of national productivity—have a vast wastage in our system, in the fundamental *unseriousness* of what our resources are put to, a wasting not only of materials but of men. We burn out talent on frivolities.

But if Russia is a more durable and respectable competitor than we once considered it to be, I think we need be in no doubt about which system is preferable to live under. Outside their borders the Communists have spread the conviction that they have a creed which offers far more than ours does, a creed that appears dynamic and is proclaimed to be irresistible. Communists talk of welcoming a peaceful trial of strength of our two systems, while we sometimes sound as if we fear one; yet surely we have less reason to dread open comparison. After a ruthless thirty-year tryout of their agricultural theories, the Russians have had to admit that their farm output is lower than it was in Czarist times. Poverty, discontent and shortages dog both Russia and China. When people speak of the superior appeal of the Communist creed, they cannot mean its appeal to those who live under it. It is not our side that must rule by terror, purge, forced labor, work camp, relentless propaganda and suppression. We alone have the strength (and the misfortune) to exhibit our weaknesses. We suffer by comparison, not with the Communist reality, but with Communism's specious promise.

Our ideological war is therefore not against those living under Communism, who do not revel in it, but for the favor of those who are dissatisfied with their own lot and, not having lived under Communism, credulously believe that Communism would serve them better. They do not want to be told which system produces more electric dishwashers; in fact, there is a point in our bragging about our material riches where we lose our listeners because our circumstances seem to have no relevance to theirs; they want to know which system can help them industrialize faster, and the Communists have made their experience seem more useful than ours.

All over the world today peoples are making the exciting and dangerous discovery that they have in their hands the means to attempt vast ambitions—means that other nations, in first developing, learned to mitigate with counterbalancing restraints. Communism did not create this problem but only exacerbates it and increases the urgency of finding solutions. We now have a foreign policy which counters the Communist but does not address itself to these specific situations on their own merits. Our propaganda makes a certain amount of sense when it says "Fear the Other," but it is less instructive when it says, "Follow us," for we are not sure where we are heading. We ask other nations to aid us in our purposes but do not think in terms of theirs.

It is not within our powers to control the thermostat of the cold war, though we can sometimes moderate the heat or insist on recognizing the chill. Diplomatically, we are involved in a poker game in which we, as a democracy, must play with all our cards face up, while the Russians do not have to show their hole cards. But we must put up with this condition and might as well accept it. We waver from contentment to despair: if only we could achieve a steady concern that was confident of the end but did not lapse into lackadaisical optimism, that besetting sin of democracy!

If Russia has the robust dynamism of a new nation flexing its muscles, there is no reason, I think, for us to believe that any pseudo-scientific law of history can make tyranny perpetual. If a Russian Marxist dictatorship "works" as a police state, it has not yet shown itself capable of meeting the needs of its people. Its internal struggle for power is not ended. Its new technical elite, knowing itself needed, will not long be satisfied with privations and coercions and will thus force moderations in the system, which the Communists will reluctantly have to agree to. It is sometimes argued that one faction or another in the Kremlin is more moderate than the other (and should even be encouraged) but I think that this kind of journalistic speculation is largely waste effort: the disagreements are primarily over tactics, and all of the leaders on the top rung have had to be ruthless to get where they are and are ready to be ruthless again. A sterile way of saying this is that leopards do not change their spots, but this irritating profundity ignores the fact that we are not talking about leopards, and that even animals are capable of craftily adjusting to their circumstances. I think that we should not look for any softening or change of heart in the Kremlin leadership, but should recognize that any liberalization that goes on in Russia is the product of tensions in the system which can be appeased or resisted but not denied. And I think a continuing scuffle for power between men who are pressed into rivalry but also locked in common complicity can safely be predicted, for Communism has no more solved the problem of succession than has any other autocracy.

If Americans seem to lurch from an easy optimism about Russia to a panic that does not weigh all these weaknesses in the other side, I think our journalism is partly at fault. It is trapped by a commendable desire to print only what it knows to be true, and is therefore condemned to printing only half the truth, and making this half seem to be the whole truth. I have sometimes wished that a newspaper might preface its coverage in this way:

The news we bring you today is a melancholy collection—murders, frauds and accidents; bickerings between politicians who exaggerate our differences; racial tensions that dishonor the Christianity we profess; failures in productivity and quarrels among allies. From the half of the world that is Communist we are able to bring you only their own boasts of strength. We do not know what fights are going on there that might be far more deadly than any disagreements among allies. We print a photograph of one Negro cuffed to the ground in Alabama but do not know how many people were herded off to "voluntary labor" in Tientsin last night. While our reporters bunched themselves around a German courtroom to see one G.I. tried, we do not know what miscarriage of justice went unmarked in Bokhara or what betrayal of the human spirit took place this morning in Smolensk. If we could bring you the rest of today's news, we might not think less of our own failings, but at least we would not think them unique. And we might find tyranny more evil than we knew, and less sure of itself than we thought. So forgive us our omissions, but keep them in mind, for we have done only half our job.

And if we had that other half of the news before us each day, we might find ourselves reassured by the fumbling and inefficiency of Communism, the immensity of catching up it has before it if it is ever to provide even a minimum standard of living for its people. We are so prone to think of the Russian leaders as chess players, men so subtle that everything they do, even that which works against them, is done by design. The fact is that they are skilled at exploiting what they are stuck with, which is quite another thing. Since they seek to expand and we only to hold, they may have an air of superior dynamism, but the history of the past twelve years is full of their mistakes, as well as of ours.

In the last days of his career, Bismarck told the Reichstag: "At the end of a life devoted wholly to public affairs, and with all the experience that I now possess, I think I can see one year ahead of me. The rest is outside my competence." In similar fashion, we cannot know which of many turnings Soviet Russia may take in the future; but surely it is wrong to act as if there were only one likelihood— that of our mutual annihilation. Let us continue to plant trees and educate men.

11. Home Truths from Abroad

> "From the whole business one can derive this moral, that the man who mingles with a court compromises his happiness, if he is happy, and, in any event, makes his future depend on the intrigues of a chambermaid. On the other hand, in America, in the Republic, one has to spend the whole weary day paying serious court to the shopkeepers in the street, and must become as stupid as they are; and there, one has no Opera."
>
> —STENDHAL

Every American who travels in Europe has one experience sooner or later which, depending on how many Europeans he comes to know, may be repeated over and over. I well remember the first time I ceased to be affected by it.

We were sitting in that spectacular setting, the Piazza San Marco in Venice. That beautiful square, large but not overwhelming, settled in style but not too symmetrical, surrounded by shops and sidewalk cafés but dominated by that gaudy Byzantine jewel, St. Mark's, was at its twilight best. The pesky pigeons had scattered, the night was mild, the street lamps were lit. From a distant café bandstand came pleasing and uninsistent cocktail music. Waiters in white jackets moved from table to crowded table, bringing apéritifs. The count, with whom my wife and I were seated, saw in our eyes that we were taking in the scene with delight and contentment and

138

thereupon launched into what I have come to call "The European Speech."

You see, he said, how everyone is enjoying himself; how relaxed they all are. Rich or poor, they know how to make the most of life. Their wants are simple—fresh air, a little *pasta*, a little wine.

His hand extended toward the campanile and the cathedral. How beautiful it all is, he said, how restful. We move among beautiful things, and have time to enjoy art and music. Then began the familiar attack. *This* is life, you see. But in America, you are always hurrying and scurrying. Where are you going? Why do you bustle so?

I had heard the speech before, with local variations, and had each time cheerfully accepted the implied national reproach: our hurry *was* mad, our newness was often slapdash, and here was great beauty. But this time, though I nodded again—it was too languorous an evening to dispute about anything—my mind began considering what had always disturbed me about The European Speech. And it occurred to me that two things did not go together: the leisureliness of the café life and the building of St. Mark's Cathedral. The cathedral and the square around it had been built by ambitious and bustling men, not musing café sitters; vulgar, bourgeois merchants and shippers had lavished their fortunes and jostled for place in building those ornamental *palazzi* on the Grand Canal. There might be much to be said for sitting at sidewalk tables (and there is), but it was not the spirit that built high naves, conceived colonnaded mansions or even financed them. The count beside me, whose own living was quite modest, was in effect having a free ride on a past European culture, just as (I reflected) I, who don't know the difference between a generator and a dynamo, get a free ride on the world-wide assumption that all Americans are mechanically gifted, and geniuses at tinkering and fixing.

Contemporary Europeans have largely inherited—not built—the glories of the Continent. They live in, and often indifferently keep up, their old houses, making patchwork improvements, installing running water and sometimes plumbing. They rarely build new homes, and those that are built are often of inferior workmanship and design. We may be grateful for their delight in settled ways, and their pride in living where generations before them have lived; grateful that they treasure and preserve the old, which is often downright uncomfortable to live in, though it may delight the eye. But they do not live in deliberate discomfort to be custodians of culture: in many cases, they do not have the money for, or choose not to spend it on, improving their houses. The situation is changing: the postwar improvement in European economies (begun under the Marshall Plan) has made it possible for millions of Europeans to have gadgets in the kitchen and motor cars out front; they are not so much philosophically opposed to these modern amenities as delayed in enjoying them. One of the indictments that genteel Europeans make against America is precisely this invasion of American objects, or their European adaptations—the Coca-colonization of the Continent, the arrival of the motor-car mass market, the spread of electric coffee grinders, the questionable gift of the loud-speaker. The countryside was prettier when the poor had only draft animals and not motorscooters or buglike automobiles.

The splendors of Europe are largely survivals. If one levels off what has been done in America by his own generation, and sets against it what has been achieved in the same period in Europe— in architecture, art, music or theater—I do not think that Americans need be uncomfortable with the comparison. If much of our culture seems harsh when set against the old, the new that is not just persistence in tradition always seems so. There is an *élan* in America's music, its architecture, its art, which, as it develops, may in time be preferred to that which is comfortable but unoriginal in European culture: ours may not match the best of the old, but it outdoes the derivative. John Maynard Keynes once tried to establish a parallel between economic high points and artistic peaks—to show that not only did wealth provide portrait commissions for Dutch and Flemish masters and patrons for architects of great country homes and town houses, but that something in the air during periods of expanding economies and speculative explorations, in the Renaissance, in Elizabethan England, in the high point of Spanish glory, stirred artists as it stirred merchant-adventurers. America may yet provide another example for this thesis.

Yet if Europe is primarily a museum, its contemporary art lively and still dominant but uncertain in direction and narrow in ambition, its musical genius perhaps more conspicuous in performance than in creation, its architecture more distinguished in adaptation

than in originality, I no longer, as I once did, depreciate the mere
custodianship of culture. Taste may be of a lower order than creation, but it is an essential preservative of creation. It must be active
—for Shakespeare, Molière and Beethoven live by performance—
and it must be discriminating, in appreciating which paintings,
which murals, which houses deserve saving. It may be easy to mock
those who have taste but not talent, but taste is a talent too, and
our world would be poorer without Europe's past and Europe's
present jealous desire to preserve it.

All of this now goes through my head when I hear The European
Speech. And when I hear that patronizing appendix to it, that
Europe is Greece and America Rome—that wise old Europe, with
its serene and moderate wisdom, must now guide that powerful but
clumsy adolescent, strong but insensitive America—I am prepared
to accept the comparison if it is made exact: that is, if Europe is
really ready to compare itself with the fallen Greece of slaves and
schoolteachers in the era of Roman greatness, rather than with the
creative earlier Greece of Pericles. On these terms, I am not sure
that Europe would welcome the comparison, and we need not insist
upon it.

It has been my lot, as a foreign news editor, to see many places,
and my luck to see them—even in brief stays—with an intensity of
experience, thanks to the efficient forehandedness of foreign correspondents who were on the scene and made plans, handled
arrangements, scheduled interviews with rulers and ranking ministers. In this day of roaming Americans, many have seen much more
of the world than I have, but I count myself fortunate to have seen
so much, and have often enjoyed a freedom from the harassments
of travel that is in marked contrast to my first poor and hungry
honeymoon trip to Europe at 21, when my wife and I wandered the
length of Europe from Sweden to Greece for six months on $750
each. On that first trip we trudged down long city streets carrying
our own luggage to save money; we ate in grubby back-street cafés;
we slept on the cold, third-class benches of milk trains to save hotel
bills. We traveled deck passage down the wintry Adriatic, bounced
around among the only other tenants of the deck—sheep, goats and
cattle, who were no better sailors than I. We lived on one hot meal

a day and were indifferent about how we looked.

Where once we knew only *pensions* and youth hostels, we have since, like many Americans, come to know the grand bars and balconies overlooking the Bosporus, the Grand Canal or Cap d'Antibes, and have often spent on one lavish meal as much as we then spent in a week. Though I would not trade the memory of the one for the comfort of the other, I confess to enjoying the absence of a nagging parsimony, and prefer good food and service to bad.

Nowadays if I should long to see Petra, "rose-red city, half as old as time," a correspondent and friend would be there to charter the one-car Toonerville Trolley to cross the Jordanian desert on the creaky tracks that T. E. Lawrence's Arab rebels used to dynamite, to rent the automobile and then the horses that would get us to those deserted ancient temples carved in radiant rock which survive in a spectacular canyon setting like the American West. There have been occasions in such out-of-the-way places when, enjoying this more-privileged latter-day state, I have longed for the simplicities of the earlier anonymity. Announced as the foreign news editor of an important American magazine, I have been mistaken for a distinguished person and forced to act the part, been conducted through schoolhouses like Richard Nixon himself, nodding approval at the handicrafts of shaven-headed little boys, asking to see the kitchen, and trying to remember appropriate phrases of gratitude and courtesy. It would never do to smile and confess the fraud, but I am not the kind to review troops impressively, even troops of schoolboys.

Making trips to new places as an editor is fascinating to the man, if disturbing to his preconceptions and sometimes embarrassing to his posture as an expert: one's firm grip on correct opinions slackens when he finds himself ogling the strange and exotic; at such times he is an innocent, a sight-seer, a relaxed man, the First Tourist; then suddenly he must accompany the American ambassador to the palace and, putting on the mask again, confront the prime minister with questions about his country that will not reveal either frivolity or ignorance. One longs to ask about what he has seen in the streets, or about the ways of rural maidens, but asks instead the proper questions about crops and armed forces.

Such visits unsettle the coherent attitude one gets about a country by merely reading about it: squalor can be accepted comfortably as a statistic but is a shock in the reality; and the Middle Eastern parliament that seemed so normally democratic in a news dispatch becomes, when one actually sees it in operation, a restless congeries of pashas and landlords going through the borrowed rituals of democracy as required by the times. One returns from such trips to pursue new curiosities of reading and, if not made particularly wiser, at least becomes vividly aware of a jarring contrast between the United States and the rest of the world. This jarring contrast always strikes me more forcibly than what flows from it, that anti-American sentiment that so many journalists love to expatiate upon. To me a certain amount of anti-Americanism abroad is inevitable.

If we as a nation are not liked as much as we once were, the fault lies only partly in our own manner. We are no longer the nation that asked nothing of the world, and provided a haven; we have become an intervening power, and our motives are subject to the subtle misrepresentations of our enemies; we have become the richest nation in the world, prey to the envy and jealousy of others, who sometimes mistakenly assume that we must have gotten that rich at everybody else's expense and should give it back. We have displaced as great powers those who find it hard to accept the ascendancy, not of a conqueror but of an ally, and sometimes feel that their demotion came because they exhausted their lifeblood and their soil while we only spent our money. If we must be mindful of others, and have much to learn in international behavior, I doubt that such self-improvement would in itself end anti-Americanism, for much of its vigor comes not from what is amiss in us but from what is awry in the circumstances of others.

It is easy to see why we should appear to be a Rome, and why others should want to wear ancient Greece as a cloak to cover their fallen state. I find perfectly understandable the classic British Tory resentment of America; but I find harder to justify the tiresome anti-Americanism of left-wing British Socialism, inflicted on a working people who are so hospitable, individually, to Americans. It seems to stem from a Marxist habit of mind, jealously clung to as a sentiment the more it proves unfeasible as a guide. The adherents of this mythology choose to regard America as a citadel of enemy capitalism rather than as a place where working people have emerged from an inferiority of status, and enjoy conditions of work and a fortunate living standard that should be a goal for left-wing British union leaders were it not that our graduated differentiation of income would blur their sterile debating arguments.

But much of what is called anti-Americanism is in reality, I think, a European resistance to Europe's own changing world, to a spreading of goods and liberties which, on an overcrowded continent, results in a congestion of highways, resorts and shops. Symbols of differentiation (to use the jargon phrase) lose their value, and the new mass market of objects to buy—cheap, efficient, stamped out— shows an American influence. America is thus not so much thanked for multiplying conveniences as damned for debasing standards.

The many varieties of anti-Americanism are not to be erased by gigantic publicity campaigns. Nor do I think that we can lessen anti-Americanism by being overly touchy about it, for this is to give the attitude a value that gratifies it.

But such manifestations of feeling do not fascinate me so much as the actual differences between ours and other cultures. Before we all go the same way, made more and more alike by the increased accessibility of each other's products, travel gives us the chance to examine other cultures to see what in them we lack and might profit by having. This opportunity decreases every year, for the spreading amenities of travel, having a deadly international similarity, take away the individuality of what is to be seen. Travel compels us to make comparisons, and we can learn alike from those nations whose past may be an inspiration or whose present may be a portent. And in older nations, the traveler can see two levels side by side—that which is and that which was—and can thus travel in time as well as space, in history as well as in geography. In particular, I always find myself, when in England and France, aware of much to envy, not in their politics but in some ingredients of their living. These are qualities contrary to our own impulses, and I enjoy them, knowing that they will never be our ways.

Historians recognize a feeling that they call "historical homesickness." Gibbon concluded that "if a man were called to fix the period in the history of the world, during which the condition of the human race was most happy and prosperous, he would, without hesitation, name that which elapsed from the death of Domitian to the accession of Commodus." Yet Tacitus, who lived in the earlier years of that Roman era, was forever sighing for the happier days of the Republic; and the aged Talleyrand, looking back, was to say of Gibbon's own day that no one who had not lived through it could know what contentment was.

Those of us Americans who find much that attracts in England are perhaps drawn to it by historical homesickness. We are drawn by qualities that survive there. We find ourselves forever being impatiently told by Englishmen that what we celebrate in their country, or what we deplore there, is really quite changed now; but we persist in seeing more evidences of its existence than they will allow.

We all carry in our minds a vision of old England—the England of pomp and circumstance and panoply; of roast pig, and jovial conversation over the port and beside the fire; of riding to hounds, and curtsies at gala balls; of a land of humble servants and God-fearing squires. It is a world that exists nowhere but in the mind, put there by Merrie England Christmas cards, whisky ads and 19th Century novels of manners, for it leaves out all the crudities—the England of Fielding, debtors' prisons and hangings at Tyburn gallows; the raucous, loutish Gin Lane of Hogarth; the venal Parliaments and the gross royal behavior of the first Georges; the child labor and dark factories of Dickens' England. Yet if it never existed in pure form, free of dross, there is a recognizable English way of life—mostly upper-class—that survives to this day in Robert Adam's ceilings, in country estates now open to the public for half a crown, and in the character and deportment of a certain kind of Englishman. Its best is high indeed, and excites our envy.

I do not think that we can match the best products of English disciplining and schooling: those Englishmen with an accumulation of knowledge, range of taste, probity of character, and such ease of manner that they give the impression of having already lived once, with no need to learn more of dress or behavior. If sometimes lanky and frail in appearance, they have usually in wartime proved their stamina, courage and resourcefulness. They speak well. Americans often feel an uneasiness in the presence of this superior articulateness, for as a nation we have convinced ourselves that skill in speech and writing probably goes with an inability to *do,* and that being fumbling and inexact of speech is a sign of sincerity. On their own terms and in their own territory, members of the English educated class can be awesomely impressive, and there are times when an American must admit that his own slovenliness of speech, his carelessness of manner and his clumsiness of behavior justifies their low opinion of him; this is most galling when one is compelled to concede that they themselves do possess the qualities one lacks. Fortunately for our self-respect, we can sometimes find them deficient in the qualities they pride themselves on, or else so given over to them that they are deficient in other qualities which we consider vital. And if we are ready to pay spontaneous homage to the best kind of educated and well-rounded Englishman, we demur as soon as he adds snobbery to his other attributes: then, I feel, we would rather contrarily be plain, awkward, naive and crude.

But since it is snobbery's nature to feel self-sufficient, an American visitor does not find himself often in snob's company; instead, in London, he is frequently gratified by the cordiality of the welcome to a stranger, and suspects that it may be easier for an Englishman to meet an American for the first time than an Englishman, because with the American he does not have to go through the tiresome status game of pegging one another's place. An American may even hear a lively curiosity expressed about his own country, but it is not so much our foreign policy that attracts as our musicals. Something fresh, energetic and slightly larger than life in America is what recommends it to those circles of Mayfair that are as knowledgeable about New York as St. Tropez or Portofino, among those international samplers of culture who take their ideas of art, food and fashion from France and Italy, their belles-lettres and tailoring from London, and their pleasure where they find it.

What impresses Americans most about a certain kind of London living is the civilized diversity and range of interests united in one company: a politician may talk well on wine, ballet or Persia, and be knowledgeable as well on more humdrum matters which he will not inflict on his companions. In such company, allusions are quick and nuances often lost on an American who speaks another language (the nuances of his own origins being of no use to him here). It takes a while for the American to discover that some of the topics have been gone over before, and that the darting introduction of new subjects sometimes involves no more originality than that of the American cocktail-hour magpie trading in borrowed straws ("Did you see that cartoon in *The New Yorker* where. . . ?" "Yes, wasn't it wonderful?"). And after long immersion in brittle smartness an American comes to wonder whether an early British preoccupation with the debating skills of wit and thrust does not produce a preference for effect over sense.

In the "Westminster square mile" of London, in the domain of Parliament, an American discovers a candor quite unlike anything he has known. In groups which meet Yeats' standard of "a society where a man is heard by the right ears but never overheard by the wrong," a journalist accustomed to American off-the-record confidences can still be surprised, as I always am, by the gap in England between what is solemnly proclaimed and what is privately said. It is not valuable information that is thus confided, but an intensity of private feelings: an American politician or cabinet secretary would not be so free to near-strangers with the violence of his prejudices about his colleagues. Perhaps this intensity of feeling results from the fact that members of Parliament have often known each other from childhood—I have heard one member in the House speak of having been caned as a boy by another M.P. two rows down—and know each other too well. I suspect that the crowding for place in a tight society and in a narrowing pyramid is what makes for a style of conversation so edged in malice (I have sometimes heard an American congressman dismiss a colleague with a coarser expression than an M.P. would use, but he would never take the trouble to refine so woundingly what offends him in the other person). I sometimes leave such company unsure whether I am more exhilarated by its cleverness or dismayed by its spite.

"When I was young," said Yeats' father, "the definition of a gentleman was a man not wholly occupied in getting on." In novels, biographies and autobiographies without end we have all read how English gentlemen were created: how cold baths and stern instruction qualified them for later privilege; how they were sent from home at an early age to lonely schools and hated the ragging of the elder boys; how they were taught a superiority to servants but also a paternal responsibility for them, for the servant class was pardonably unintelligent; we have read of kind nannies and aloof parents, and have seen how sons of good English families were bred for character and schooled in civilized rather than practical knowledge. "But did you ever notice," an M.P. once said to me, "how many men in the House of Commons stutter?" If the British system produces a fine top level of character, it exacts a heavy toll on those of whom too much was demanded.

In England, L. B. Namier has said, history is made by families. And it was a member of one of the most prideful families, Lord Robert Cecil, who observed: "It is better to have second class brains than second-class character." One knows what Lord Robert meant, yet when character is taken to mean—as it so often is in England— a certain kind of origin, then one finds second-class brains of proper "character" taking up most of the best places. Room must be found for those who got the discipline but did not measure up, whose inner inadequacy, combined with a training in outward assurance results not in authority but only in haughtiness. Clubmanship in London sometimes strikes me as a form of self-defense against the more talented, who, feeling unfairly excluded, can be counted on to disqualify themselves further by seeming too pushy.

The trouble with England, it seems to one American who finds so much to admire in it, is that there are too many reserved seats. And this applies all the way up to the gallery. A member of the upper class may feel no need to assert his superior status, because his symbols are everywhere with him—his speech, his dress, his manner. But it is in the middle range—among those less sure of status and the more insistent on it—that Americans find themselves most put off by the labyrinthian gradations in Britain ("I don't like middle classes," Melbourne told Queen Victoria. "The higher and lower classes, there's some good in them, but the middle classes are all affectation and conceit and pretense and concealment.") To an American, the gradations seem to descend not only from earl to baron to knight, but on down to chief clerk, clerk, doorman and char. Even the institution of royalty seems largely designed to petrify status and exalt distinctions. "What differentiates man from the beasts that perish," Sir Arnold Lunn has written, "is his respect for the conventions of a hierarchial society." It is also what most differentiates American from Briton.

To most Englishmen I have met, all of this seems a stale argument: they say that the shared humanity of the blitz and the Labor revolution changed all that, and they may be correct when they say that some things that assault the American eye and ear are only the surviving artifacts of an old battle. After all, millions of Britons live lives sufficient to themselves, not much concerned with their place in the pecking order, reading of the peccadilloes of the well-born without envy, and finding in the royal family not only a symbol to respect but an absorbing soap opera to follow (complete with spicy uncle, fun-loving sister, earnest mother). And if Englishmen otherwise qualified in business are still prevented from advancement there by their giveaway accents, I am aware of the blunt self-confidence of a new generation of English businessmen, scornful of class (to an Englishman they may seem very American; to Americans, some of them have a repellent brassiness). There are other signs of change. The recent journalistic agitation against the Establishment (by which was meant some sort of interlocking directorship of palace, Anglican bishops, lords, dons and the higher civil servants) was a hoot and cry against old ways. Who takes the House of Lords seriously any more? Not even half the membership, which rarely shows up. Similarly, the Royal Family has felt it better to appear near and democratic than remote and mystical. It is also argued that the postwar playwriting rage of England's "angry young men" is evidence that an intelligentsia—a new group set apart by education from society—has at last emerged in England, similar to the "superfluous man" of Russian literature. Where formerly educated people in England were by definition members of the ruling class, the postwar revolution, as David Marquand, a young Oxonian scholar, says has "given university degrees to people who have cut themselves off from home and family in order to get them, who are obliged when they return home during the vacations to talk a different language from the language they talk at university. Such people are banished from the class from which they come. But they cannot just accept bourgeois decorum, patiently acquire the table manners and speaking voices of the languid young smarties they meet for the first time opposite them at the Oxbridge* dinner table. To do so would be treachery to their own backgrounds and

---

* English shorthand for Oxford and Cambridge.

their own earlier selves. More: it would be treachery to their own values—for what the upper classes so often fail to realize about the lower classes is that they're glad they're not the upper classes." There sounds the rebel note!

The "news" about England, we are thus told, is not the thrust of individuals to rise above their origins into the ranks of the privileged (that has always gone on) but the self-confident assertion of the generality of the people that they are what England is about, their sturdy conviction that the old way not only must go but is going. In this loosening of the moorings of English society, there are many who fear a drift toward an American-style egalitarianism, but despite all the British alarm over the spreading Americanization by television, films, gadgetry and advertising, I think Britain will turn into something quite different from us. It is not so much heading toward us as being driven in the same currents we are.

An American in England can find himself perversely enlisting in societies for the preservation of the old ways, anxious to save what was distinctive and English against the spreading international lowest common denominator. But though Americans instinctively sympathized with socialism's urge to end the unfair discriminations of the old society, I am frequently disturbed by a get-even vengefulness in Labor's leveling attitude, which may be an unavoidable blight from a past that has no equivalent in our country.

If in some ways British life drifts reluctantly toward ours, I think we might wish ours to move toward values which are still esteemed in Britain and too little celebrated in the United States. If we sympathize with those Britons who wish an end to the unfair dominance of privilege, we might recognize that something valuable in the standards and traditions of an elite is often missing from our own way of life. Privilege was often selfishness secured, but at its best felt an urge to uphold character and to acknowledge responsibility. The democracy of equals has not yet learned how to prize quality and distinguish merit.

An American enters the settled cosmos of Europe like some wild comet out of orbit. The contrast in standards of living enables him to enter it at a higher level than at home. His money gives him entrance to public places where others present have, along with their money, accepted similarities of experience: these Europeans may not be wiser, nor half so generous, nor one quarter so well-intentioned, but they are accustomed to habits of ordering, habits of eating and habits of gathering that are alien to us; be an American ever so discreet, so quiet of necktie or so black of dress, he is still an intruder.

He is usually on vacation in Europe, and dressed accordingly. He is prepared to spend a little more since he may never pass this way again. He would never think of wasting his money by eating at one of the two or three most expensive restaurants in New York, but wants to eat in the best place in Paris. He may feel a little uncertain in doing so, and is apt to guarantee his escape by leaving too much of a tip, and this is all the more galling to the parsimonious well-to-do around him, who see their standards of *pourboire* being senselessly inflated. The American has gained admittance to public places, but finds no one around him cordial to or even interested in him; and he may for the first time encounter that kind of aloofness which is able to say "I am sorry" in such a way as to make plain that one is not sorry at all. Not only is there a barrier of language abroad but often a threshold of reserve higher than his own; and Americans frequently return home complaining that the only ones friendly to them were those who had something to gain by it. Europe was not quite what it promised to be.*

The American also encounters, and is not enthusiastically welcomed by, fellow Americans who "have been here before" and who are scornful of those plainly arriving for the first time who talk loud, dress loud and carry cameras (they can be a sight!). Veteran travelers like to feel, because they are more at home in the landscape,

---

* Someday a monograph should be written on the psychological deceptions of travel ads. Where other ads feature only the young, trim and beautiful—as they smoke, drink or eat—travel ads always include at least two old people well up front, kindly, ample and white-haired, having the time of their lives, surrounded not by other old people but by the happy young who have obviously included the old in their festivities. There is usually a young girl traveling alone too, and as the train pulls through the Rockies, the others are including her in their ecstatic enjoyment of the Vista Dome scenery; in the cocktail lounge aboard ship, though alone, she is the center of things, and the pianist seems to be playing just for her. The old folks shown getting out of their carriage in Rio or standing before the Vatican are as unrumpled and neat as if they had just stepped out of their own front door, and as if no problems of laundry, language or the other hazards of travel existed for them.

that they are more inconspicuous in it, though I suspect that, to the local people on the scene, all are equally foreign. But even if there are no toreador pants or dazzling neckties to forgive, it is a common enough experience to find the glaring presence of one's own countrymen abroad an intrusion on one's solitary immersion in foreignness. I have heard Englishmen and Frenchmen equally ashamed of the look or behavior of their own abroad, eager to avoid them—and if they do not want to be spoken to I know none who can be so effective as the British at looking it.

A certain kind of American abroad so delights in the homely smells and crooked streets of European cities, and the tranquil harmony of the countryside (billboards seem not quite so glaring in another language) that he comes to romanticize Europe and to deplore everything American. He marks the agreeable serenity of landscapes of red-tile roofs and pastel walls, where proximity of materials has given an entire village—church, factory, houses—an affinity of texture and plane. He wanders down streets where buildings jut forth at random and have a pleasing uniformity of shutters along with welcome grace notes of individuality: if these buildings were once nakedly new and not specially remarkable, they now have the common sanction and unity of age. He sees a countryside that the special vision of painters has made familiar and beautiful to him. He applauds the inexpensive pleasures of a coffee on an outdoor terrace, where the customers are free to stay as long as they please to watch the passing scene. Who can blame him for falling in love with it all? He notes the practical economy in simple things: the pinafores of the school children, the aprons, the universal dark-blue denims of the French workmen—simple, renewable and durable uniforms; and when all of this has rushed in on him, he is apt to reach what I think are exaggerated conclusions.

He may be heard to proclaim that the simplest of French girls has a certain flair in dress when using the plainest of materials, though this is easily refutable. He may also say that the poorest French peasant has a purity of taste superior to an American's, and adduces the spare simplicity of the French landscape, though it was not taste but poverty that determined that utility of appearance we now regard as tasteful. If anyone wants to celebrate the instinctive good taste of the European, let him first look into the gimcrack-crowded room of any *concierge,* or observe what are the prevailing fashions in religious statuettes. When a Frenchman does have money, let it be noted what hideous kinds of ornamentation he can deck his new house with. For there is nothing so universal as vulgarity, though its manifestations be everywhere different. An American who looks too closely at the comic postcards of Brighton or the bathing beaches of Italy may even find himself preferring his own country's vulgarity—and pained to see that the worst of American vulgarity seems to have the greatest appeal abroad.

We are told that the French are individualists, self-centered and thrifty. They are indeed thrifty in small things, and even in squandering: in fashionable shops one notices how the lavishness spent on effect ceases immediately the minute the effect is unnecessary (as contrasted with the increasing American trend in business to make office and back shop equally attractive). But if we acknowledge the thrift of the sharp-eyed French shopkeeper and the prudent shopper, how improvident in time and money can be French eating habits, and how much of their income must go to food, and how much of their labor force go to supplying and serving it! It is a country rich by nature, that prefers to squander its francs not on electric blankets but at the table, eating well. The Frenchman, eating out, must spend four hours a day at table. The result is a glory of cuisine, and a dedication to the rites of serving food, that is a pleasure to participate in. But oftentimes, sharing that Lucullan bounty, I have wondered how a country which elects eating to be its national pleasure can speak so disparagingly of the materialism of America.

But there is a danger in speaking of other peoples as *they,* and of including everyone in that country in the indictment. *They* may be a convenient shorthand among nations, indispensable to journalists, but it is at best only an approximation. Thus, we may say that if *they* (the French) are so lucid and intelligent, why can't they set up a stable government? If *they* are so devoted to honor, why don't they pay their taxes? And if *they* talk so much of *fraternité,* why can't they get along with one another? The trouble with *they* is that it ignores those among the French whose honesty, patriotism and civic-mindedness are the match of ours, and whose political skill may be superior.

It is a natural instinct in us all, I think, in making comparisons with others, to discount their virtues and to take comfort in their lapses. But to do so is to risk becoming like Jack of Dover, who roamed the world over looking for a greater fool than he was, and did not find him. The glory of France is not its regime but its way of life: it is selfish, but also self-sufficient; and in insisting on the right to go their own way, the French are prepared to let their fellow citizens (or strangers in their midst) go theirs, and the result is that happy encouragement of independence in thought and behavior that so attracts an American escaping from what is too centripetal in his own country.

This stubborn insistence on individuality has its immense civic cost. What paralyzes France politically is often not indifference but the very thoroughness and ardor of political convictions. A contending of prideful factions has canceled out community responsibility; too often the celebrated French intelligence has been applied only to the skillful maneuverings of selfish interests. Thus an American may find that the French individuality of temperament has made France a delightful place to live in, but is glad that he does not have to contend, as the inhabitants do, with the humiliating impotence or desperate expedience of French statesmanship.

The ineffectuality of intelligent men is perhaps at the root of that familiar French intellectual mood of eloquent despair. It is the despair of men conscious of values gone, or disappearing, and of their helplessness to prevent it, for they find themselves as an elite, or even as a nation, an insufficient unit to control their own destiny. "It is not what separates the United States and the Soviet Union that should frighten us," the Catholic novelist François Mauriac has written, "but what they have in common. Those two technocracies that think themselves antagonists are dragging humanity in the same direction." The French feel themselves overwhelmed by Russia and America, and outranked by Britain; they even see an ascendant Germany being preferred to France, and will not recognize that those who would have preferred an association with France found no echoing responsibility there.

But the despair of France, and of European culture, goes deeper than politics. It speaks to the weary knowledge of the hatefulness of man, to the depths of savagery they have found beneath civilized

European man in two devastating world wars and in the bestialities of concentration camps and Algerian prisons. They have learned the inadequacy of the well-intentioned; worse, they have become so philosophically convinced of the evil in everyone that some hesitate to distinguish any longer between degrees of good and bad, for fear of developing spiritual pride.

French intellectuals so often seem to dislike the present, to fear the future and to deny the hereafter. They believe only in disbelieving, and not only reject but despise optimism as if it were a bourgeois fantasy, and feel so well-dressed in funereal black that they regard cheerfulness as an adolescent frivolity unsuited to man's state. An American, accused of easy optimism, is often tempted to reply: "Don't you think we know defeats and disillusionments too? Don't you think we also know death?" But if the riposte temporarily silences the European, it may not fully satisfy ourselves: do we in fact know death as the European does, as that young village widow does who elects to wear black and to live in solitude all the rest of her life? Or do we not insist that grief must not be persisted in, and solitariness must be avoided: "Come out of yourself, come join the crowd, and live a little?"

One must ask whether European writers like Camus and Sartre see deeper and therefore truer; whether the awful experiences Europeans have lived through are a sounder guide than ours, and despair the ultimate counselor. Or, as most Americans instinctively seem to feel, has the European experience corroded and perverted European intellectuals, so that, being rendered color-blind, they see only black objects and gray shapes? In Europe, pessimism has been made a fashionable cult; it deserves to be left to the philosophers, free of the poseurs who make of their disappointments a cosmic unrest. American optimism may be founded in some final sense on illusion, or on pursuit of wrong values; we may be protected by good fortune from the worst knowledge of ourselves; but I can only think that our attitude is natural to us and our circumstances. One might as well ask the Siamese whether they have a right to look so happy: don't they know about disease and death and The Fall? The Siamese might answer: "Yes, we know, but don't you know about the sun, and love, and beauty?"

For though despair creates ready enough proofs of its own thesis, it is a carping guide to everything else. As for ourselves, if we acknowledge a disquiet in what Dr. Tillich calls our "ultimate concerns," we are a practical enough people to realize that the making of anything better in our condition must start with the hypothesis of hope. We may sometimes feel frustrated, but we do not feel defeated: that much at least do Americans feel in control—if not in full control—of their fortunes.

Those who travel the world by air can now go around the world without seeing anything. From pressurized heights, one looks down on cloud banks instead of villages, and if able to peer down to earth, sees only geology, not geography. The speaker crackles and the pilot announces that those are the Alps below; through cracks in the clouds one sees only whitened mounds, like the salt maps I used to make in school as a boy. One puts down in odd countries to refuel, and is locked in the waiting rooms of their airports, with only a few gaudy dolls in local costume at the newsstand, amidst all the bric-a-brac—the ubiquitous filigree jewelry and stale chocolates—to distinguish one country's culture from another's.

The ambition of each country seems to be to have an airport indistinguishable from Chicago's. One can stand in the Istanbul airport and be assaulted by the same scratchy-needled barrage of jazz that he heard at the Denver airport; in fact, Middle East airports give the impression of having been ordered entire, and everything put to use without clear knowledge of its function. The music of the loud-speaker deafens, but the dull-eyed local officials pay no attention to the booming racket, seemingly regarding it, like the signs on the wall in English, as put there for some incomprehensible utility of the travelers. Thus spreads American culture—the saxophone and the chemical toilet.

Over Calcutta one is served not a curry but a piece of internationalized chicken said to have been prepared at Maxim's, and by some mystery of refrigeration served warm now. Lest one feel contaminated by proximity to the Orient below, even the silverware comes wrapped in cellophane. But the outside world insists on breaking in, and Pan-American might take you safely to Southeast Asia, but could not prevent a war from being fought there in Indochina, whose ugly last days I fleetingly saw; or could not clean up for you the congested, odorous cities, or keep from sight those frail-bodied, impassive-faced coolie women, working like animals and treated like animals, carrying burdensome loads.

And then, after the Far East, comes Honolulu and the shock of encountering one's own. Now comes that subtle transformation I have often noted in myself and in others on trips abroad. I have been seeing foreign lands with American eyes, and I return, full of the contrast, to see America freshly, as a foreigner might. The experience can be disturbing, and in no place more so, I think, than in Honolulu. First come the absurd getups of American old people, the men in garish "aloha shirts," the Middle West women in bright *muumuus*: decent, self-respecting people if one talks to them, forgetting their outlandish appearance. Even more jarring, I find, as do many who approach the U.S. from Asia, are the young American girls in Honolulu—fit, tanned, self-possessed and confident, yet somehow, so soon after one's arrival from Asia, looking too self-satisfied. I am left divided of mind. I certainly did not wish these open-faced girls humbled, subjected, or made miserable, yet had to concede that among the Far Eastern women I had just been among, I sensed a dolorous and wise dignity that is missing in these strapping and buoyant girls.

The shock of America is to be met with again in the airline stewardesses. So trim, so trained, so nice looking, frequently so pretty in a poster way, and yet with a sameness. How can one object to that pretty smile as she leans solicitously low to ask whether you would like more coffee? Would you prefer a slightly tatty, or slightly harried and probably most plain English stewardess? For me the choice would not be hard, yet there is a lingering case to be made for the English girl, who is apt to be too efficient and brisk, or too remote, or perhaps not groomed well enough: but the human being, because of these rough edges, cuts through.

The smiles of the American stewardesses are genuine: they *mean* to please, and do. This amiability, when not self-seeking or too intrusive, is one of the engaging American qualities. Perhaps, I reflect, as our plane throbs across the Pacific, one's objection is that stewardesses shouldn't *have* to be so unrestrainedly, so wholesomely, so wholeheartedly giving of their personalities, so that the smile they give their boy friends at night cannot be much more attractive than the one they give the fat, bald, sleeping man in the seat up front. In fact, it may be less of a smile. Stewardesses probably appreciate most in their boy friends a willingness to let them be themselves—that is, sometimes tired, sometimes irritable, sometimes unsmiling.

Salesmanship and service—in their extreme American manifestations—make, I believe, too heavy a demand on the human personality in the name of commercial necessity. In a certain kind of businessman it produces a hypocritical use of blandishments, kidding, familiarity and "likeableness" in their dealings with customers and "contacts." Even the final serious act of sealing a bargain must be joshed away: "Put your John Hancock here," one is told, on what is no good-humored arrangement but a legally enforceable contract. And in a certain kind of serving employee, such as the airline stewardess, the smiling American business code requires too much of a surrender of personality, even if the surrender is voluntary and unselfconscious.

This surrender of the private rights of personality, I have often thought, extends further into American life than the moment-of-purchase relationship between seller and buyer. It suffuses a wife's relationship with her husband's business associates, and with their wives: a relationship that must be at once cordial and careful. It affects one's conduct in shops and buses, and his posture in the community; it even transfers itself to so private a rite as the sending of Christmas cards—not only to one's intimates but to long lists of associates who come to expect, and are even careful to check off, the mailed good wishes of those whom they may care little about. We Americans have, I think, too much blurred the distinctions between affability, manners, affection and friendship: often using the stronger word, or the brighter smile, when the least emotion is involved. Perhaps this is why the British and French quality of seeming coldness, indifference or reserve (when it is not the rudeness of asserted, but unproven, superiority) often attracts at the same time one is being excluded by it.

We do not have that hard and fast European separation between what is business and-no-mistake, and what is private life and not to be invaded: we take our business so seriously, and it engages so much of our energy, that we have learned to find our pleasure in it too. We have coffee breaks at work, as well as working lunches and "business entertaining" after hours, so that it is sometimes hard to tell the tax collector honestly which of our engagements were free of pleasure, and which were free of business. That inward-turning quality of Europeans, firmly walling off what is theirs from general sight, refusing any engagement with strangers around them, feeling sufficient to themselves and at most possessed of a curiosity toward others that rarely seems sympathetic: all this is alien to the American, who by comparison is prodigal of his personality to all and sundry.

When I think of those nations where distinctions and suspicions of class and family have been transmitted through generations, like legacies, I am aware of how honest and unhampered our business seems, how unviolent our labor, how tolerant our politics. This is not the whole truth about us, as we know, but a foreign vantage point makes me realize that our criticisms of ourselves are the complaints of prosperity and take much good fortune for granted. We have a society where the gap between richest and poorest is immense, but where the gradation between them is so gradual that no abrupt division exists, walling off one class from another, perpetuating differences of education, manners and outlook. These are our blessings, and most of our difficulties stem from them.

I know that other nations have much to teach us, but in the end our condition is unique, for no other place confronts our peculiar mixture of handicaps, advantages, advances and stresses in quite the same way.

III.   My Own, My Native Land

12. The American Image

Just as the sky over a city, when seen from afar at night, is lit by a reflected luminosity that is the merged glow of the city's many lights, so does a culture give off a halation. That halation, which is not a true sum of all its parts but only a visual effect which can sometimes be misleading, might be called its image. What is the American Image?

I think that it is first of all an image of immense energy. On the day of Pearl Harbor, when Americans themselves were stunned by the blow, Winston Churchill was in quite a different mood. He thought of a remark that Edward Grey had made to him more than thirty years before—that the United States is like "a gigantic boiler. Once the fire is lighted under it there is no limit to the power it can generate." With such an ally, and no longer condemned to fight alone, Churchill went to bed "and slept the sleep of the saved and thankful." In the few short years since Pearl Harbor, our capacity to generate power has increased in strides that in turn appear to be but timid, mincing steps compared to what scientists intend for us.

A rich and prodigious giant, we seem impulsively improvident to those peoples whose barren hillsides yield a hard living, or whose crabbed space requires a meticulous tilling of terraced hillsides: we dust crops by plane, reap by machine and think in vast acreages. Much of what they call our wastefulness we regard as a mere excess

163

of our energy, and if we are sometimes prodigal of resources, we are also cognizant of how much science has multiplied the energy of our waterfalls and the usefulness of our coal, and of how much a seeming squandering often returns far more than was spent. This knowledge of our productive wealth inhabits our characters and influences our conduct; it makes us so generous a people. We are freed by our wealth from that pinched, selfish and guarded outlook so prevalent in Europe: the foundation of our generosity is our belief that "there's more where that came from." In Palm Springs live men who consider themselves only a little better off than most, but who outdo ancient kings in their holdings. Our awareness of plenty governs our restless quest for more; we are not dulled by a sense of limitations nor made grasping by a feeling that we are all taking from a diminishing pile. The way to great wealth in America is not to be a Tiffany to the few but a Henry Ford to the many. Part of the dynamism of the American capitalist (and the reason he is more esteemed than despised) is that he is an energizer whose ambition multiplies opportunities for others. This is a far cry from the view put forward by Karl Marx, of an inevitable and squalid conflict between classes for a share of the common wealth; Americans are apt to find Marx not only a pernicious guide but a bad prophet, even if his theories were perhaps explicable in the practices which he saw in his day and which still persist in other parts of the world. To read any classic American 19th Century success story today is not to be left aglow with admiration but appalled by its avarice. We no longer believe in squeezing nickels, but in rotating dollars.

The American lives in waste and accepts the principle of the discard pile. We can chance; if we fail it was "worth trying"; we have a margin. The American credo holds that activity has a value all its own, and that corrections can be made along the way. This pragmatic optimism—the spirit of it-can-be-done—helps explain how much does get done. The easy American confidence is sometimes mistaken for bragging by those who miss the humor in our self-assurance: hyperbole is our style; our folk stories are tall tales, not small ones.

To the wider world, to which every nation makes its useful contribution (Britain, its political institutions and trade patterns; France, its cuisine, its style of living and thought; Germany, its science and commercial impulse; Russia, its military might and political influence), America contributes organization, efficiency, commercial imagination, dynamism and optimism. There are defects to these American qualities: an overriding and sometimes insensitive propulsion to change often takes insufficient account of the values of habit, comfort and simplicity in the old ways, and our missionary-minded enthusiasm is sometimes determined that others must imitate us. But we bring to the world an inventive spirit, prepared to try anything: a boldness that can be seen in our engineering and heard in our jazz. Our science may not be as inherently creative as the German, but it achieves more by being linked to great organizations and vast resources. We bring attractive business practices: openness of wallet and openness of mind; a random experimentalism that prizes new ways: our builders casually make cost estimates on the backs of envelopes as they go about their jobs, and corporals and sergeants in our armies may be restrained by their instructions but always feel free to improvise.

A vital working confidence is the essential American trait, but its sunny outlook has become clouded over of late, because of increased doubts over what use our energy is put to, and fears of an uncertain future. Exuberance is no longer our national image as a people; politically, the halation radiating from us, as seen from abroad, is of selfishness threatened, and inclined to panic. It is an image that does less than justice to us. The capacities that produced our turbulent creativity are still there, and still being used: our productive dynamism has not dried up. Our trouble, as a people that has always been given to anxious self-examination, is that we have begun to doubt our ends.

It was simpler in the 19th Century, when so many massive tasks confronted us—wildernesses to be settled, slums to be torn down, poverty and malnutrition to be conquered, illiteracy to be overcome. If some of the ardor that went into attacking these evils was too expectant, if enthusiasts believed that literacy would make men enlightened, prosperity would make them unselfish and education would make them virtuous, we can be grateful for what, less than the dreams, was achieved. Those immigrants who struggled and denied themselves so that their children might lead better lives may have been avaricious and clutching, but was it their children who gained most, in inheriting it all—or the immigrants themselves, who along with their drudgery and saving were also pursuing, as their children perhaps are not, a goal beyond themselves?

As a nation we have worked hard—for we are not a lazy people —for goals that are nearly in sight. Easy Street now stretches from coast to coast, even if it has its rough spots, and our economy its lurches. The President's Council of Economic Advisers talks of a "diffusion of well-being," which may be another way of saying that our goal has become a life of amiable sloth. Once we chased happiness; our national ambition now seems diminished to life, liberty and the pursuit of ease. We once talked of the greatest good of the greatest number, but now think of the greatest pleasure of the most people, and the distinction is significant. We have television for those who do not even actively seek pleasure any more but are satisfied with distractions. (What is so deadening about mass entertainment, as compared to a past age's aimless conversation and card playing, is that it is all intake and no outgo, involving no effort of response.)

Working at jobs that often do not require or inspire our best, we demand the right to relax as we will. Is the tension of incentive disappearing from our lives? When, like Chinese peasants in a paddy, one must work all day, rest becomes necessity and one does not worry about "what to do with the time." The American woman, freed from an arduous day of preparing food as her grandmother did, is not fully satisfied with the time saved, and elaborates her meals and her preparations to take up the slack, pursues curiosities of cuisine and "balanced meals," is busy in the community or taxiing her family about, and giving luncheons which must look as if they were no work at all. Or else she ceases to struggle. See her now "slaving" over a hot rotisserie with a prepared chicken inside while the dessert needs only thawing from the deep freeze and the automatic dishwasher waits at the ready and the TV baby-sits for the children; then comes that time of day known as "the children's hour": mommy and daddy are having their martini. And ahead, after a lifetime of this, what awaits—a vision of gray hair, rouged cheeks and tartan slacks, drink in hand, playing the slots at Vegas? Or for the quieter ones, shuffleboard and bragging on a Florida park bench?

We are the first people to be freed from the need for overwork: before, there were only individuals, or a class, so freed—and either they became indolent and declined as a culture, or took on duties and responsibilities in return for their privileges. Will it be said of us that we had the greatest of opportunities, and merely enjoyed them?

Few Americans are marked any longer by the 19th Century relentless quest for money. We want to get a little, and then take it easy; the more ambitious want to get a little *more* and then take it easy. We no longer think of our life span as a steady, desperate accretion of money, but more as an arc, after a certain point tapering down into easy retirement. No longer compelled to struggle for necessities, we find ourselves on a rising plateau of demands. Parents find themselves saying that they need all of this—this neighborhood, this car—to set their children's school and college career off properly.

Though our tragedies and disappointments remain individual, all that can be alleviated by society—illness, ignorance, poverty, those ancient evils—has been largely overcome. It is not even necessary to be confronted any longer by society's remaining unfortunates: we have charity by check, and organized benevolence, which is a tax-free and well-paid industry. We have largely eliminated the Dickensian horrors of childhood—of cruelty, misery and sternness— which crushed many while sharpening a few: the tendency now is to provide our children with as carefree a childhood as possible, free of the frustrations we knew. But will this produce a generation of strength and character, or is our disbelieving and leisure-happy generation failing to transmit the qualities of duty and responsibility, so that many of our children are suffering from malnutrition, an insufficient absorption of good things?

We are in danger of becoming a vibrating and mediocre people. Who can say of us that goodness and generosity inevitably triumph? That talent prevails and honesty pays? Who would say that quality is in any phase of our culture outracing the spreading debasement? Have we sold our souls for a mess of pottage that goes snap, crackle and pop? Such doubts arise in us all, at least on our off days, when in impatience and anger we see our entire nation seemingly bereft of rectitude and character, satisfied only to make money and gratify wants. But we know that our anger spreads itself too unselectively. In a nation of 170 million people, the exceptions to almost any generalization inevitably number in the hundreds of thousands. What is statistically true of even 98 out of 100 Americans must statistically exclude three or four million of them. And though it is possible to talk of Americans' bland self-satisfaction, was there ever a more self-examining people? If we are patronized for this soul-searching quality abroad, by those who inherit their grandfathers' way of life, we ourselves know our need to be continuously self-critical, we who are changing so fast.

We are often accused of being lazily complacent, and we are also accused of being in too big a hurry. Perhaps the first of these charges reflects an attitude of mind and the other is a matter of pace, but the accusations remain somewhat contradictory, and if an indictment of us as a people is to stick, I believe that it must be more carefully drawn. To talk of our fatuous indifference as a people is to leave out the many who read Freud or Bishop Sheen, and who seek out psychiatrists who are salvationists, or salvationists who are psychologists, to overcome an emptiness in their lives; the many who, caught between responsibility and inadequacy, become mentally disturbed; the many who are anxious, who take to drink or tranquilizers; to leave out all the widespread dissatisfaction, the feeling of lostness, in American life; to leave out all the earnest searching to understand desires and ease frustrations, all the longing to understand what we are here for. It is to leave out the decent, the modest, the selfless—whose avoidance of the spotlight makes them, despite their large numbers, so barely visible in the halation given off by the American Image.

For the image we make as a nation is largely set by the kind of person who is driven to want to play in the center court. Perhaps this is why foreign visitors, seeing us all and not just the pushiest among us, often find us to be a more attractive people than we had seemed from afar. Yet those who do most to create the American Image are often only exaggerations of our nature; we may deplore their methods but do not sufficiently examine our own ends; and so long as Cadillacs are our prevailing standard of success—and no questions asked—our condemnation of these others among us must be relative.

I think that our difficulty as a society lies often not in its goals but in their unreckoned side-effects, for what we pursue so single-mindedly often has a double aspect that we are only half aware of. Not villainy is our trouble, but ambitions that are unregarding. Once this is understood—once it is seen that our bad is often a concomitant of what we consider good, and is intertwined with it—then we may be freed of the notion that all our ills are the faults of *others* among us. Too often the American discontent, the kind that gets expressed in self-righteous and querulous Letters to the Editor ("What's become of America?" "If we want to catch up with the Russians, we should think less about baseball and more about science," etc.), assumes that others must start or stop doing something, and does not scrutinize what is amiss in us all.

Why is it that we as a people tolerate what we at the same time lament? I think that in the double aspect of our objectives lies the explanation of some of our most respected lunacies. Take our appearance, for example: what we have made of our cities and done to our countryside. We may deplore our jerry-built look, the wastage of building up and tearing down, the lack of standards—but the other aspect of our appearance is that we prize variety and newness, insist on liberty, and resist regulation.

Economic advantage, not aesthetics, determines the thrust of our cities. We have no dictator, no king, no Baron Haussmann to decree wide boulevards and parks, but only traffic pressures that create vast highway cut-throughs. We do not build for the ages, or to gratify a royal vanity; our buildings, which must conform to a profitable expectancy, have impermanence built into them. They are planned to be torn down. We assume changing needs and changing tastes, and know that the city may move on and leave a building isolated in a less desirable neighborhood; we anticipate the perfection of new materials: it would be economically unsound to project any structure's existence too far. Conscious that even in a building's brief life it may become functionally out of date, we now equip it with movable internal walls, for nothing is here to stay. What else can we do but plan for impermanence, when an urban hell like Los Angeles grows at the rate of 600 new residents a day, and for every three who come to stay two leave?

Part of the American urban ugliness, and its provisional and unfinished look, then, stems from the rootless knowledge (unlike Europe's) that we do not intend to remain long in this particular place. We intend to move on, and to improve our lot (there may be another group moving because it is coming down in the world, but we do not talk about that). As a nation we are a volcano that is still heaving and puffing; it is asking too much to expect us at the same time to be conserving and prudent: perhaps when we reach the state where we are decently solicitous of what is being destroyed, decadence will have begun to set in—for creativity and custodianship are often warring qualities.

We pay a sentimental homage to the old, but do not really prize it. As a nation, we conceive of ourselves as having started from scratch; we did not build over Roman glories but slashed down trees and made squatter's cabins, and the feeling that we are "improving" sites, even when we are not, makes us slight the old: we may mourn the passing of something old and comfortable, but concede that its right to a particular patch of ground is economically untenable. Aesthetic regret, in the United States, is never a match for economic ambition. Depredation is always organized; preservation almost never. It might be formulated as a law of public pressure that the strength of interest is as twice the strength of numbers: those with a vague and intermittent goodwill are helpless against a sleepless and consuming want. The finest house, the handsomest street, is therefore at the mercy of any casual promoter who wants to tear it down. We are like an animal that casts off its skins too quickly: no wonder we look scraggly.

Progress is a hard word to fight in our land, and there are no exacting definitions of it. But though we may damn the despoilers and plead our helplessness, we are unwilling to limit impetus or to restrict variety to what a design commission will allow us. Americans cannot convince themselves that a frozen mold of the past—whether Beaux Arts Roman, baroque, or timbered English brought up to date—can outdo for our uses something that we can think up for ourselves, and the price of our license (which accounts for the happy audacity in the best of our architecture) is our random look, and the proliferation of bogus-modern or bogus-ancient by those who take a prevailing style and adulterate it. We do not believe in dictatorships of taste, and therefore must put up with Taj Mahal orange-juice stands, and roadside joints named the Leaning Tower of Pizza. The modern Voltaire would tell Helvetius: "I do not approve of your taste, but will defend in principle your right to make a buck as you see fit." It's a free country, isn't it?

We may wish to discipline the anarchy of competing ambitions, but how? At this point we become aware of our dislike of controls. We have decreed ineffectuality in government, preferring that it be inadequate rather than overbearing.

Government is usually pictured as big and bad, running all our lives. It is big, all right, but clumsy, and rather than being too full of plans, goes panting after the unplanned actions of millions of energetic souls all at work at projects tangential to the national interest. We have made the decision that spontaneity in our society should reside outside the state, and from this decision we receive unique advantages, but pay a price. We regard bureaucracy as survival of the unfittest, and among public servants give a careful respect only to judges and tax collectors.

We ask government to regulate our society, not to organize it; we ask it to register our patents, copyrights and freeholds, but we will do the inventing and buying; we ask it to provide for the common defense and common sewerage and any other odd jobs that are too big or too uncongenial to make a profit from. Increasingly the role we ask of government is that it play the Rectifier. We do not want it initiating too much. We ask that it be weak, yet capable of making an equilibrium in the country, through such levers as impetus spending, tax rates, and the money power. A rectifier's task is to build highways where congestion compels it, and if possible to foresee the direction we are all about to go; it is to build schools but not to run them; to level slums so that others may build on them; to erect airports that private companies may fly to; it is to subsidize science or agriculture but not to control either; to carry our letters and papers, but not to monitor them; in short, by regulatory commission or by the power to tax one endeavor heavily and to subsidize another, to impose some social order on the millions of impulses at work in society. We don't want government erecting barriers against our energy, we want it only to dike channels in which that energy may flow—channels that should conform to our common wishes but not be so narrow as to prevent a healthy, or even an unhealthy, diversity.

We have contrived a government that is strong of limb but weak of will, and have limited it for what we consider good reason. The greatest flaw in our system of government, therefore, is no longer the temptation it offers the strong man, but the latitude it allows the weak man to do less than is necessary. But if we have decreed limits to our political power, and if the weak in office use these limitations as an alibi rather than as restraints to be kept in mind, isn't there a power outside government that determines—and can be held responsible for—the course of our society?

We are often told so. We hear of interlocking directorates of powerful men, press lords and corporation presidents, who are a "power elite." But if, as will be argued later, there are indeed fragmented elites in the United States, quite powerful for single purposes in narrow areas, I think the notion of an America dominated by taste-makers and power-wielders is erroneous—another way of shifting responsibility for what we dislike to a They, rather than finding it in ourselves.

What is unique about American democracy is that wealth and culture are not synonymous: those whose hands are at the controls of our mighty engines of production usually do not have the time to acquire culture, but only possessions. They (or their wives) import decorators to furnish their homes, and hire gallery owners to make sure that the art they buy is a good investment. They do not consider it their duty, as an aristocratic society once did, to be preservators of culture and arbiters of taste: they would be humble before the task—and appalled by the notion. They feel no such responsibility. If they think at all about their debt to society, they think it discharged in their work: they are not indolent people required to justify their leisure; they labored and *made jobs*. They are a prey to ulcers and heart attacks: what more can be asked of them? They work hard, and when they play they want diversion: to read a detective story, not Dostoevsky. They think that wealth entitles them to be honest about what they like. They are caught up in a swirl of competition, and need no other stimulus: it is their life's blood, and requires a great deal of it. Even the golf course or the yacht becomes merely another setting for thinking of their jobs, or for consciously trying to shake off their work. They talk a business idiom at all times; they write badly because for their purposes effect is all and grace nothing—one hires someone else when artful fluency is required. And if they may be men of a subtle knowledge of market forces, or gifted at organizing and administering, they are often plain by nature: they pride themselves on common origins, and would think it dishonest to want to be other than what they are. They are like everybody else, just richer.

This elite of so-called captains of industry, men of a hard pride in their vitality and with a quickness to dismiss whatever they do not consider practical, are (except in their limited fields) hardly the pacemakers of our society. Only a handful of them are known by name even to conscientious readers of newspapers. They are too busy in their own pursuits to set a tone for anyone else: they are not so much uncaring as driven men.

Most of us may envy but few revere these titans of business, for we no longer have heroes in American life: instead we have invented celebrities, who are an inferior democratic substitute. Celebrities form our nearest equivalent to a group that sets the tone and stirs the imagination of the anonymous many. Celebrities may be defined as those who get the best tables without (like wealthy girdle-makers) having to tip heavily; they enhance a place by their presence, be they ever so gauche.

The essence of the celebrity condition is that there, but for the breaks, go I. We don't worship celebrities; we consider them equals (or even inferiors) who have been favored by special advantages. They—the starlets, the ball-players, the comedians—are ourselves, with one talent (or a bosom) writ large. They are not aristocrats with a whole set of values we could not learn in a lifetime; they are not scientists whose brainy triumphs would make our heads ache, but someone like us, who enters the night club and spends freely, indifferent to the check, or builds a garish home with swimming pool as we might like to. And since he is us—plus the artificial life of riches and notoriety thrust suddenly upon him—he will probably make a mess of his marriage or of his life and provide us with an interesting morality play to read about as well. Hollywood starlets not only act out make-believe stories, they live them, and have lately taken to describing their expensive misfortunes and drunks in ghost-written books that in turn become further movies. We must be able to believe the worst about them, for if their lives were as common-place as ours we would not want to read about them, and it must be confessed that we read with some satisfaction when they fall. A certain kind of gossip journalism has mastered the art of smacking over sin, so that it can be enjoyed vicariously and disapproved in the same breath.

Celebrities, with their popular skills or acknowledged beauty, play somewhat the same role in a nation's life as court circles once did, except that they are courtesans to the public. They must remember to be obliging to autograph hunters, and to smile into the television camera.

We have come now, I think, to one of the principal reasons we Americans are as we are. It is the notion of equality. Most of us (I confess it in myself) feel superior to much of what we see around us. In private conversation, we condemn eyesores and deplore pre-vailing popular tastes. But we hesitate to draw the natural conclu-sion of such thoughts, for we recoil as if from an immoral proposal at the idea that we are anything but practicing democrats. Of all the characteristics that set the American way of life apart, respect for the appearance of equality is the most dominant. All who would be in the American mainstream must pay homage to that appearance, and those who defy it must choose to lead a life somewhat apart. It accounts for our most attractive qualities, and most of our short-comings. It invades every area of our life. In this we differ from those European societies which, though politically democratic, have islands of privilege that dominate their country's culture even though they are no longer its most dynamic economic or political force. And we differ also, in this emphasis on equality, from the Communist societies, though the Communists talk a more exagger-ated democratic lingo than we do. Having chosen to imitate democ-racy instead of monarchy, they raise their right arms in their obedient parliaments when they might as appropriately bend their knees, for tyranny is their actual form of government: they do not really ask public consent. In the United States, more than anywhere else, the practice of democracy and the assumption of equality are in every man's mind. Everything, sooner or later, gets referred back to the public.

Since the appearance of equality in American life is often contrary to the fact, we are enmeshed in humbug and that well-intentioned hypocrisy which is also so apparent in the American Image. Equality requires a special language, from the studied "he don'ts" and "ain'ts" of the politicians to calculatedly ungrammatical advertising campaigns; "associates" are told to use the side door, but are no longer referred to as employees; and lucky is the man who can go through life without being told that he is a valued member of The Team. Nor is this jargon confined to crude business men, for one has only to give a plaque to a scientist or professor to set him off into a speech: "I can only say that you have honored me more than I deserve. I accept this award not for myself, but on behalf of all my associates, who really deserve all the credit." Sometimes, just to be thorough, he adds his wife to his list of credits.

Hollywood, which knows its market, has a shrewd affection for fables of equality triumphant, in which the prideful get their comeuppance and plain people embody all the virtues. Bing Crosby made several millions of dollars by proclaiming, in a dozen ways, but with one unvarying theme, that he preferred not having much, and with but a pocketful of dreams was the happiest man alive, for the best things in life are free: it may be presumed that at contract-signing time his agents saved him from the pitfalls of carefree indiscretion. Character actors have spent their entire Hollywood careers playing hauteur unbending before the new equality; the camera finds them in the front row, in white tie and tails, at those concerts where the hero works himself up into a lather conducting, or banging his piano through, some puffed-up tawdry jazz concerto. Mr. Hauteur at first looks uncomprehending at the enthusiasm breaking out all around him; then, as the music continues to engulf us all, he too is apparently won over, and is shown turning to Mrs. Hauteur as if to say, "This is *really* good. How wrong I was!" The ordinary has triumphed again, and we can all go home happy, wiping the popcorn butter from our lips with the back of our hand.

We all know better: Life is not like this Hollywood fable. Against the egalitarian trend in American life exists the natural hierarchy of disproportionate achievement and unequal rewards. The cynical might think that this hierarchy, then, more closely represents the American reality, and that all talk of equality is but necessary pretense. They argue that the true business of our society gets done in spite of the democratic trappings. But I think that they ignore how much equality permeates all sectors of our life, in ways and places that we do not normally acknowledge. Many who most proudly flaunt the banner of their superiority are often unconsciously accepting the disciplines of equality, and could not prosper without it.

Equality is a trait we preen ourselves on, and when we violate its spirit we practice a careful hypocrisy, but I think we are its servant more than we know, and more than we should be. Equality requires a closer look.

13. Equality and the Profitable Middle

One of the prevailing characteristics of American life is our sentimental confusion of equality with democracy. Equality is denied by every means of observation: people are not equally clean, equally ambitious, equally honest. Our preoccupation with equality is what produces much of the cant and demagogy of public life: democracy has its own justifications and should not take on the impossible burden of defending equality as well. That all men were created equal is one of the great fictions of all times, and would have been so regarded by most people throughout history. The circumstances of parentage give one a head start and another a handicap; the color of one's skin gives him an advantage over another. It might be possible—through a violence of political activity—to see that all parents had equal income, and to legislate a compassionate falsity about color and race; there would still be the inequality of being born to loving or unregarding parents, to those who had a gift for raising children or did not; and the children too would still be unequal by birth: some born with great talents, some dull-witted and some deformed. All men are *not* created equal: nor as they become adults are they equally intelligent, equally caring, equally informed.

But once we exclude children and lunatics from the franchise, we are in difficulty in our politics if we would devise tests of exclusion and inclusion. We all know of educated fools, and at the other end of the scale, among the ignorant whom the Walter Lippmanns regard as hardly worthy of the Good Society, live those who in time of national crisis freely give their lives with a simplicity of duty and patriotism that confounds all who would deny them air to breathe.

Since life must move on assumptions, we thus assume equal democratic weight to the responsible and irresponsible, and presume that if a man be only literate, he is informed; democracy also requires that information be made available to everyone but that no one shall be required to use it. Franklin Roosevelt, Groton accent and all, reached perfection at saying confidently to us, "*You* and I know . . ." In fact, many did not know, and democratic apologists hate to acknowledge that in matters of serious moment many people not only don't know but don't even *want* to know. More attractively stated, they don't presume to have an opinion—they leave that to the experts. Their modest estimate is often the correct one, but it is the democratic pretense that if only journalism were better, or education better, this would not be the case. It is a sentimental and unproven assumption.

The sum total of the undiscriminating democratic method—adding together, at equal value, the votes of those with some idea of issues and those with none at all—can hardly be regarded as a scientific exercise in political wisdom, but only in temperature taking. It is a justified makeshift, because voting makes everyone a participant in society, and helps establish a sense of order and well-being. The democratic assumption has also proven to be a more responsive index of the State of the Union than might reasonably be expected, for each person is "well-informed" about his own condition and is the best judge of whether he thinks his wants are being met by those elected to serve him. But in foreign affairs, where the uninformed can have no awareness of disturbance until it is already upon them, and are then apt to demand wild lurches of policy, the democratic process is a less sure guide. It is in fact a dangerously inadequate guide, and in the increasingly sensitive area of foreign policy our complacent toleration of a system that works, though faultily, is an immense risk.

We are saved, when we are saved, by those politicians who understand the principle of *representative* government, and are prepared to act with measured audacity. Charles Curtis, who was Herbert Hoover's vice president, was of the opinion that most things get done in American life between opposing forces. "There is no such thing as self-restraint in a people," he said once. "What looks like it is indecision." Faced with this indecision, the artful politician knows that politics is about fulcrums.

He understands instinctively that he must anticipate opinion, and that if he acts, his actions will create a new climate. He constructs operative fancies, and acts *as if* he had prior consent. Americans know the art of delegation, and have decreed a representative government; a politician has in his hands a set of unexercised options, and is free to use them imaginatively, realizing that he must be prepared to defend his course if an indifferent public later takes an interest in what he is about.

Stanley Baldwin, who may not have been a great prime minister but was a good politician, used to say that it was not so important to know what the House of Commons thought on Friday, but what it would think on Monday: "I have always believed in the weekend," he said. "But how do they do it? I don't know. I suppose they talk to the stationmaster." The English weekend, during which people in clubs and country houses were presumed to make a consensus, was an excellent institution when caution was needed; it was of less help when imagination was wanted, for it is—like its American equivalent, the public-opinion poll—most useful when nothing needs to be done: often the easiest crowd to assemble is the "don't knows" and the "don't ask exertions of us." A weak president uses public indifference to justify inactivity when, if that public were sufficiently informed, it would be aroused. For this reason, our weak and likeable presidents often enjoy a contemporary popularity, only to suffer an angry whiplash from posterity.

Politics, said Valéry, is the art of making possible that which is necessary. The possible is harder when we must ask the consent of the governed to that which restricts them. But if hard, it is not impossible: all the reasons advanced by weak men for their incapacity to do something are present to the strong man who does it. The capable politician knows that decisions cannot be demanded of a mass, which does not have all the relevant information even if it had the interest: what is required is an endorsement, and he will have taken public prejudices into account in appealing for a verdict. He works to reduce the complexities of issues to the simplicity of a choice, a push-button registration of satisfaction or dissatisfaction; and thus we must endure the paraphernalia of parades and slogans and shouts. Out of such means is consensus reached.

Something like this taking of responsibility, subject to later concurrence, was the original Constitutional intention of representative government. Checks and balances and the placing of certain powers beyond the reach of transient majorities were devices meant to limit the absolutism of the popular will. Rights carried obligations. This inspired conception was sensible and successful, but it was not the same thing as saying that any passing mood of the public must prevail because the people are right, whether right or wrong. In presuming a mystic wisdom in the collective will of the many, we have reversed the old notion of a pyramid society, and have sought to make of ourselves something that is all broad base and no apex.

The classic thesis that the king could do no wrong did not mean that he was entitled to absolute whimsicality. Revolt against tyrants has always had moral sanction: "If you do justly, you will be king; if not, not." We tend more and more, in loose popular thinking, to set up the sovereign will of the people as an absolute, an equivalent of the divine right of kings; but the absolutism of the popular will must also find its sanction in the wisdom of its acts. That the people can do no wrong is not the message of democracy, but a monumental perversion of the doctrine that government shall be with their consent. There is often no worse tyrant than a majority. "Democracy as I understand it," said John C. Calhoun, "requires me to sacrifice myself *for* the masses, not *to* them."

Man often continues to fight battles already won, and fails to see that the extent of his victory has created a new enemy more dangerous than the old: the hardest enemy to spot is the one disguised as an ally. Where once we fought to free ourselves from servitude, we won such a victory that we are now cramped by the bonds of equality. For the legal fiction of universal equality is a denial of the truth of an inequality of merit; but worse, it is also a repudiation of the value of unequal effort, and we may wonder how many American school children have demanded less than the best of themselves for fear of the unpopularity that goes with wanting to excel. They are early confronted with the accusation that to show oneself better is to prove oneself conceited, and few sins in the democratic catechism outrank conceit. This restricting, leveling spirit frequently persists into adult life, where men who require public favor learn not to display their knowledge but to affect a stance of "regular guy" common sense. Of all the wastes in American society, not the cutting down of forests but the stunting of intellectual growth is our most costly squandering of resources. The democratic heresy is to value slag more than coke, simply because slag is more plentiful.

The effect of equality in our political life is, if not always admitted, well understood. In our economic life it seems to be denied by gradations of authority and differences of income, but exerts a powerful influence if we look beyond the internal hierarchies of our business world to the markets they serve, and how they go about it. One of the reasons Americans are individually powerless against the false leveling of equality in American life is that the most powerful element in the community—the dominant economic elite—feels itself required to turn *to* the public in order to be free, in private life, to turn *from* it.

The world of business, like the politicians, must flatter the public, and knows that its continuing prosperity depends on winning spontaneous new majorities of approval every day. If there are certain checks and balances that restrain its submission to the public will, business will rarely be heard to admit them. Businesses, like government employees, affect to be "servants" of the public, and while we may be grateful that some do instruct their employees in manners, their hypocritical profession of desiring only to please *you* can sometimes be almost beyond bearing. It was an Australian air line, but perhaps an American adman, who coined the slogan, "The most important thing in the world to our stewardesses is your smile." We are flatteringly assured that every man is king, and though we knew it to be an impossibility politically when Huey Long first said it, we may be less alert to recognize the demagogic falsity of "your majesty, the public" when it comes to goods and services being offered to us.

So often the profession is allowed to substitute for the fact. When we are assured constantly that something is being done "for your greater convenience," what annoys is not the phony hearty tone of it (which disturbs only purists) but the fact that the expressed regret for public dislocation usually excuses doing too little about it. The American restaurant hostess, that paid dispenser of wholesale charm and substitute hospitality, is another exemplar of this substitution of word for deed. When, after one has eaten an undistinguished assembly-line meal carelessly served, and is then greeted solicitously by the hostess with "I hope you enjoyed your dinner," though she obviously doesn't care at all, the grouch in us all wants to shout "No" to escape from being smothered in false gentility. But then one realizes that she is the poor, desperate end of a system —probably a widow driven to this life of black dress, tired feet and pasted-on smile.

Beneath the surface mannerisms of this public courtship, which can be cloying and annoying, lies the truth that American business is in fact a captive of public demand. By the free enterprise system, Henry R. Luce has said, "We mean a system where the consumer, who is Everyman, is able to register *what* he wants and we businessmen and entrepreneurs are *forced* in seeking our own gain to serve the public will."

The result is a business system that has produced a material plenty unparalleled in history, and diffused its blessings widely: no other society anywhere, however dedicated in theory to "sharing the wealth," can claim like success. And this has been possible because of the simple American discovery that wealth must be multiplied, not divided. Well do we celebrate our flair for perfecting useful and attractive products, and by mass methods distributing them widely. Sometimes quality is leveled down to what can be stamped out cheaply and design debased to what will have the widest appeal, but the *spread* of good shoes and stoves and chinaware is wholly admirable. Great skills go into this achievement, and sometimes the least of these may be the actual mechanical act of manufacturing: there must be a continuous and restless concern with product design, manufacturing techniques, cost analyses, market research, prudent inventorying.

The American product must be priced right (with allowance for profit). It must be merchandisable, portable and uniform. It should also be durable *enough*. We live in the age of the standard size and the replaceable part; we have learned the art of the module and the pre-fab. Articles of great bulk must be made easy to assemble and to install; articles of great complexity must be made as simple to operate as throwing a switch. And since there is a dynamism of competition for public favor, there is a constant upgrading of expectations: no manufacturer may depend, as many have in England, on setting one style and one model, and staying with it for years. The living museum of our business creativity is the American supermarket, that vast and bewildering cornucopia of packaged appeals to the appetite: here jostling for favor are all the goods that have learned to compete in that best of markets, the largest one.

But in making of the consumer an Everyman, business finds itself under the spell of a force as powerful as gravity, a force which might be called the pull of the profitable middle. It is a force that creates an irresistible impulse to uniformity of product. Under the pull of the profitable middle, an American restaurant owner, who sets out in the beginning to please everybody, soon learns to reduce his menu to the four or five most requested entrees and the three or four most accepted vegetables; and if this alone is not enough to take all individuality and style out of American cooking, the owners of restaurants and diners (those pre-fab huts serving pre-fab meals) also play scientist too, and serve teabags and plastic-wrapped gobs of jelly to insure what they call uniformity of "portion control." In America competition engenders two kinds of response—making a product better, or making it cheaper.

The pursuit of the profitable middle goes far beyond store counters and cafés—it is the measure of all economic life in the United States. It determines the content of our magazines and newspapers. It provides our hit tunes (many songs are recorded, but shrewd publishers concentrate their promotion on what looks like a winner). It accounts for the sameness of our television programming, for so great is the disproportion between hit and expensive also-ran that if quiz shows, variety programs or Westerns are adjudged the most popular, all effort will be bunched there. In having to produce art, music, drama or even political commentary for the greatest number, men learn to cultivate clarity and simplicity, and to avoid esoteric aridities, but they must often sacrifice subtlety and nuance. The process of writing down to an audience, or succeeding by broad stroke, also results in an erosion of development in both those who give and those who receive.

The situation is not so bad in the printed word: though we have newspaper publishers who aspire to call at every door that the garbage collector calls at, we have magazines that assume varying levels of taste and knowledge; and finally, in book publishing, there is a chance for the individual voice to be heard. But television, with its excessive costs, has found no such gradation possible: it must always aim low to hit the most. Minority tastes are accommodated in off-hours known as "the intellectual ghetto," and if the intellectual minority must turn on their sets at 10 A.M. Sunday morning to get a program to their taste, it is no wonder that it is easy to prove that they don't. The point is not that there is a big "slob" audience, and a limited choosy one, but that there is a scaled gradation of knowledge, taste and interest in the United States of many degrees of depth and range which the law of the profitable middle is often driven to treat as one.

In many operations, then, the majority (or the majority's presumed taste) dominates the scene more than even its numbers entitle it to. There is no right of proportional representation on television, and in buying automobiles, a minority taste finds itself forced to choose among several designs it may not like, if it would have a new car, and is thus recorded in favor of one or the other, while actually happy with none. The pull of the profitable middle thus works to increase the distortion of the American Image, for it seeks out, and accents, the sameness in us all.

Confronted with rising costs, all who sell to the public are driven to increase the number of their customers, and to decrease the amount of individual attention. The American manufacturer cares about his customers—but only in bulk. Something resolute and unpredictable in the consumer keeps this tendency from going too far: in goods and furnishings, manufacturers are compelled to have a complete "line," varied in style and color, for the American people will not let the momentum of uniformity make of their homes or their clothing a dull identity. Even the builders of assembly-line houses are compelled to paint the front doors in different colors, and to vary an unbroken line of cheap-Jack cottages by adding a dormer here and switching a garage there.

Beyond these marginal differences lies a market of those who insist on something out of the ordinary, either because they have the money to gratify an individuality or because they are determined to be distinctive. They must expect to pay more for something else (whether of good or bad taste) for they lose all the advantages of mass merchandising, and in this era of declining craftmanship can never be sure that something individual will be better made than what large-order ingenuity can provide: the best designers have likewise gravitated to the profitable middle where money and power in their trade is. So rich are the resources of those who capture this middle that they are often able to offer better value with their "large economy size" than those whose units, though individual, must be small and uneconomic, and thus the middle swells at the expense of the top as well as the bottom.

The result has been a remarkable increase in the taste of many popularly designed articles; if we would analyze our dissatisfaction, it is often not the design we object to, but its ubiquity. Furthermore, if enough people want something different, a market will reach out to them: those who play badminton instead of baseball, buy *espadrilles* instead of gum-soled sneakers, or prefer Vivaldi to Stephen Foster will find another entrepreneur seeking a profitable middle inside their specialized tastes. Compared to other nations, America's diversity of available goods at an acceptable price is one of its productive triumphs.

But so often quality suffers. The need to find variations in a product—a process that must not be too complicated or expensive— is one more difficulty plaguing the manufacturer, who is caught up in an unending war between high cost and salable price, and in the end turns out not the best that can be made but its most profitable approximation, for the best is apt to be uneconomic. He calls in the advertising man to assure everyone that a mass product is really "custom built" and that goodhearted Charlie, who runs this vast chain gang, may have gotten big but is really still thinking of you. ("Today's banker is a helpful merchant of good will . . . the modern bank has a heart as big as a vault.") Publicity men, who fancy themselves "engineers of consent," step forward, offering to provide a good name for the product before it could possibly win one on its own merits. They, and the advertising men, justify their services by saying that mass production requires mass merchandising, and demand must sustain the rate of production.

Advertising nowadays hopes to do more than persuade us of a distinction between soaps made of the same fats, or gasolines that come from identical refineries. It also presumes to tell the producer in advance what the public wants. The modern adman, like the augurs of old, with much occult mumbo jumbo and crafty searching of entrails, also promises to foretell the most propitious moment for launching profitable operations. Advertising agencies have erected vast empires of research, and deploy brigades of opinion samplers, market testers and misplaced psychologists to tickle the public's fancy, feel its pulse, recoil from its breath and probe its psyche. But if their intentions are often unworthy, I think these pseudoscientists are not nearly as effective as they or their critics believe, who make the mistake of taking these "persuaders" at their own inflated valuation. It is argued, for example, that the adroit packaging and merchandising of Dwight Eisenhower as a presidential candidate in 1952 "put Ike over." It might better be asked whether anything could have stopped Eisenhower from winning in 1952. Could such expensive cajolery have merchandised an Adlai Stevenson or a Thomas E. Dewey into office *against* a public trend?

Nonetheless, fortunes turn on the promises and hunches of advertising specialists. Millions of dollars are involved as high-priced executives listen anxiously for the "feedback" from the public, and in this echoing process fancy themselves manipulators of opinions. They develop an understandable contempt for a public that can be diverted from one brand to another by the sight of a pretty girl or a sly hint that one cigarette is less unhealthy than another. But perhaps the public is not so dumb as these manipulators take it to be. Perhaps it can be diverted from one soap or cigarette to the next precisely because it never took seriously the advertisers' previous nonsense, and considers most standard products to be more or less alike. And what are we in turn to think of these manipulators, who have no standards of their own but will merchandise one product or another indifferently, who feel so superior to us, the dumb public, and who spend their lives in this fashion?

Yet I do not think the advertising man is the villain of the piece: he is only more visible. Perhaps there are no villains. The fellow who at work writes ads that debase others as well as waste his own gifts may at home be a considerate father and on the golf course a friendly companion. He is as apt to be as disturbed as anyone else about something awry in the values of our society, and perhaps in his own community seeks to offer his persuading talents to worthy enterprises. He sustains his pride either by thinking that all human activities have their disabilities and their price, and asks accusingly who then is entitled to criticize him or, more positively, by persuading himself that he is essential to keep the production lines at full pace, the trucks rolling, the cars sold, and the economy going —as in fact he is.

The result of all this attempt to flatter our ear and gratify our whims, of this immense manufacturing and marketing mechanism in which we take our places alternately as participants and as receivers, is the society that gives off the American Image. It will be seen that this image is made, not so much by ourselves as by those who would reach us. We are under daylong assault of those who would exploit us, and who address our most common motives. We are being done in by irrelevancies, leveled by palaver and coated with sham.

Saturated with canned music that follows us wherever we go, to drown out our shuffling or to fill our silences, berated, enticed and warned 24 hours a day, Americans are to be congratulated for remaining as individual as they are. Meaning themselves to do right, they give others the benefit of the doubt, and are indulgent—often too indulgent—of those who would steal their attention. They accept the principle of "free" entertainment—that is, they recognize that television programs could not afford their stars, or newspapers and magazines their luxurious plenty, without the advertising sponsor who in return demands "one word with you." And most people would rather have expensive entertainment with advertising than routine programming without. They are content to argue back at commercials, to develop an immunity to them, or even to take a sporting attitude toward them, and like hockey goalies, dare any to get through that can.

The irresistible, said Justice Brandeis, is often only that which is not resisted. We are so caught up in the complexity and clamor of our way of life that we do not realize how much all of these powerful efforts to attract or divert us are a tax on our spirit: they do a double harm, in the triviality of what they offer and the fatigue which they engender, that keeps us from doing something more profitable with our time. Even to screen out that portion of our culture that we do not want becomes an effort of will. Simplicity of life is no longer ours to begin with, as it was in the days of remote farms, and of school lessons written on the back of a shovel. In a world of congestion, shattering noise and an infinity of seductions, we must, in the midst of a carnival, find and insist upon our own decent simplicity.

14. Fragmented Man

Let us now turn from such a society to the man who inhabits it.

The poor earnest American spends his days importuned to keep to the right, to curb his dog, move to the rear, watch where he is going, dim his lights, throw trash here, not smoke there, fasten his seat belt, face the front, not stand in this place or park in that; he is asked to remember the blind, the helpless and Pearl Harbor; he is tempted with fattening foods and warned to watch his weight; he is urged to think this and told not to think that; he is solicitously invited to go into debt to pay for a car, a TV set or a vacation—and urged to be thrifty; he is asked to consider the Jews, reminded of Arab refugees and cautioned to be kind to minorities; and he is asked why he also doesn't relax.

He is told that everything is done for his listening, smoking or dining pleasure. He is the end man of all production, the object of every politician's affection. And yet, if he subconsciously feels that there is something wrong in American life today, something for which he may be partly at fault, he feels helpless to correct it. No wonder that critics find significance in the fact that his favorite character in fiction is the lone cowhand who goes his own gait and is in control of his circumstances. The legendary cowhand is a man of common sense and good heart, shy with girls but attractive to them, slow to wrath but quick on the draw, fond of solitude but capable of leading, minding his own business except when justice requires his intervention to put things right. He is the unfulfilled American dream.

Latter-day sociologists now divide Americans into three handy sizes—the "tradition-directed"; the "other-directed," who by a process like radar get their direction from those around them; and the "inner-directed," who get their stability from a gyroscope inside themselves. According to what we learned in our copybooks, we should all prefer to be inner-directed. But David Riesman and his fellow sociologists* hesitated to brand one group sheep or to honor the other as goats. Other critics have not been so prudent. The hue and cry about conformity that swept the United States in the mid-fifties was an outcry against a nation of sheep, and no commencement speaker could be in fashion who did not denounce conformity (commencement speaking being the conforming art that it is). I have never taken much to this denunciation: it is usually invoked by the timid trying to console each other for their timidity and hoping that they will soon discover that they add up to a safe majority. I believe that conformity is often confused with uniformity —a different accusation. When so many experts are at work on the American consumer, studying his wants in order to gratify them, is he to blame for conforming to what is made to fit him?

The trouble with the conformity cry, with its appeal to the individuality of the old frontier—though not to the disapproved individuality of the industrial buccaneer—is that it asks an impossibility and thereby increases the common frustration. We can no longer go it alone as individuals any more than we can as a nation. Perhaps we never could. Our frontier history is as instructive in cooperative activity (the quilting bee, the house raising, the common stockade) as it is in solitary resourcefulness. And far more than in the days when a family grew its own food and shot its wardrobe, we have become a collaborative society. We are dependent on our benefits. Others grow our food, make our clothes, build our houses, provide us with heat. Our collaboration goes deeper than that: almost everyone in America today is, in his work, con-

---

* It is a sign of the times that *The Lonely Crowd*, as a treatise on the plight of individual man, should be signed by *three* authors.

structing something that is only part of a whole. We are all in harness, and feel the trace galls.

We are part of what we can only partly control, whether in factories, design rooms, law offices, theaters or city rooms. In our domestic lives, we are in a similar collaborative relationship. Our schools, our shops, our golf courses, our highways and our railway schedules depend on forming communities of need. We are caught up in this condition, and accept more of it than we want. In this important sense, the good and bad of our way of life have been, though willed by us, not wanted by us.

We have become like stacked rifles, standing together and incapable of standing alone. The very technology that makes our living simpler makes our society more complex. The more efficient we get, the more specialized we become, and the more dependent. So many knowledges must go into all our operations these days that the ablest is driven to specialize; the more specialized he becomes the fewer jobs there are to be had; and the more helpless he is to do anything else. He tends to find his friends among those who share the same interests and reassuringly esteem the same skills. He often develops great pride and derives much satisfaction from performing his limited tasks well; sometimes he even makes of his tasks a cult, or a closed shop.

Interdependence in our life is readily acknowledged by those who put together component parts. It is not so often recognized to exist in jobs that have the sound of power and authority. I think of my own. To be foreign editor of a magazine with several million readers perhaps suggests the opportunity for spectacular movement, lavish perquisites, sweeping judgments and a curt nodding acquaintanceship with destiny. The practice is much more modest. If I have the power to set afoot great odysseys, or to pursue curiosities of interest, I must in the end justify their expense and earn their space. An editor in New York may have the foresight to dispatch a man to Kenya or to Algeria in anticipation of trouble, but he must finally rely on how well the correspondent covers the story, and how well the staff in New York handles it. Furthermore, he must convince his managing editor that his own interpretation of the event is the correct one. The decisions that one makes are always subject to the modifications of his colleagues, or to the sabotage of their limited enthusiasm. In our craft, discussion is professional and amiable, but lively. I have come to learn that the more command one has, the less whim he is entitled to. One enjoys a corner office, a secretary, freedom from punching a time clock (which usually means the right to spend much more time at the office) and an impressive view, high above the New York streets, of sunsets reflected goldenly in the windows of distant buildings. But he becomes the voluntary slave of his responsibilities.

In Montaigne's definition of rights, so different from the popular view of them, one has the right to be free to do what one ought, and free not to do what one ought not to do. As an editor, I have no unlimited drawing account on caprice or errors of judgment. I have the right to be right most of the time. This is, I think, the inevitable fix of fragmented men in collaborative undertakings. They cannot doze; they must constantly dare, but they are granted independence only in so far as they continuously justify it.

The legend of science is the lone inventor; we now have laboratory teams. Once a stage director and a playwright were enough; we now have show fixers and play doctors. Physicians have divided the body into a dozen divisions, and men who today know everything known about the brain know next to nothing about the spleen. Most of us even have little knowledge of how many subdivisions science has been splintered into, let alone any awareness of the complexities in each category. It has been estimated that 30,000 scientific articles are published throughout the world each week: even to keep abreast in one's own field is a heady enough task. So much is there to explore that no man, though he set out as confidently as Francis Bacon, can aspire to encompass it all.

Unbalanced specialization, complained Ortega y Gasset, has made scientists hermetic and self-satisfied within their limitations, and he argued that if there are more scientists today than in 1750, there are fewer cultured men. Specialists are apt to become efficiently pointed, like a projectile, but not rounded enough to be human; and their proper humility about what in other fields they do not know sometimes becomes an evasion of responsibility for the effects of their labors. Many of our best people are tongue-tied by diffidence: they hesitate to make judgments about what they do not know well (who knows one thing well knows how little he knows) and therefore leave a no man's land to those who do not hesitate to holler out their ignorant claims.

Our science is becoming in some respects as Alexandrine as poetry once was: the very precision with which scientists use words makes them more unintelligible to the layman. Philosophy now pursues terminology, not content, and disclaims, in the words of one English philosopher, the "ability to discover in the ultimate nature of reality some source of ethics"; political scientists treat of forms and decline to make moral recommendations; historians hope to get the past straight, but do not pretend to draw lessons from what they learn. We have not only narrowed our explorations but have narrowed our ambitions.

Specialization and fragmentation do not end with the technologists. It is understood that comedians have joke writers, and assumed that movie actors do not write the testimonials for the products they recommend but do not use. But the president of the United States also has ghost writers—to whom he may or may not outline his ideas in advance; and he has a public relations man to guide him to tactful answers to press conference questions. In the name of efficiency, all this is useful, like those multiple pens that enable a president to sign a dozen documents by writing his signature once. Yet the result is the creation of a bogus *persona*. How is the historian of the future to measure a modern president's thoughts— by searching out the marginal corrections he made on what someone else wrote for him?

Fragmentation is a perfection of the parts: it has such obvious economic utility in our society that no one can withstand it. It reaches into sport, where it results in the specialization of offensive and defensive teams: football's ancient sixty-minute iron man may have been more of an athlete, but he would be no match today for a succession of fresh players trained in specific functions. In after-dinner speeches, football coaches now celebrate as the virtue of their sport the teaching of subordination to a common effort rather than individual excellence.

The trend to fragmentation spreads throughout our society, and may be further observed in our public personalities, our commentators and our corporation presidents, who are often an artificial synthesis of separate skills, producing a whole that is more than human. They seem slightly larger than life not only because publicity has swelled them, but because they are in effect a holding company of several talents: more is done in their name than one person can do, for three or four persons, or an entire retinue, labor at sustaining one inflated personality. Much effort then goes into concealing this effort.

In the course of selling us whisky, the admen have provided us with their notion of the "man of distinction" contemporary society is presumed to consider ideal. He is a bronzed man of action in elbow-patched sporting jacket, who wears his clothes casually and his learning lightly: he recognizes the slow movements of difficult quartets and the lyrics of Herrick, yet is never seen in apprenticeship. Culture descends on him like a mantle, intact, entire. If such a creature exists, he is apt to be unphotogenic, and a $30-an-hour model would look the part better. He too is symptomatic of the inflated artificial personality put together out of separate parts. I remember once, in more trusting days, attending with some anticipation a small luncheon given by *Life* for a famous stage star who excelled in sophisticated comedy. His arch manner, his dry delivery of scathing wit was celebrated from coast to coast. At our lunch, all of us listened eagerly every time he opened his mouth, ready to admire, ready even to be crushed by his wit if only to enjoy it. His timing was expert, and so was the manner, the delivery and the assurance. But out of his mouth came only commonplaces. Without his author, he was a clothes dummy and a trained larynx.

So it is today with most of our contemporary celebrities: spontaneity is studied; one person achieves an emphatic and compelling voice, another gives the voice something to say. A man with a handsome face and knit brows may earn several hundred thousand dollars a year on television because his unforced reading of something he doesn't understand makes him seem so calm and reassuring. We have rewrite men to make an author sound more like himself than he himself could. We stitch and patch taped music, so that a sour trumpet note can be excised from a Toscanini performance, and a new one put in. We once had, and thought it bad enough, radio programs where the announcer held up applause cards to stir up an audience to laugh and clap on cue to pay for their "free" entertainment; we now insert recorded laughter into television films from past programs, so that one man's hilarity at a pie-throwing episode five years ago may still be heard howling through a pantomime a century hence. One wonders about juvenile fans these days, wanting to become successful and admired like their hero: do they know what a synthetic echo-chamber composite he is, or do they feel hopelessly in awe of his effortless and many-sided talents?

Most of our public arts now require a platoon system of inspiration; our sophisticated magazines shine with mechanized urbanity. We have division of labor, and become replaceable parts (the danger in taking vacations on many jobs is the discovery of how dispensable one is). Yet no one of us set out to be a replaceable part in life, or to be simply a valuable cog. Our youthful ambitions were round, like the world.

Even before management became so skillful at fragmenting us, in order to get the most efficient work out of each of us, there always existed that compromising need to settle for what was closest to our ambition and yet paid well, simply to earn a living: the secondary part of one's nature is often the most useful commercially. And so there are the writers, working on newspapers and magazines, or, in a shade less pure fashion, in ad agencies and publicity jobs. Ballet dancers weary of eternal practice and slow promotion, and drift to Broadway or television, where the pay is better and stardom quicker for less exacting performances. Girls training for opera, but wanting to enjoy luxury too, sing anonymous radio commercials (who knows what jingles you sang on the way up, they might ask, as the loose woman asks, "Who misses a slice off a cut loaf?"). Our youthful ambitions survive as a taunt. Some people later comfort themselves by overvaluing the jobs they settle for, in that American addiction for puffing up titles. Others become cynical about their work and coin depreciatory names for it, feeling that this is at least to have salvaged their honesty.

Our civilization has become so complex that it requires interlocking skills: whether as auditors, clerks, foremen, editors, lab technicians or administrators, we contribute our fragment of talent and effort to a whole, and yearn for reassurance that what we do matters. For many, even, fragmented work permits a preferred concentration: they can work at a specialty without thought of its bookkeeping necessities; they have but to ask for what they want and it arrives "through channels." We all develop a merciful selectivity in appraising our daily work, satisfying ourselves with the good we have done, or the effort we have taken, and passing over the triviality, the rote, and what was unworthy of us. But some of the dissatisfaction with our lives, and one of the reasons why the United States is superior to its image, is that so many people—whether designers, machinists or salesmen—are better than the product they work at, which must be rounded off to have wide appeal, made simpler to be operated more easily, and made of economical materials to insure a salable price: this multiplicity of individual disappointments in our collaborative society is the price of our collective achievements.

We would tire of nothing but piano solos, but he who takes up the bassoon must resign himself to a lifetime of playing in ensemble.

We are apt to be spiritually dissatisfied in our work, but not materially discontent, for the essence of our many individual bargains with Mephistopheles is that our wants are usually well taken care of. Once corporations had to be prodded into looking after their help, but they now sometimes outrun the unions in suggesting benefits. First the wartime labor shortage, and then the later need to hold onto specialists, got companies into the habit of solicitude for key employees. Where personnel departments formerly existed only to recruit workers, they now developed a new specialty, that of devising attractions to keep people on the payroll: retirement plans, annual bonuses, educational schemes, medical insurance, hospital benefits, bowling teams, psychological counselors. The employee must feel wanted, and benefits were contrived so that if tempted to move, he would be reminded of his stake in staying.

In a turn that Karl Marx did not foresee and many of his successors do not concede, capitalism has become a collection of city-states. Like those Italian medieval families with armored and crenelated domains, it has its retainers and its warriors. These city-states develop their own patriotism, and display house flags; their rulers long to be known as Good King Harry or William the Just. They take care of their own wounded, and watch over their families: in fact, this enlightened benevolence toward workers makes the employed in America feel less need to seek redress through government, and may help explain our political indifference in settled times. Desires which begin as political demands made of the state often end in being gratified by the employer, for the American tendency is to work out health insurance and similar schemes through the employer, not the government. It is a mutually agreeable arrangement; the employee is gratified by corporate munificence but accepts it as self-interested, and feels no need to tug at his forelock and say "Thank you, master." Social programs in turn strengthen companies. But they are also one more centripetal force in our society: an individual working on his own time labors without provision against sickness, accident or other contingency, and finds himself drawn toward work that will assure his family against misfortune.

Like city-states, corporations continually joust with rivals, make brief pacts of convenience but are driven to compete. Sometimes their warriors put sugar in the tanks of rival tractor makers at demonstrations, but usually the stratagems are subtler. They war with sales charts, territory grabbing and secret discounts. There is a momentum of growth in any ambitious company; it cannot stand still; it operates aggressively, and develops a belief in itself which permits people on occasion to do bad deeds in its service. The instinct to preserve the institution—that instinct which in nations and in churches has led to mistaken zeal, to cruelties and inquisitors—also operates in a corporation. It does things to keep its "competitive position" secure, and out of fear of falling behind; and as in all patriotic undertakings, men sometimes acquiesce in deeds they would not do in their private lives.

Primarily, however, these city-states long to be liked, or at least respected, and they covet goodwill. Corporations are no longer the "heejus monsthers" of old; and the biggest are frequently the best. They have earned their rightful place in the American scene, though in individual cases it can be an insecure and shifting one. Even the leaders of big corporations now find their movement confined by the vastness of their operations, and, if allowed to construct fantasies of individuality and encouraged to consider themselves adventuresome, find themselves deterred by institutional inertia and caution. They are surrounded by advisers on how to design their product, how to promote it, how to market it, how to transport it; they hire experts to guide their labor policies and others to tell them what attitude to assume in public. They are even counseled as to what to say in speeches, warned against their natural promptings or given wings for their banality of thought. They are beset with advice against seeming to be the bosses they are. To quote one management textbook: "One cannot expect the employees of an organization to have a real sense of being a full member of the team in good standing if management flaunts the trivial and superficial aspects of status in their face." If they took seriously all such mock-scientific advice, they would not dare to drive up to the factory in their gadget-filled, air-conditioned Cadillacs with backseat telephones.

Socially, the modern corporation is of threefold benefit to us: in the standard of living it provides us, in the employment it creates, and in the diffusion of power it represents, so that we do not owe everything to the omniscient state. But this last advantage is also responsible for some of the weakness in our society. Providing us with so much, corporations take the place of what in other societies would have to provide more. They suffer from the disabilities of all city-states: each being so strong, they war against the possibility of a unity above them, and the result is the absence of some of the advantages, as well as avoidance of some of the evils, of powerful and integrated communities. A corporation is responsible for what it does, but cannot be held responsible for what it is not required to do. The north of its ambitions is a magnetic north, and not true north. Since profit-seeking is its ultimate function, its science must first seek utility and cannot always afford purity of search; its advertising may prefer to be truthful but is required to sell; its product may aspire to be the finest but must be first of all profitable. A corporation may take steps that are sensible in its own terms, which are not necessarily so in society's. And though increasingly responsible, it is not finally accountable to any outside agency for much of what it does. The harm it does is often peripheral and usually unintended; if there is violence done to society it is usually guilty at most of negligent homicide.

In some respects, the jagged skyline of New York perfectly mirrors our corporate society: reflecting our technical proficiency and feverish energy, reflecting also our many individual ambitions, each thrusting up the distance it dares or can afford to, and the whole having a certain fortuitous beauty in the right sunlight—a chance harmony that is largely unintentional, and never tranquil for long.

In fashioning a society where corporations are the source of so much of our energy but do not have full accountability; in counting on the competition of rivals, the demands of unions and occasional interventions by the state to moderate so vital a power, we must pay the price of a haphazardness in the community, and a feeling that we are not in full control of ourselves, and that no one else quite is.

15. The Poverty of Plenty

After dinner, over a cognac, the purser of a French ship was telling me one of those neat little anecdotes that ships' officers seem to keep in open stock, to stop any passenger from saying something vital about politics, religion or national divergencies. Once, the purser said, his employers decided, as a morale-building gesture, to invite the crew's families aboard ship while it was in port, so that they might see where their husbands or fathers worked. The captain's young son took in the luxury of his father's quarters, the sweep of the grand salons and the splendor of the dining room where the captain's was the head table. When he had seen all of this, the boy asked, "Daddy, how can you be as rich as you are, when we are as poor as we are?"

The gap between the manner of living at work, and living outside it, is a familiar anomaly to many Americans. It exists particularly among those many men who have been granted that priceless boon, an expense account, and who learn to live in one style on it, and much less grandly off of it—among those anxious souls, that is, who do not simply swindle their private expenses onto the company's bills. Even without this special privilege, work in America has steadily become more agreeable, insofar as shorter hours, better quarters, scientific lighting and two-toned walls can make a difference. We have had a constant upgrading in working conditions, a process that is quite independent of the product itself, and in no way reflected in it—except in the price.

Just as in the modern army the ratio of men behind the lines to the man up front continually widens, so in the modern corporation is there a trend toward continued expansion in the carpeted echelons. As the making and marketing of goods has become more complex, new jobs have foliated in every company—dispatchers, accountants, staff nurses, mail-room supervisors, consumer representatives, market testers and form fillers. What they have in common is white collarness, and a wish to work in the front office.

This tendency—more than the inertia of workingmen—may account for a stagnancy in our productivity charts. Fewer people now want to be *making* the product: all want to be on top of the process, marketing it, packaging it, distributing it, with congenial surroundings to work in, coffee breaks as a matter of course, and expense accounts if possible. Soon in many plants still another operation must be set up, employing a new group of experts skilled in reducing the cost of materials or in economizing in the manufacturing processes to offset the increasing expense. Sometimes great ingenuity goes into this effort, without being evident in the product itself. We have progressed from simple labor-saving devices to elaborate automation plants where several women can baby-sit machines and ovens that bake 4,000 cakes a day, though the cakes taste no better. Engineers not only work to take the labor out of using a product—and develop automatic transmissions and power steering—but also to take the labor out of its making. We have thermostatic controls and magnetic memory drums. Who wants to do hard work any more? And why should a man strain his back, when a fork-lift truck can lift a load so much quicker, easier and cheaper?

The result has been a proliferation of service industries—those who sell, those who distribute, and those who handle the personnel forms of those who sell and distribute. Everyone is engaged in the pursuit of jobs that do not require "dirty hands" and are not considered degrading. No wonder there is lessened pride in homely jobs, or that coal miners and stevedores and grease monkeys see in a son's schooling his chance to escape his father's fate. It is not alone heavy jobs that are considered degrading: jobs which involve "waiting" on someone else have come to seem undemocratic. The serving class no longer feels the need to defer to anyone, and is willing to do so only if well tipped, to show that its labor is not lightly volunteered. Tipping has become no condescending rite, but a toll.

When we talk about the dignity of labor ("after all, we all work for a living") we mean a dignity that is felt, not granted. A welder feels it, for though he has to wear work clothes and a hard hat, he is not required to smile at anybody. Smiling is for climbers. We may be pleased that in America no one need any longer feel servile, but in a housemaid who resents her mistress's leisure or a waitress who dislikes serving others, emancipation often expresses itself in the right to be sullen, rude and slothful. They are protected in their jobs by unions and the knowledge that there are other jobs to be had, but they also know that they are in work that society requires but does not highly value, and they reserve the right to get back at society. For if we have come to depreciate, we have not learned to do without, certain jobs.

Only what society values will finally be done well: in France, where so many people are dedicated to a morose perfection of appetite, a waiter's job, like a chef's, is an honored one; the best of French waiters manage to convey an impression of pleased anticipation, as if they know better than you what a treat is in store for you in the kitchen. The deference of a French waiter would be intolerable to an American waiter, yet the Frenchman finds in his work a dignity of conferred respect. For an American, any service must be without a feeling of inferiority. A mechanic works for others but does not feel menial, for though he may be greasy he is doing something that those who hire him probably cannot do, and this gives him self-respect.

But as America becomes more and more a land of high wages and short hours, of labor-saving devices and of bulk manufacturing processes, we are confronted by a decline in craftsmanship. Men no longer learn trades, they learn to assemble and install. We live in the age of the repairman, and products are designed not to require a long apprenticeship of him: he must be able to fix a number of brands, and will be heard to abuse any product that requires too complicated an effort of him. With mass production, we all can have a standard good product (perhaps not as good as its advertising promised, but good anyway) at a price we can afford—so long as it does not require too much individual attention and craftsmanship.

In the old days a cobbler took pride in his craft and in the visible satisfaction of his customers, among whom he lived. The task of today's shoe manufacturer is also to make shoes, but his mission is to make money. What craft pride can the lathe operator, the box inspector and the credit manager look to? At best, they contribute to a process that makes not the best shoes that money can buy, but *good value for the price.* How stimulating can that be? And thus we have the desperate effort to keep men interested in, and gratified by, routine work.

Unions, righting old wrongs, have made the workingman feel protected in his job, but the burden of their indoctrination is that a job is a right. Unions exist to extract benefits from employers, not to encourage initiative, which in some places is defined as a selfish and unfraternal effort to get ahead. Unions preach loyalty to the trade, not to the employer. All such reasoning has a melancholy reality to it. I remember my first awareness of unions, when I was a boy and my father would take us by the hand and lead us across the street so that we would not pass close by that headquarters of nameless evils which in Seattle was called the Labor Temple. Later I became child enough of the Depression to watch companies lop off loyal employees and to see white-collar employees, always the most devoted, suffer the most, because they had no contractual protection. But now, so embedded is unionism that in large factories workers even have a say over how they are spoken to, and foremen learn not to appear too taskmasterly. When supervisors are judged by their capacity to get along with those who work for them, they can hardly be blamed for not wanting to be regarded as black bosses. This "nice-guyism," whether insisted upon by unions or volunteered by superiors who want to be popular, makes work easier, but often at the expense of care about details.

Despite our much-boasted productive genius, the fact is that many of our products—automobiles, radios, TV sets—are now often slovenly made and carelessly assembled. And who has not returned some expensive but defective automobile or appliance only to be told by a disinterested foreman, after hearing the defect described: "Oh, they all do that"?

In Europe, though American products are still admired for ingenuity of design, they are no longer regarded as the last word in manufacturing. Prosperity, in eliminating worry, has too often eliminated care.

As wages go up, manufacturers seek to hold their prices steady by installing machines that make more products with fewer hands, or to find materials that will be cheaper but serve almost as well. And as this process continues, as the number of expert advisers and their secretaries and sword-bearers multiply in any operation, an employer worried by his "unit cost" discovers that only so much time can profitably be spent on any individual item or customer. "Special handling" by well-paid employees becomes one of a product's costliest charges. This fact applies not only to those working at hourly rates in the plant, but to those out front who are less aware of the "unit cost" of whatever they do, but know that they can only "waste" so much time on any one customer or devote only so much effort to each prospect. The exceptions to this condition are not so many as they seem. If the commission for selling a substantial order is to be large, more time can be spent in wooing a client. If the product is to be reproduced many times, more hours can be spent in designing it. When people at work say that they have done what they could, they generally mean that they did their best considering the importance of the task and the time that could be spent on it. Such rationed competence is not to be confused with excellence: it is its profitable approximation.

The modern executive oversees so many kinds of operations that he has to have his own built-in regulator of how much time and energy he can allot to any one of them. He rarely sharpens his own pencils, not because the work would demean him, but because it would be an uneconomic use of his talents. Office work is efficiently fragmented so that men do only work scaled to their rate of pay. What a man does is apt to become less visible the higher up the ladder he is: sometimes an executive sitting at his desk seemingly does nothing but encourage one course and discourage another: he grunts through his day. If it thus becomes harder to measure this man's triumphs, or to discover his shortcomings, life has become no easier for him: jobs that do not have measurable utility are apt to have more fitful tenure. The less a job makes physical demands on an executive, the more nervous demands it makes. Life on that high plateau requires a confident character to begin with, but since so much often rides on one decision, easy confidence frequently turns into desperate uncertainty, speaking with a hollow assurance. At those heights, breath becomes shorter and life more precarious.

The fragmenting of effort, and the compromising on profitable approximations required in most jobs, means that men of good heart and good will find themselves, at their desks or their design boards, busy at work that makes full demands of their energy but sometimes less demand of their best. The most frequently heard complaint in American business life is the desire to "escape the rat race."

Considering the nature of their work, most people feel rushed.* Creativity itself in such a climate must account for its time, and often cannot wait on inspiration but must adapt what is close to hand. We thus tend to take a decorator's interest in other cultures—ransacking museums or far-off places for combinations of colors or design motifs we can borrow from them—and no wonder that we "use up" these other cultures so fast and move on to something new. Fashion can never stay long enough to discover what a culture was really about, but moves on restlessly like one of those crop-picking machines that whooshes across an entire field, gathering in its claws all that it can profitably pick up and leaving behind what would have been uneconomic to pause over. This year a Polynesian theme; next year the Etruscans. The present temper of the arts, to satisfy people's longing for something more than the bleak and efficient functionalism of our uncrafted homes and offices, runs toward

---

* And since our pace is what it is, we then have soda fountains, which are another form of profitable approximation: we must have speed and therefore accept clutter; we demand economy and must tolerate crowding and rapidity of turnover. Drugstore counters are a hurried substitute for restaurants, and the American, understanding their function, puts up with their annoyances. While a counterman slops an egg into a pan and whips up some ready-made tuna mash, an adman—at a low unit cost—has been at work on the menus, spreading his crispy crunchy promises that have no relation to what will be delivered: for it is the American custom never to acknowledge a lowering of standards in service or product, but to deny stoutly that anything has been lost along with what has been gained.

diluted borrowings (simplified Victorian, etc.). The designer's task, in adapting a past elegance, is to see that what is intricate be made simple, or capable of easy reproduction, for we no longer have time to be original or thorough: we adapt, we imitate and we multiply, and are becoming a society of tomb robbers.

More than a century ago, Tocqueville, that perceptive young French critic of American life, observed that private life in an egalitarian society "is so busy, so excited, so full of wishes and work, that hardly any energy or leisure remains to each individual for public life." As compared to Europeans, we live our businesses—not only executives, but almost everyone—with such intensity, accompanied by such urban strain, that we relax nervously too: drinking, watching thrillers or fights, listening to hectic music. Public service, like culture, is something we delegate to others who are paid to take their time at it: we are content to register a push-button approval or disapproval. We often ask that even our leisure pleasures be screened first: we demand that theater critics—those tasters for the king in a democracy—return a definitive one-, two- or three-star verdict on plays; we do not want to waste time or money on promise, or the half good—we want the sure-fire. Best-seller lists guide our reading and hit parades our listening. To some extent, our pace compels this attitude, but it also results from the complexity of choice put before us.

A century ago, in the country society of England, it may have been possible for a few to have a familiarity with books, music and painting, along with the external manners and skill in dancing and in French that Lord Chesterfield prescribed, joined with the ability to preside over a manor and ride to hounds. This state of things presumed first of all a kind of leisure class that does not exist in America. But it also existed before the modern proliferation of culture (good and bad); before radios and phonographs multiplied the amount of music available to be heard; before photographs and films and reproductions multiplied the amount of art and architecture the well-informed are expected to be aware of. He who would now have a cocktail-hour fluency in the arts is expected to have a smattering familiarity with Persian miniatures, Japanese lithographs, African masks and contemporary ceramics, as well as Byzantine mosaics, Viking prows and Romanesque stained glass—though he need know little about any.

In trying to encompass all, we may end by understanding nothing and, like Buridan's ass, starve to death not knowing which pile of hay to reach for. Psychologists speak of our brief attention span. We no longer wish to read long books with leisurely descriptive passages: our literature is pell-mell in style; television programming rarely dares go beyond an hour, or at most ninety minutes, if it would hold an audience; we have become a land of digests, of quick summaries and of "briefings." Our picture journalism specializes in telling us "all you need to know" about Aztec civilization in five pages—and so resourceful is American ingenuity that the job is often quite competent, representing the splurge of time and money that used to go into those gilt-lettered volumes made for a king. In laying out the pages, the editor judges by his own viscera how much he thinks readers can endure of the Aztecs, and how this topic must fare against the competing attractions of shapely Miss Tillamook Cheese and an article on the revival of Christianity. He knows that if he wants to keep five or seven million restless readers he cannot saturate them with Aztec culture. So another fast foray has been made into "understanding the world we live in." Many have labored "to keep a drowsy emperor awake" and their majesties, the American public, can feel themselves well served. Their foreshortened attention span then turns to something else.

To say that we pursue a false set of values is to give us more credit than we deserve for conscious self-direction; progress has us in its tow, and sets so fast a pace that we do not know how to let go. Out of our riches has come a kind of poverty, the poverty of speed and saturation, and a bewilderment of attractions. Movies, sports, books all compete for our time, and do so in a ratio of impact measurable not by intrinsic worth but by the amount of high-powered collaborative effort that went into attracting our attention. In sport, fragmented professionalism drives out the clumsier amateurs. Spectacular movies drive out the more modest, even though sex and splendor, whether in Biblical or Renaissance dress, have a flat, expensive sameness. The immense resources of our big glossy magazines crush the gentle art of the essay. The ease of travel to everywhere and anywhere in the world makes us discontent with the near and familiar, so that in our rush we no longer see flowers or valleys individually.

A century ago Ruskin, who could not be consoled "for the destitution of a London suburb by the softness of my own armchair," saw the timid beginnings of speed, and did not like what he saw. "No changing of place at a hundred miles an hour, nor making of stuffs a thousand yards a minute," he warned, "will make us one whit stronger, happier or wiser. There was always more in the world than men could see, walked they ever so slowly; they will see it no better for going fast. . . . As for being able to talk from place to place, that is indeed well and convenient; but suppose you have originally nothing to say. We shall be obliged at last to confess what we should long ago have known, that the really precious things are thought and sight, not pace. It does a bullet no good to go fast; and a man, if he be truly a man, no harm to go slow; for his glory is not at all in going but in being."

He lived in a slowpoke age, and could not foresee that progress itself would not be satisfied to keep a steady pace. Now, before we have time to absorb what we have, science and invention have accumulated new wonders, at a rate that accelerates every year, for we are in a cataclysmic breakthrough in every field of endeavor except human conduct. Progress moves with a momentum that is not our own; we are left protesting that we cannot help it, because in making better bottle openers or guided missiles, competition is a demanding spur. It is all very exciting and exhilarating, and it's great to be alive. But despite the multiplicity of advantages and advances, it sometimes seems to me a bleak, wind-swept tarmac we occupy on the airstrip to the future.

16. The Barracuda Waters

So far, if I have muttered harshly about the defects of our contemporary life, I have also assumed the existence of a kind of American innocence, in which evil was largely an unintended side-effect. I have suggested that the American Image is a distorting mirror because its surface reflects not us so much as those who would influence us. I have argued that there is a lack of coherence in our society because no elite exists to set our standards, and under our democratic conception of equality, one would be resisted if it presumed to.

I have further argued that the dominant economic groups which are in their own fields something of an elite, do not seek to erect standards for our society but set their course toward trying to please opinion. They do not want to change the world, but only to sell to it, and are content to anticipate and minister to taste rather than to reform it. They are not so much seeking to inflict vulgarity as pursuing another goal, and would as soon (as some do) produce what is uncompromisingly first-rate, if this can be shown to produce profit similarly. These immense industrial or commercial enterprises, which in many ways provide so well for us and those they employ, are too big to be subordinated yet are in themselves neither completely free agents nor fully accountable. And finally I have suggested that the nature of our intricate and interlocking society has made us all live fragmented and dependent lives, and for this

reason, it is hard to persuade most of us—except in emergencies—
to make common cause about anything.

We are thus, unless there is to be a drastic and unlikely change
in our national habits and ambitions, up against forces as impersonal
as rain, and against our dissatisfactions can only open our umbrellas and wear rubbers, or stay indoors. The villainy of a few
individuals or even of a class cannot be blamed for the way we are.
Impersonal forces hold too great a sway.

But all this being true, we must not leave out the enrichments to
our culture contributed by villainy.

Perhaps the subject of villainy should be tactfully prefaced by the
assurance that the resemblance of anyone hereafter described to
any real person living or dead is purely coincidental. But I do not
really need such a qualifier: my knowledge of the commercial
world's villainy is largely an onlooker's. I have not in my own working life sought my satisfactions where the knife edges of competition
are sharpest. Like most Americans I have found my closest friends
among those I work with, who know my shortcomings, quirks and
lapses as I know theirs. Their interests touch mine, and their dry
and offhand praise or censure—because it is knowing—means more
than unreserved compliments or denunciations from outside. But
one can hardly live and work in the center of Manhattan Island
without being aware of another kind of daily life—centered principally in a more unrelenting kind of business, in the discount
houses, in the go-for-broke agencies, the networks, the stores, the
sales departments, the garment houses, the national headquarters
of big corporations—where one man profits by another's fall, and
where men plead the necessity of business for engaging in a cordial
but unremitting warfare. Particularly in those situations where big
rewards and lucky opportunities coincide, where success is more a
matter of the breaks than of steady preparation, where one may
quickly win much or lose all, where every favor has its price, does
villainy find its most natural habitat. There lie the Barracuda Waters,
where victories are worth a few casualties, or a few enemies.

"You're in the big leagues now. Get wise to yourself, boy."
The barracuda waters, red-stained and turbulent, are mostly in
those deeps where the most ambitious and energetic go (though they

are sometimes to be found closer inshore too). In these perilous waters the big game fish sport and attack the weaker, and not only do the big turn on one another, but there are those lesser contests where liberty for the pike is death for the minnow. These spots are sometimes deceptively tranquil to the outsider's eye, for though an angry urge may be as intense now to a proprietor as it once was to a cave man, his means of gratification has been moderated under capitalism's civilized demeanor. Where once heads were lopped off, men are now merely severed from their jobs; where once there were eye-gouging contests, there are now competitions for vice-presidencies; where once losers were banished, they are now sent to branch offices. A moralist might see no distinction, except in degree, between banishing a man to Siberia in fact, or merely "putting him on ice"—but the victim may be forgiven a preference.

Having made due allowance for the universality of man's depraved nature, it must be admitted that life sometimes gets primitive in our wall-to-wall-carpeted jungles, where the rapacious stalk between mahogany desks and panelled walls, or forage over executive luncheons. There are some who thrive on the power game, and find pleasure in it that others get from shooting birds or kicking cats. They master the rope-jumping skill of making little intrusions at staff meetings, delivering an innuendo and darting out again, undetected except perhaps by the victim. The business jungle is often more treacherous for seeming kind: for if we must be like animals, it is a pity that we did not develop tails like dogs, which wave only when friendship is genuinely intended.

"Sit down, won't you? I've been meaning to talk to you. We're reorganizing around here—and I hate to tell you—but I'm sorry to say that you don't fit into our new plans. We have to make room for new blood. I expect the same thing will happen to me one day. You're not as young as you used to be, you know."

Schooling in the barracuda ways begins early, and there are many textbooks. Stendhal's duchessa, in *The Charterhouse of Parma*, advising Fabrizio on how to prepare for the violet stockings of a monsignor, tells him: "Believe or not, as you choose, what they teach you, *but never raise any objection.* Imagine that they are teaching you the game of whist; would you raise any objections to the rules of whist? . . . Bear in mind that there are people who will make a note of your slightest objections; they will forgive you a little amorous intrigue if it is done in the proper way, but not a doubt. . . . Do not give in to the temptation to shine; remain silent: people of any discernment will see your cleverness in your eyes. It will be time enough to be witty when you are a bishop."

Men have become office managers in the same way, needing no duchessa to guide their instincts.

"We'll make it up to you. We're not going to let you starve, or just dump you out on the streets. We're not that much bastards. I personally have always enjoyed working with you, but I just don't have full say around here. God knows, I put up a fight for you."

At an early age, American boys are taught the laws of competition: be a sportsman, but win (alumni praise athletics but honor only victories). They learn the art of pitching—"don't give him anything to hit"—and reconcile themselves to the notion that one has to lose if another is to win. They learn not just the individual urge to excel, that lonely demanding of the best in oneself which is the mark of champions, but the vicious edge of combat. They hear that "nice guys finish last" and observe that any coach or manager who does not take advantage of every wile permitted under the rules will be outshone by one who does. Later they discover that some businessmen, like baseball pitchers, are not above throwing an occasional duster or beanball at a competitor, not meaning to kill, but just to jar him up a little. Young men, naïvely entering the business world with the belief that ideas will be treated on their merits, and that everyone else is interested only in seeking the company's best interest, soon find themselves among men who say "Let's keep him waiting a while," or "He's getting too big for his britches," which is the way seniority (and mediocrity) often holds its ascendancy.

"We won't do anything quick, so you'll have a chance to shop around. And if there is anything I personally can do for you, just name it. No—I'm afraid there's no point in trying to see the old man. He's awfully tied up, and he asked me to talk things over with you."

Many executives pride themselves on an aggressive stance that keeps people "on their toes," which in practice means living on their nerves. They understand the art of playing off one ambition against another, and believe that making a man a little uncertain, and a little hungry, is good for his work, lest he get to feeling indifferent—though of course they would not want him to have ulcers or a heart attack. As places narrow and the competition increases—out in the big game waters—the sport gets rougher, and victims are then required. Employees on the outer edge of these treacherous waters become expert readers of the battle communiqués which issue from time to time, and know that fulsome praise of some poor fellow in an interoffice memo probably indicates that whatever his new title, it probably reflects a demotion.

"Well, you asked for it. I wasn't going to let you have it, but now that you're acting this way, I'll tell you straight out. You've had it, brother. Nobody wants you around any longer. You haven't a friend in the place."

And then there are the farewell dinners, those hypocritical occasions when they pass the poisoned chalice and sing of comradeship. After many drinks, a few insincere remarks and a set of golf clubs, everyone appears equally a good fellow, and the victim may even become convinced that it had to be done, and probably hurt the other fellow to do it. The laurel is for those who came in first, and the myrtle for those who finished second; beyond that, no prizes are awarded.

I have sometimes wondered why such practices seem more prevalent in America than elsewhere. Perhaps it is because Europeans seem to expect no favors on their jobs, and the relationship is colder and more guarded. The American business habit of being accessible to one's office colleagues, and of seeking their affection as well as their respect, requires an executive to dissemble more than would a European businessman, who believes that affection's place is in the home, if anywhere. The smiles of American business are part of our open ways: sometimes indicating pleasure, or courtesy, sometimes signifying nothing, sometimes disguising dislike. The palship practice of business (which makes it more embarrassing for both when the moment comes to fire someone) are sometimes misunderstood by Europeans who, being greeted heartily, think they have made a quick conquest of the simple Americans. They may later discover that a blistering candor is also part of the American way. Underneath smiling exteriors, distinctions are being made, and understood by others, all the time, and when justice at last overtakes someone who had it coming to him, his associates agree that it could not have happened to a nicer fellow.

Perhaps this is why men who have gone up in balloons report that the last sound heard from earth is the barking of dogs.

I would not argue that deadly competition is more widespread in America than everyone knows it to be. For most people, the place where they work must be congenial or they will not stay: the camaraderie of fellow workers cannot be legislated by union contract, but exists. They must be able to grumble together over the weather or the boss's latest mistake; they watch with critical eye men around them who rise by flattering the boss, or women who prosper by semaphoring with their hips. In the bullpen, the backroom, or at the water cooler, judgments are passed by the severest of American juries, one's peers. The left-behind, the passed-over, the misunderstood, the deficient can count on sympathy in this spontaneous forum, and the man rising from the ranks can count on—at the most—temporary probation until he proves himself fit to rule.

The nature of our competitive world obliges everyone to arm himself to some extent, if only with defensive weapons. An innocent's success will still provoke the malice of the jealous, and even in monasteries, among dedicated men, favoritism and envy exist. There are some in any group who practice the cruelty that must unmask, and allows no one his desperate pretenses. There are those who condemn most violently in another what they most deplore in themselves, and exorcise their own demons by denouncing his. If victory has its roughshod ways, failure has its vicious rebuttals.

I would not even argue that in America only the pushy get the prizes. In the end, merit generally wins, but usually only after it has "gotten sophisticated" and learned to temper its protests and to measure its opportunities. Some who succeed preserve a kind of power innocence, totally indifferent to rivalry and incapable of maneuver. Like good half-milers, they win by setting their own pace. Others are not so self-sufficient: they jockey for position, and those around them must learn to fend and endure. In New York City the pushy get-ahead quality is at a premium. Its end result may sometimes be observed there too, among those older men in an office who have had to give way to springier-legged younger versions of their own breezy breed, and find themselves drinking a little more, and believing a little less in what they are doing, though ready, like an aging boxer, to go on "hustling." It is this metropolitan ingathering of the ambitious that gives New York City its metallic brilliance.

There are degrees of villainy, and of intent. Those with an "instinct for the jugular" glory in it; others are at unhappy moments driven to it. So often all of us, in our necessary entanglements, have to make collateral decisions, choosing between cutting a thread entirely and accepting a choice we do not like in order to continue a relationship we think on balance to be worthwhile. We face constant conflicts of loyalty. Society grips us like a web; money holds us, and most of us are prisoners of the kind of specialized talent that requires us to pursue our tasks with the help of others. We are not always as we intend to be, and our actions are capable of being misunderstood. We comfort ourselves by private explanations, and count on our friends to make allowances, knowing the gap between what we seem to be and what we wish we were. A severing impulse in us fights society's persuasive voice: "Put up with this and you won't be sorry," "What do you care, you're getting paid, aren't you?," "We all have to give in sometimes," "You'll soon get over this," "You'll find it's like this wherever you go," "You can't have all the benefits without paying the price," "None of us wants to do this, but it's got to be done," "You're being stubborn: how can you be so sure you're right when everyone else is against you?," "You're talking as if you're the only one with moral principles around here." Or, the simplest of all: "Why don't you get smart?"

Relationships among beasts of the jungle are said to remain constant through the centuries: no giraffe grows up thinking that because he is taller and particularly daring, he will become king of the beasts. Whatever the form of society throughout the centuries, ambition, greed and hate find their mode of satisfaction. Toadyism takes many forms: a man who righteously condemns a Russian composer for dedicating his opera to Stalin finds it easy to address a memo to his colleagues: "B.W. made a speech last night to the Executives Club of St. Paul, and I thought it so fine a statement of his principles that I knew you would want to have a copy of it too." Nepotism is a true international, making Junior the board chairman, or Stalin's son the top flying officer over Moscow.

Nor are all the barracuda traits confined to business. Envy's spiked tongue guides the professor's qualified praise of a colleague's work (that is, if the two are not engaged in an unspoken understanding to feather each other's nest). Actors, singers and authors trade testimonials for mutual advantage, and the public be damned. Thus do men live in the world-as-it-is. And a little off to one side may be described those authors who write novels about heroes like themselves, straining for integrity in a dishonest society, and loading their plots with the sure-fire tricks of beds and bourbon and the big money, to enable themselves to continue to enjoy the corruptions they righteously denounce.

Sometimes it seems as if the wrong people nowadays have all the self-confidence. They are the ones who make mistakes only of the heart, rarely of the head. They are the successful men, small-souled and energetic, who are full of tough certainties. Or they are the ones on the make, who, because they love puppies or their own children, think their jostling and pushing excusable: if only the others knew it, they resolve to be better *once they get theirs.*

Men become expert in what they "can get away with," slickly consider that "what others don't know won't hurt them," and talk of the necessity of "looking after Number One." Many businessmen prosper by proclaiming the highest moral standards while knowing when to suspend them, and how to cover their naked ambitions with a fig leaf of legality. Law, in fact, has staked out its own little splashy preserve in the barracuda waters. A lawyer knows that courts deal not in the wide question of guilt but in the narrower one of guilt according to the evidence. Some become specialists in recommending what will be barely inside the law: what "you can probably get away with;" what can be done on the assumption that "they don't dare go into court with it," or if they do sue, knowing how the case can be sufficiently muddied. They know what can be safely charged off, written off or passed over. Law often sets a minimum code of conduct which in fields that are fiercely competitive quickly becomes the prevailing code, for it takes an extremely principled—or impractical—businessman not to take all the competitive advantages permitted by law. It would not be fair to say that in our culture Anything Goes, but it can be said that for pay, someone can be found to justify almost anything.

A voracious subspecies of our marine life includes those who exploit desperate situations, who capture control of companies and milk them, who hoard a scarce commodity until someone will pay dearly for it, who force another to the wall and ask, "What's the matter, can't he take it?"; those who give short weight, misrepresent ingredients, or substitute shoddy materials; those who muscle in to get an undeserved cut; those who conspire to mitigate frauds by the public relations device of "slapping a fresh coat of paint" over them, or who as lawyers worm a scoundrel out of his difficulties; those who lie but in no illegal way, who steal but cannot be indicted, who cheat but get away with it.

The cut and thrust of combat in the barracuda waters, of the big eating the small and everyone on guard against sudden attack, takes on a peculiar coloring under our economic system, but must not be thought indigenous to it. We are talking about something that began with Adam. The sins of wrath and greed and pride are as old as the hills of Galilee, and have prospered and been condemned through every known variation of society. But only in recent times has it become fashionable not to condemn our sins, but rather to deny them.

If cupidity is universal as the sun, it is unfortunately conspicuous in our society for two reasons. One is that we tend to measure success by externals, and externals often provide little clue to their acquisition. Sellers do not ask where one got his money, but whether he pays his bills; neither money nor mink betrays how it was earned, and Cadillacs are indistinguishable.* So long as a society conceives

* The Cadillac people, in their advertising, like to suggest that such a fraternity of Cadillac owners exists that merely owning one of their cars provides an entree to Society. But in making this short-cut-to-success appeal,

as its end the exalting and rewarding of selfishness, and admires the adroit seizing of opportunity, it finds it a little hard to condemn short cuts. So attractive are the rewards of a money success, and in a mobile society so easy are the standards in determining the welcome of a well-heeled newcomer, that men can easily escape the scene of their crimes. A Sunday school teacher is thus hard put to prove to her pupils that evil does not pay, and can only fall back on Emerson's remark that success must not be judged by the standards of the market place.

The second reason cupidity flourishes so in a society like ours is that, in our modern day, we tend increasingly to cover everything with the goose grease of rationalization, including in the same protection the good, the bad, and the not so bad. Since Communism questions our values, no one else must: fearing that someone may lose faith in our system, we redouble the publicity in its favor and discourage any questioning of it. Anyone who introduces morals into any serious business discussion is apt to feel prudish in doing so: he should save that for Sundays.

Apologists fall back on the assertion that *most* people in business are trustworthy and considerate. Being anxious to establish that they themselves are not taking a high moral line, they point out that businessmen gain *pragmatically* by honoring their commitments and their word. Ethics does guide many decisions: lawyers despise ambulance chasers; doctors deplore fee-splitters and those who exploit rich old ladies; merchants scorn price-cutters and would prefer not to be challenged to meet their prices by debasing their own services; reputable manufacturers insist on purity of product and honesty of labeling. Companies may have to make deals with dishonest jobbers ("He's a bastard—but he's *our* bastard") and to live with venal union officials; they may develop private rationalizations about expense accounts and juggling income taxes, but they prefer aboveboard operations, and the esteem of their employees, their

---

they are also afraid of losing the trade of the respectable, and are sometimes discomfited by the way gangsters, black-marketeers and other dubious characters seek Cadillacs in their quest for an unearned parity of esteem. In the company's jargon, there is a category of Cadillac owners known as "the newly rich of deprived origins."

competitors and their public; and they sometimes sigh over what competition forces them to do.

But they do not fundamentally question the *right* of someone to make a "fast buck" as opportunely as he can; business is business, they say; if they form trade associations with elaborate proclamations of ethical codes, and liken themselves to bar associations or medical societies, they usually do not require that every member be made strictly accountable, for they do not want to be "policed" by their competitors. In this way, I think, the good in our society unwittingly protects the bad. The cheaters have a way of implying that since everyone is a little corrupt, degrees in corruption do not matter, and in such comparisons the worst find their immunity. Mutual associations often turn into cliques of craft that condemn wrongdoing but in practice give miscreants respectability against outside criticism.

The lines are further blurred because the best of business corporations are rarely content any more to be what they are. In our contemporary inflation of self-esteem they must avow that they are spreading the American way of life, and exist only to serve the public. They talk the language of ideals but in practice obey their necessities. If public relations men ran their board rooms, and did as they talked, many a company would soon be out of business. But corporations feel the need for this kind of pretense, for it would be too naked to say that their *raison d'être* was simply to turn a profit (Marx has made everyone so self-conscious). Yet when they address their stockholders, they make it clear that no lesser motive guides their thought. In the days of the Spanish conquests, one of the conquistadors, Bernal Díaz del Castillo, proclaimed that his men had set out *a service a Dios y a hacernos ricos*—"to serve God and enrich ourselves." Nobody talks that way any more.

The common blurring of motives—the immense gap between what is professed at the highest level and practiced at the lowest—is further confused by the blathering efforts of publicity, which knows how to make less sound more, and is often paid highest when its task is most uphill. So much of its effort seems a harmless puffing, like a carnival barker's spiel, or an understandable selectivity of what facts it chooses to exploit, but the result of a thousand dishonesties is a false picture. Perhaps it would be preferable to acknowledge that the bad in our business society has to be put up with, on the valid grounds that it cannot easily be corrected without introducing greater dangers, than to pretend that the bad exists only in carping minds. It was better when things went by their right names.

17. Measuring Rods

So unsparing a portrait of our failings as the one I have just painted concentrates too much on the grays and ignores our healthy pinks. I admit it, but we have had too much flattery about our good points, which we already know.

A further objection might be made that it is easy enough to counsel perfection, and to criticize everything in sight, without stating the basis of one's comparison. A critic should show us his measuring rods. Is our way of life being judged against some abstract ideal, against some superior period in the past, or against some possible alternative? Let us take up the comparisons one by one.

Few Americans any longer have any real curiosity, as Americans had during the Depression, about the relative merits of various economic "systems"—capitalism, socialism, Communism, syndicalism, the corporate state. We may not think ours the best of all possible worlds, but we think it the best of all likely ones. We may acknowledge Communism's capacity to organize its might, but we want no part of its ways. Terms such as syndicalism and the corporate state have dropped completely out of currency. Socialism, we think, enlarges government too much: we generally find that those who over-organize the state in the name of liberating the individual have yet to bring their objective nearer, and have intruded new obstacles. We have also come to realize how supple our own economy is, so that it is possible continually to tinker with the amount of statism we want, altering the mixture to suit our needs. We have not exhausted, only neglected, the range of possibilities inside our order. But in fighting off the propaganda of other systems, and in abandoning all lyricism in our own legislating, we have more and more let other systems appeal *in the name of* qualities we once uniquely spoke for—peace, opportunity, equality, social justice.

In examining what it is we overemphasize and what we nowadays understress in our own way of life, we might begin by searching our own past for clues. "Let us return to the old ways," said Verdi, "and that will be progress." It is not a very American remark, but it provides us a beginning.

In our despairing moments, as we get older, we often think that rectitude is disappearing from public life, and that our society is losing the most valuable of those attributes of character that we respected in our parents' way of life. Few of us would, however, go so far as Horace, who proclaimed, "Our fathers, viler than our grandfathers, begot us who are even viler, and we shall bring forth a progeny more degenerate still." We are apt to dismiss this awful outcry of a man living in Caesar's day but before Christ's, as a judgment not valid for all time, but the product of special circumstances, the desperation of a man witnessing the first warnings of his own culture's decline.

We may no longer believe so trustingly in progress as we once did. But we are aware that people who suffer from "historical homesickness" for a past glory are usually too selective in recall. They may envy a Georgian style of living, but forget the brutish bucks who swaggered in it, the "dark and satanic mills," the grimy children in mines, chained like dogs to a go-cart, or the wretches in debtors prisons sleeping on straw. Or if they romanticize 19th Century America they are apt to forget the Tweeds and Goulds, and the scandalous greeds that followed the Civil War.

Dyspeptic critics match us against the best of all past cultures, minimizing what was evil in each. In doing so, I think they are as misleading as those jaunty moderns who make the opposite mistake of dismissing the past entirely, who consider improvements in plumbing a conclusive test of progress and regard every sophomore the superior of Galileo because he has been taught where Galileo went wrong. All those in this second group, who smugly invoke the past to prove their present superiority, need to be reminded of that caution put forward in the 12th Century by Bernard of Chartres, that all of us are "like dwarfs seated on the shoulders of giants; we see more things than the ancients and things more distant, but this is due neither to the sharpness of our own sight, nor to the greatness of our own minds, but because we are raised and borne aloft on that giant mass."

With both these warnings in mind, that we should neither romanticize nor slight the past, most Americans would, I think, regard as a high point in our own past the era of our constitutional forefathers, and would freely admit that we have no such corps of disinterested intelligence presiding over our own society today. Even after the debunkers have picked over their bones, we find in these first Americans noble aspirations happily harmonized with political wisdom.

If we would ask ourselves what has gone wrong since then, we must start with what was different in their circumstances. "We, the people," for whom these men contrived a government—and only afterward asked popular approval—amounted to an electorate of less than 5 per cent of those who lived in the United States at the time the Constitution was assented to. In 1791, the United States was a nation of but four million people, who were not yet subjected to the bewildering advantages of telephones, television, airplanes, unions and big employers.

The men who designed the Constitution were men of the Enlightenment, and some among them assented to the watered-down theology of deism, but they lived in a time more aware than ours of moral precepts. "It is impossible," wrote Hamilton, "for the man of pious reflection not to perceive in [the Constitution] a finger of the Almighty hand which has so frequently and signally extended to our relief in the critical stages of the Revolution." The framers were certain that "once an efficient national government is established, the best men in the country will not only consent to serve, but also will generally be appointed to manage it" and they erroneously conceived of the United States as "for the most part exclusively addicted to agriculture, and likely from local circumstances to remain so." They did not foresee the day when two thirds of our population would live in cities, and only one in seven would be self-employed.

Perhaps, in their eagerness to escape from a past tyranny, the framers of the Constitution failed to see that a government which was to be made strong but not overbearing, and which was to regulate but not dominate its society, was not likely to be a magnet to the most dynamic forces in the community, who would have other ambitions to follow. But the men who wrote the Constitution had to argue against those who wanted an even less forceful federal government.

Our present age characteristically doubts the practicality of men it considers noble, and doubts the nobility of those it considers practical. Perhaps for this reason the *Federalist Papers,* those pamphlets of propaganda that were written to "sell" the Constitution to the public, are not much read any more: they suggest a Fourth of July patriotism. We would prefer to honor than to read them. But in fact the *Federalist Papers* retain a relevant vitality to this day because they speak not in the high-flown humbuggery of contemporary oratory about the Constitution, but with a clear-eyed and refreshing knowledge of the weakness of man. Hamilton, who wrote most of the *Federalist Papers,* put this undeceived attitude most plainly. "The supposition of universal venality in human nature," he wrote, "is little less in error in political reasoning than the supposition of universal rectitude." Contrast this tone of public voice with the cant of any modern presidential State of the Union message, carefully worked over by those skilled in giving no offense to any bloc, and if required to condemn a few, always taking care to congratulate the many. What public figure today would suggest the "supposition of universal venality in human nature" as a sound guide? It is instructive to follow this thread of honest self-knowledge throughout the *Federalist Papers:*

"Making the proper deductions for the ordinary depravity of human nature," Hamilton argues that "men are ambitious, vindictive and rapacious. . . . Are not popular assemblies frequently subject to the impulses of rage, resentment, jealousy, avarice? . . . Is not the love of wealth as domineering a passion as that of power or glory? Have there not been as many wars founded upon commercial motives, since that has become the prevailing system of nations, as were before occasioned by the cupidity of territory or dominion?"

The Federalists had few illusions about their place in the world: "We are rivals [of European nations] in navigation and the carrying trade; and we shall deceive ourselves if we suppose that any of them will rejoice to see [ours] flourish." John Jay, worried by the danger of America being fragmented into thirteen or even "three or four" independent governments, asks in a manner that still has relevance to contemporary West European alliances, "Would there be no danger of [these separate governments] being flattered into neutrality by specious promises, or seduced by too great fondness for peace to decline hazarding their tranquility and present safety for the sake of neighbors, of whom perhaps they have been jealous, and whose importance they are content to see diminished?" And he adds, "Although such conduct would not be wise, it would nevertheless be natural, the history of the states of Greece and of other countries abounds with such instances." Hamilton recognizes that "there is perhaps nothing more likely to disturb the tranquility of nations than their being bound to mutual contributions for any common object which does not yield an equal and coincident benefit."

Would we today not denounce, if we heard put forth by another small nation, Hamilton's prescription for an American navy able to play off both sides so that it may seek its own advantage? Hamilton favored a navy "which if it could not vie with those of the great powers, would at least be of respectable weight, if thrown into the scale of either of two contending parties. . . . A few ships of the line, sent opportunely to the reinforcement of either side, would often be sufficient to decide the fate of a campaign, on the event of which interests of the greatest magnitude were suspended. . . . By a steady adherence to the Union, we may hope, erelong, to become the arbiter of Europe in America; and to be able to incline the balance of European competitions in this part of the world, as our interest may dictate."

Always the key word is interest: people of any country "seldom adopt, and steadily persevere for many years in, an erroneous opinion respecting their interests." A proper conduct can be expected of chief executives because "we may . . . count upon their pride, if not upon their virtue." Madison thought that in public affairs "the causes of faction cannot be removed, and that relief is only to be sought in the means of controlling its effects. . . . If the impulse and the opportunity be suffered to coincide, we well know that neither moral nor religious motives can be relied on as an adequate control." And in providing against power-grabbing, Hamilton observes that "the provision for defense must in this, as in all other cases, be made commensurate to the danger of attack. Ambition must be made to counter ambition. . . . It may be a reflection on human nature that such devices should be necessary to control the abuses of government. But what is government itself but the greatest of all reflections on human nature? If men were angels, no government would be necessary."

Viewing human nature in this way, the *Federalist* authors repeatedly argue that in the control of affairs "the means ought to be proportioned to the ends." Hamilton recognizes that "there are particular moments in public affairs when the people, stimulated by some irregular passion or some illicit advantage, or misled by the artful misrepresentation of interested men, may call for measures which they themselves will afterwards be the most ready to lament and condemn. . . . So numerous indeed, and so powerful, are the causes which serve to give a false bias to the judgment, that we, upon many occasions, see wise and good men on the wrong as on the right side of questions of the first magnitude to society. . . . Ambition, avarice, personal animosity, party opposition, and many other motives not more laudable than these, are apt to operate as well upon those who support, as upon those who oppose, the right side of a question."

Only in one fleeting, condescending mention by Madison is there any reference to that majority of the population so below the salt that it was considered unfit for the franchise: "I take no notice," he wrote, "of an unhappy species of population abounding in some of the states, who, during the calm of regular government, are sunk below the level of men; but who, in the tempestuous scenes of civil violence may emerge into the human character, and give a superiority of strength to any party with which they may associate themselves."

Usually, the writers of the *Federalist Papers* take a less rancorous, if yet cautionary, view of their subjects. "The republican principle," said Hamilton, "demands that the deliberate sense of the community should govern the conduct of those to whom they intrust the manage-

ment of their affairs, but it does not require an unqualified com-
plaisance to every sudden breeze of passion, or to every transient
impulse which the people may receive from the arts of men, who
flatter their prejudices to betray their interests. . . . The wonder is
that they so seldom err as they do, beset as they continuously are
by the wiles of parasites and sychophants, by the snares of the ambitious, the avaricious, the desperate; by the artifices of men who
possess their confidence more than they deserve it, and of those
who seek to possess rather than to deserve it."

When we seek to examine why we do not seem to have public
discussion at this level of sanity and honesty now, we might conclude that 18th Century times simply called such men forth, and
that the United States at that crucial moment was singularly blessed.
Or we might think that privileged position in the community gave
them the opportunity to talk as they did, and we might be inclined
to blame all subsequent decline on the extension of the franchise.
But perhaps we might also recognize that what has gone wrong in
America is an increase in a lazy tolerance of wrongdoing, because
we find it easier and more agreeable to call things by their wrong
names than to correct them.

It might be asked: Are there men in our nation today who are the
equal of our constitutional forefathers? If so, politics does not often
attract them. And if they exist, they certainly do not exert such a
dominating influence on the community. It may be that we have
simply become too big for any small group to preside over us. The
work of our best people is dissipated, fragmentary and complex; except in their own fields, they tend not even to know one another.
Sometimes a war will call them forth, but generally they have other
pursuits besides politics and public affairs, for whose necessities
they have a distaste.

Granted all of these explanations, the fact is that quality no
longer puts its stamp upon the image of America. Others speaking
down to America do.

Still another way to measure a society is not against the past, or
against its contemporaries, but against its own standards of the
good. And when we do this, we must come to the subject of religion.

America's early statesmen believed in the separation of church and state, but did not hesitate to inscribe on their coins "In God We Trust."

Perhaps a majority of the most determined critics of our contemporary society are men who themselves give loyalty to no church, though they may be prompted by ethical longings. They often accuse religion of being incapable of doing battle against the mercenary and the misdoers because the church is too busy cultivating its rich parishioners. It is only a partial answer that a church cannot be responsible for the hypocrites it attracts; its mission is to sinners; if bedeviled by those who quote scripture against it, the church may have to answer: judge not, that ye be not judged.

If I understand Catholic teaching correctly (which is a hazardous assumption), it regards itself as in a basic quarrel with capitalism. This quarrel, which frequently mystifies Americans—who think the Vatican an even more conservative bastion against Communism than the White House—is not with riches, but with the means of their acquisition, with the failure to acknowledge the duties of wealth, and with the setting up of any domain which is not answerable to spiritual authority.

If I now hesitantly take up the subject of religion's role in American life, the hesitation comes from a conviction that one's own religious beliefs are his private affair, and besides I can pretend to no authority.

My own religious views have had a hard time getting off the ground. Religion made a melancholy division of my childhood. At my state university in the unbelieving thirties, religion was not so much avoided as ignored. Where the instruction was not undisguisedly skeptical it was in the manner of phenomenology; that is, it confined itself to self-sufficient scientific descriptions of the known, eschewing interpretations and evaluations. I called myself agnostic then, and was enchanted by a phrase of Remy de Gourmont's: "Though dead to the faith that assured me of God, I mourn to the end the delights of belief." But to say I then mourned would be to describe my adolescent indifference too grandiloquently: I felt superior to those who needed religion as consolation, and could quote Bertrand Russell to the effect that philosophers had no more duty to return an optimistic answer than an accountant to bring in a favorable balance. Trusting by default in the discoveries of science, I learned only gradually that each age's certainty in science is the next age's ridicule; that the hard-won deposit of scientific knowledge is but a small part of the whole of knowledge, and not much guide to the unknowable; and that though we all dread credulity, most of us take more on trust from science than we do from religion. I believe in the ibex but not the unicorn, though I have seen neither.

Other inhibitions held me back from religion. Abhorring cant, I disliked selfish behavior more when it was joined to sanctimonious moralizing. I could not envision heaven. (Did it have electronic swinging doors or was it more old-fashioned? What did one do with his time there?) I was caught up in the familiar inability to reconcile an all-powerful and all-good God with the evil and pain in the world. I could not accept John Stuart Mill's notion that God had put evil in the world just to test us and to keep alive our powers to struggle against it; for the testing was often so unfair: why so much pain to a crippled child, while scroundrels and lechers prospered? And, perhaps, I had too many selfish desires to gratify before wishing the restraint of faith. I might have echoed that honest youthful prayer of St. Augustine: "Give me chastity and continency, only not yet." For, as St. Augustine admitted later, "I feared lest Thou hear me too soon."

There came times when in the night I asked the void to take shape. Where others become unsure in their faith, I became unsure of my lack of faith. If I were now to know this to be my last moment, I might call upon God, saying, "I accept you," and would count on Him to know that half of me was ready long ago, and the other half not hostile but only (such is our age) inattentive, unwilling to be inconvenienced, and convinced that its inability to believe was at least honest. If this were my last moment, I might make such a confession, yet cannot now.

"The conduct of God, who disposes all things kindly, is to put religion into the mind by reason, and into the heart by grace," said Pascal. "But to will to put it into the mind and heart by force and threats is not to put religion there, but terror." Elsewhere he adds, "If we must not act save on a certainty, we ought not to act on religion, for it is not certain. But how many things we do on an uncertainty, sea voyages, battles!" Yet to me Pascal's famous wager on belief, that we had nothing to lose and all to gain, was the worst of reasons for faith: it could not be a spur to belief but only to churchgoing. I no longer think credulous those who believe, but envy them their torments and rewards. Those who already have faith find constant verifications of it, but I do not find it easy to come to faith by reason alone, for we must finally take "on faith" what cannot be proved. But my own story is unfinished, and I cannot foretell its ending.

Even those who live with no faith live on its accumulated moral capital. If they do not worship any god they generally accept religion's notion of the good, having absorbed religion in their pores while rejecting it with their minds; rarely do the unbelieving think out a coherent set of ethics for themselves. They usually consider themselves to be as commendably motivated as those with faith, and often are; they also think themselves more honest about their shortcomings, but it is easier to be true to a less demanding standard, and in the end such people acknowledge no obligation beyond their own promptings.

American churches, especially Protestant, increasingly tend to dilute their message and diminish their demands in order to widen their audiences, on the grounds that "you can't save souls in an empty church." Many preach a bland good will agreeable to their hearers, with no hard edges of doctrine. I am not convinced that this is the best way to inspire faith: it may be the way to spread a desire for good conduct, but belief must make the demands inseparable from it: not its rigors but its reality is what many in my time have found hard to accept.

But if I find our churches often weakened as arbiters of our conduct by having become so accepting a partner in the standards of our society, I do not mean to slight religion's beneficial and substantial influence on those it guides. Society is not redeemable *en masse*; conversions must inevitably be individual.

In delirium views, or when we are out of sorts with the world, we sometimes see with great clarity that everything about us is false —no friendship to be trusted, and selfishness the world's only guide. If our considered judgment is more optimistic, if we believe that the Barracuda Waters are only the angry deeps of a wide and pacific ocean, we owe this knowledge to all those forces in our society that labor uphill against what is so appealingly easy around them, who strive to return love for hate, to instill charity, to celebrate truth and seek justice. Such people aim to be better, rather than simply better off. They aspire to "do justly, love mercy, walk humbly." If the influence of those whose ambitions go beyond themselves—who live by religious abnegation, by soldier's code, by professional's discipline, or by a combination of them all—were universal, society would be a much different place.

Those who attack the authority of religion usually do so in the name of freedom of speculation, but in winning this famous victory they have also loosened the moorings of society, and have left most people afloat in an agreeable vacuum that does not fully satisfy and does not at all inspire.

18. Elites and Other People

A melancholy facet of our times is that many who consider themselves part of the American cultural elect feel no link to the rest of Americans, and want none: they cut themselves off from the majority with a disdain that is tinged with fear. They isolate themselves in communities where they feel "understood" by one another, and are not content merely to be different in temperament but insist on brandishing their differences, as a flag of their freedom and their superiority.

I think it possible to echo their misgivings about American society and to understand their predicament without wishing to join them. Like all elites, they think they keep the faith pure—and in fact some of them do. But they are in danger of becoming a set so drawn in on itself as to pervert its original quest for freedom. Its members glory in their individuality, but respond as a group. Take a sample of their bloodstream in either La Jolla or Westport, and it would contain roughly the same mixture of enthusiasms and dislikes. They develop their own tribal tests of exclusion, and can tell by what another person drinks, reads or wears whether he belongs among them. The talents they admire are usually limited in ambition; the chief criterion of art for them seems to be that it must be anti-public: so bereft of meaning, melody or beauty, so nihilistic in design, distorted in tone or obscure in text that it could not be taken up by ordinary people. They do not so much prize achievement in an artist as cheer his effort to be different: rebellion and protest are what they ask of him, for those are the impulses they feel themselves, and the major source of their excitement. Of none are they so scornful as of one of their own who becomes widely popular.

Their need to keep ahead drives them to desperate exoticisms of taste, because they are confronted not only by the Philistines they glory to have as enemies, but by another part of the public so eager to understand and copy their tastes that it has already accustomed itself to blobs of color in art, to blasts of dissonance in music, and to formlessness in literature. As these would-be avant-gardists retreat in revulsion before the onrushing herd, they toss back after them, like bread crumbs in the snow, anything that seems about to be widely "taken up."

Pascal said of something that it "would be an infallible rule of truth if it were an infallible rule of falsehood." Similarly, to be so infallibly anti the "mass taste" as to always uphold its opposite, fleeing from the obviously popular to defend whatever obviously is not, is to be twice the servant of the mass, and to have surrendered the ability to judge any piece of art, music or literature on its own merits. We must leave it to the Freudians to determine whether such people are actually defiant of the mass or merely out of sorts with their parents.

But I think that we must be wary of making the mistake of disliking something because we dislike those who become enthusiastic about it, or to think something phony because some of its admirers may be. (One of the hardest disciplines in the world is to look at a thing as itself, free of its accompanying overload of labels, fashions and criticisms.) It is easy to mock the kind of people who gather where the martinis are driest: easy to strip their pretenses and deride their standards, easy to indict the whole for the behavior of the most conspicuous.

Some of these emancipated people dislike respectability and fashionable display so much that they regard dirty surroundings and soiled clothes as a proof of intellectual incorruptibility; disdaining gentility's falseness, they must be scatologically explicit to prove their independence. They regard marriage as a useful arrangement that one should be adult about. A conscience is something that, with Freud's help, they hope to do without. They take up causes, but as lightly abandon them, and consider a cocktail-hour bravery of mouth a sufficient substitute for having done something about anything. They dart about in their interests: they read up on the Dead Sea Scrolls without being read in the Bible, for the Bible is not new, and besides it is the property of The Others. They are often frustrated people, believing in nothing beyond emancipation; they have learned the ridiculing cant dismissal phrase for everything, and a sourness often pervades their work and a boredom their play. A sense of the helplessness of it all, a self-pity that is translated into a general statement about life, is their nearest approach to an aesthetic standard.

The danger of talking about an American cultural elect in terms only of its extremest exotics is the risk of narrowing its membership to those who are most perverted by it. But the condition of deliberate isolation from the mainstream of American life extends far wider than among those who are casual in marriage or defiant in taste. It is felt on campuses, among those literary scholars who abandon any attempt to come to grips with their times but prefer to erect safe edifices around past writers or to cultivate minor sensibilities; among poets lost in technique for want of something to say; and among that increasing intellectual brotherhood of those who get jobs with foundations and, with money earned by some millionaire's vulgar strivings, enjoy a sanctuary where they can condemn the vulgar strivings of American life.

This withdrawal is even more apparent in those who in their daily work (men in the "communications industry" and its sideshows, the ad agencies) find their living by ministering to, or adulterating, public taste. After hours, or even in the cynicism that invades their working conversation, they despise in the mass what the mass seems to require of themselves, and not alone the pace of their jobs, but their distaste for their work, accounts for the forgetfulness they seek in jolts of whiskey or vodka. The result of directing ads to the simpletons "out there," or of scoring a cheap tune for one hundred dulcet violins and a wordless choir of sopranos, is a contempt for the public that is made more bitter by the awareness of one's own self-destruction.

But doesn't that cynical adman realize that, while he cuts a figure in his own private circle by proving how refined and esoteric his tastes are, he himself can only be judged, by all who do not know him but know only his work, as part of the American lump he loathes? The They out there did not demand that he write soap jingles for them: he can drive a truck, for all they care, or write a book that doesn't sell: his own ambitions have put him in his spot.

But again, I do not want to confine the argument to extreme examples.

Intellectual isolation is felt in America by thousands whose daily work is lost in larger wholes—among law clerks, bank officers, chemists, researchers, engineers, corporation executives, salesmen, designers. Their work requires a cultivated narrow skill, and nearly all of their energy; but since it does not bear their individual stamp, it does not fully gratify them or give them identity in the public eye. Most such people, I think, tend to have an exaggerated sense of how cut off they are from their crasser countrymen: if they get along well enough with those around them, and can see the simple worth of the people they know, they feel unable to imagine a relationship with the rest of the country, except at a level lower than their best.

They do not realize that the United States is full of non-colliding elites like their own. Their difficulty is that they measure unseen Americans by what they see in the American Image—that distorting image that tries to make majorities of us by appealing to what is the same in most of us. And since a disdain is often unintentionally reflected in their aloofness, it separates them even more from their fellow countryman, who feels himself patronized and knows himself a better man than the intellectual makes him out to be. The intellectual thus does not take his full part in the American consensus. But if his vote is not counted in the American majority it is often not because he has been denied a voice but because he has failed to register: he has disenfranchised himself.

We come now to democracy's touchiest question, the problem of unequal quality, a subject more delicate than unequal advantage, a subject that bristles with evasions and subtleties, and is hard to discuss without seeming cavalier, condescending or romantic. Yet what kind of attitude one takes toward his fellow countryman—those not just of his acquaintance—is central to our good health as a nation.

As a Westerner who gravitated East many years ago, I have come to appreciate that many Easterners were schooled in nuances of taste and judgment that were no part of my plain boardinghouse upbringing, though something perverse in me leaves me with no wish to trade places with them. Not what they value, but what they ignore, troubles me. Their standards, which were once largely Eastern, are increasingly dispersed around the country. A certain degree of isolation is required to cultivate these admirable qualities, but the result is often a fatal miscomprehending of the rest of American life, which such people know of only literarily. They have a hatred of banality and make of it a distaste for people.

Many educated people find a secure footing in American society only by an act of repudiation, and I suspect this repudiation of often being too sweeping. They make a double error who deny the individuality of those they do not know, and who fail to understand how much their own actions (and inactions) are registered in a collective result they deplore. They are apt to take the same over-simplified view of the American people that the mass merchandiser uses, who levels everything to his purpose—and if this oversimplification is useful in marketing tennis shoes it is a poor way to distinguish human souls. I recognize that elites of whatever category (music, physics, literature) in our society must jealously safeguard the purity of their standards. That is all they must do, but they must do it. Sometimes this safeguarding requires defiance. More often it tempts people to create little occult tests of exclusivity, and to adopt attitudes of superior standoffishness.

The word *elite*—like the word *mass*—does not suit the American ear. Those who form isolated communities of taste may be right in their particular preferences, but their verdict on the American people is too often based on insufficient triangulation. To despise people because they are hostile to Picasso while paying their debts, doing a hard day's work and raising their families, is to judge them by too exacting and narrow a standard: a God, it may be presumed, would not make the same mistake. Baudelaire and Pergolesi may be important figures, but many a man is no less a man for never having heard of them. A too-hasty dismissal of his fellow human beings is, I believe, the prideful error of the American intellectual today, a dismissal that increases and embitters his isolation.

It is easy to understand that anyone who would be better than the crowd must first outdistance it. The intellectual achieves his level of knowledge and taste by disregarding, and sometimes scorning, the tastes of the many, for—our society being what it is—individuals do not generally start out above the pack but must emerge from it. In concentrating on his own emergent values, a process so essential to his growth, an intellectual often comes to reject everything about the run of people; in doing so, he risks missing many of their merits, and developing in himself a narrowness of outlook—and perhaps this is why so many Americans instinctively shy from using the word intellectual to describe themselves (much of the resentment toward "intellectuals" comes from those whose own role in society, correctly defined, is intellectual).

So often intellectuals, like everyone else, ignore how they themselves are counted by those who do not know them. For in making anonymous multitudes of those we exclude, and considering them inferior to our own discriminating selves, we are apt to forget that so many are the varieties of inquiry open to us, and so diverse are the treasures to be explored and satisfactions to be enjoyed, that we are all, at any moment, among the ignorant. We are all unconsciously members of majorities who are *not* knowledgeable in astronautics, frescoes or woodcraft. And while we make our own circle of exclusivity, others make another. In every small town exists the circle of self-sufficient men who fish well. They may not intend to exclude those who do not talk their language, but the barrier exists naturally: they are a fraternity to whom the outsider has no password. (Can a man who dislikes painting but is mutely content with rocks and streams and trees be considered indifferent to beauty?) We are all part of negative multitudes at every minute: the multitude not reading a book that doesn't sell, or not seeing a play that is about to close. America is not made up of a precious few with "enough taste" to appreciate the finest, and an immense and anonymous lump without taste; it is composed of people with infinite degrees of interest, knowledge, curiosity and taste who are confronted by a bewilderment of appeals. There is even a driven group of well-intentioned Americans (usually women) so anxious to "keep up," so conscious of so many interests and causes worthy of their support, and of so much to read and to hear, that they dissipate their energies in a helpless attempt to spread themselves around, and see nothing steadily and hear nothing clearly.

Furthermore, we all have interests of work or play which we pursue seriously, and in these fields may insist on severe standards; but in relaxing outside them, because the bow cannot always be at the stretch, we indulge in pursuits which others take seriously but we do not, and in these we become part of the undifferentiating majority. A widespread audience for a television comedian may include giggling schoolgirls with empty heads and lonely old women with nothing to do, but it may also include nuclear scientists relaxing.

None of us would like to be restricted to the heights of culture, and all would weary of nothing but Shakespeare and Beethoven's last quartets. We excuse our own crotchets and lapses, knowing them to be what makes us individual, but neglect to extend this privilege to those we do not know. Tastes are bound to be uneven. A man who shapes chairs of fine proportions may have banal fancies in music—or a tin ear. Women who dress badly and fill their parlors with gimcrackery frequently have a sure sense of beauty in their gardens. The businessman is deplored for his after-hours taste in theater, for his liking of *unchallenging* entertainment: pretty girls, easy music, quick gags, cheerful plots. One can't blame a frustrated dramatist for a hostility toward this attitude: any writer worth his salt wants to challenge, wants to assault life: the theater is *his* serious pursuit. But the writer, unwilling to take seriously what the businessman does, often describes him as a boor and a Babbitt, failing to see how subtle, anxious, engrossing and exhausting a businessman's own life may be, requiring ingenuity, audacity and art to anticipate the complexities of the market, and tact to handle the temperaments of those he must work with.

If we all could see ourselves plainly we would discover that while we think ourselves insistently individual, someone else is including us in a mass, if only a negative mass. In our daily lives we interchangeably become minority and mass: we walk along the street thinking our personal thoughts, and are individuals; we enter a bus, and are one of a mass whose movements can be anticipated and scheduled; a four-lane highway is not something for others—the herd—but for all of us solitaries, who together become a herd. When we go to a movie theater, producers assume that a number of us will respond to the same appeal, but some take one thing from a film and others something else (we usually hesitate to confess the lowness of our own tastes).

If, then, it were possible to free ourselves from a kind of false elitehood—or at least to recognize that the superiority of any elite does not make it in all ways superior, but only in the place where it discriminates—we might see that we are all We and at the same time part of They. Until we realize this dual relationship, we are incapable of understanding the peculiar complexity of our times or of our own place in them.

Whenever I hear a too-quick dismissal of the anonymous American people—of all those, that is, who do not conform to the notions of whatever nonconforming group I happen to be among—I do not call to mind "another America" that is like a *Saturday Evening Post* cover of a happy Thanksgiving dinner. I know that bland dinner circle too well: those clean-frocked children, all keyed up, will soon be quarreling and splattered; gray-haired grandfather smiling gamely is in reality more apt to be sobered by his infirmities and a little deaf; father is a bit edgy; and the uncle who took to drink and went bad has not been invited and is never pictured. Nor do I leap to defend those fellow Americans who have an assertive ignorance that affronts the eye and ear, who deny standards that rest on shadings they do not see, who resent manners they do not have, who invade, overrun and have no respect for beauty, solitude or privacy, who loudly mock what they do not understand, and insist that what is not like them has no right to its own ways. A good many Americans are like this, and I do not cherish them. But I think instead of people in front-porch hammocks listening to the lazy summer sound of crickets; I think of gimp-legged switchmen fanning themselves beside railroad crossings; I think of fishing crews returning with their catches, enjoying in the oil-heavy, throbbing interior of the boat the silent communal satisfaction of hard work done for the day.

And though I long to defend such people against *all* charges, because they are good as they are, it would be a patronizing sentimentality to praise in them qualities they do not have and may not want. To celebrate the instinctive taste or judgment of those who have neither is another form of the "equality" heresy. But these people must not be denied the qualities they do have. I believe that there are millions in America—not anonymous people, but only anonymous to us—whose way of life is an inarticulate protest against what they do not feel fitted for, or are unwilling to pursue, in the values of our society. Such people are often said to be "without ambition," and perhaps lack push. They don't want to set the world afire, as the song goes. But though they might not put it that way, they know dimly that push takes a certain kind of ruthlessness, that climbing takes something out of one's self besides wind and requires a derangement of personality. They have no taste for it, and are content to be what they are.

Such people are the rejectors of society, though not rebels; it is only because they are inarticulate in abstract things, or feel that they owe no explanations, that they are content to let it be known that they "couldn't care less." They are satisfied to find their own formulas of work and play. They are the kind who in the Army never want to be more than noncoms. Let others live artificial and anxious lives, it is not for them: they find themselves more at home with their own kind. In their private lives, as clerks or foremen or truckers, living in streets of identical homes, they may feel a need to keep up with the Joneses but have little desire to get ahead of them. They do not think their own qualities remarkable, nor ask to be considered noble, but they have a right not to be disregarded. To those who make no distinctions in the mass, these people may be considered part of an American herd ranged against them—but the rejectors are not so much against them as indifferent to them, and self-sufficient without them. A distaste for the conspicuous American style of success—of Cadillacs and celebrities—takes many forms: in some, a resentful discontent, in others a defiance that results in creativity apart; and in still others, a contented simplicity of living.

Monsignor Ronald Knox, according to his friend Evelyn Waugh, liked that classic division of mankind into the "drastic"—"the men of action and decision who know what they want and how to get it, who have little patience with the hesitations of others and never shrink from 'making a scene'—and the 'apathetic'—who take what is on the table when it is offered them; who suffer neglect rather than assert themselves, who hate to inconvenience anyone." The "apathetic" have a low visibility in the American Image, but their numbers are legion, and only the imperceptive scorn them.

"Both in history and in life," the British historian Herbert Butterfield has written, "it is a phenomenon by no means rare to meet with comparatively unlettered people who seem to have struck profound spiritual depths and reached the poetry of things—reached what I should regard as the very quintessence of the good life—while there are highly educated people of whom one feels that they are performing clever antics with their minds to cover a gaping hollowness that lies within." Even among those Americans who have not reached "the poetry of things" are people with qualities I respect. They have no desire to know only the right people. They are spontaneous, not wary. They are sometimes imprudently hospitable, and subject themselves to bores out of an unwillingness to wound. They do not bend their entertaining to serve their self-interest. They would agonize over a kind of ambition that required them to disregard among their friends those who do not keep up or do not measure up. They accept people "as they are." They may be silent in difficult matters and do not claim to be conversationalists, but they do not surround themselves only with those who amuse them, and they do not neglect among their acquaintances the old, the needy or the sick. In this they differ from those successful people who want to be surrounded only by success, by gaiety and malice, and quickly discard anyone who becomes an obligation. Among the dull whom the successful scorn are people whose antennae are more acute than theirs to the hurts and prides of others, and whose understanding and charity run deeper.

Americans may be assembled easily into markets but they do not fit easily into types. But it may be possible, to illustrate a point, to imagine among the diversity of Americans a Nebraska farm woman who is pious, honest and hard-working, who slaves for her children

but sometimes neglects to show them her affection, who never reads
a book or makes a witty remark. In the crises of her life she has
followed what she thinks her faith asks of her. She finds pleasure
in working in the garden and a rhythm in nature that proves her
inscrutable religion to her; in the evening she relaxes by listening
to the radio, skipping through a magazine, or watching television.
And then imagine a Connecticut broker or a California chemist
who is hep to every current allusion and is an asset to any party;
who is liberal in politics though only fitfully interested; whose hands
are skilled only at driving a car or sailing a boat, and who has
lively opinions on many subjects but few bedrock convictions. He
is alert to whatever is fresh, and brings a quick enthusiasm to the
new. The Nebraska farm wife would be distrustful of his cleverness,
and he would be antagonistic to her narrowness, but if I were select-
ing characteristics that I would want to be part of the American
character, I would take as much, and reject as much, from one as
from the other. As a nation, we would have lacked imagination had
we been confined to the first kind; had we been limited to the
second, we would have acted often on gusts of impulse, and lacked
something in solidity.

Those who are joined together by the blunt candor of their
ignorance, and by the complacent conviction that whatever they
do not understand in the arts or manners must be without merit,
can make a tyrannous majority. A petty, stolid vindictiveness can be
as destructive as clever, stinging wit. I only wish to argue that
perception about mankind or nature knows no income bracket nor
station in life, and requires no college degree. Too often America
is judged by the sameness of its front doors, which reflect a
stamping-out process so that everyone can afford a home of his
own. Behind these uniform doors live some whose life is an ordered
serenity, and others who hate and destroy one another. The miracle
is that out of such ordinary cocoons, butterflies sometimes blossom,
unmarked by their circumstances, for this is how America changes
from generation to generation.

To righteousness, cleanliness, integrity and respectability in the
American character we all pay due honor. But honor is so solemn
a duty. What I more cheerfully celebrate in the America that stands

outside any "elitehood" is something irrepressible, spontaneous, vigorous and original that constantly wells up there, among those who are not self-conscious about whether their taste is cultivated or their words carefully chosen. It is the stuff of Mark Twain, but also of second-rate night-club comics and of wisecracking milkmen. The judgments expressed are often crude, but lit by a carefree audacity that helps excuse any outrage. It should be added that many try but few succeed, and that he who would find the best must mine through many impurities—but when he finds it he has found something truly American—fresh, shrewd, skeptical and jaunty. It is to be found, amid much that is coarse and much that is windy, in the chatter of disc jockeys, in the doggerel on signposts, in the gossip columns of newspapers, in the asides of burlesque comedians and in the dialogue around garages.

It is a product of its place and its audience and dies when someone would make an art-form of it: its essence is that it be quick and unstudied. Its form is usually wry exaggeration, a skimming and cheerful mockery of pretension and of defeat; its irreverent tone is genuinely American, though not often reflected in the speeches of our Secretary of State. There is nothing cramped or cultivated about it—it tumbles forth in happy profusion, its daring reflecting the American preference for long shots.

A similar carefree spontaneity inhabits our jazz. Its excitement comes in its lyric outbursts of melancholy or sentimentality, and in its easy inventiveness, and its best has the classic virtue of freedom within discipline. Art, like God's presence, can be anywhere, among the lowly and the untutored, while denied to the schooled and tasteful, whose refinement sometimes holds back their spontaneity. This inventive spontaneity is, I think, the first claim of American jazz. When it allows itself to become symphonic, grandiose or pedantic it loses the freshness that demands it be taken seriously. Jazz risks being frozen to death in concert halls, risks crumbling to dust when enshrouded with footnotes of turgid social comment. Nowadays certain jazz styles and periods (New Orleans in the first World War, Chicago in the thirties) are considered admissible by those who collect respectable tastes. I confess myself more depraved than that: he who really likes American popular music finds himself less selective, and prepared to endure much that is bad in order to hear the rare, unforeseeable good burst forth, and has a sneaking fondness for much that purists abhor. For myself, though in listening to string quartets I find a tranquil pleasure that may go deeper than a liking for jazz, I at other times and in other moods still love the company of earthy saxophone, the steely edge of trumpet, the irreverent intrusion of drum, the tawdry songs whose banal simplicity gives the musicians an easy, familiar ground on which to meet and diverge. I plead guilty to a random taste in music, and may be like that musician described by Gide, who loved good music, but did not sufficiently detest bad.

Most of us know what we are expected to like, and sometimes persuade ourselves that this is what we actually prefer. I, for example, "know" that Verdi is of a higher order, but it is Puccini who can make my throat catch. Sometimes we affect a degree of interest in a subject that does not really interest us out of an eagerness to be in step with the times and in tune with the future; we sometimes sheepishly conceal preferences that we know to be held in low esteem. This presumption in favor of what is approved is an artificiality, yet I prefer it to the blindness of those who, in fields they do not understand, deride all established reputations. (I can remember as a high-school student believing that I was the only one honest enough to know that Shakespeare was overrated, though I later learned that the emperor *did* have clothes on.)

In fields where our own judgments are not certain, or not yet matured, it is natural to follow guides: so often the best of art, of poetry, of music, like the best of wines, prove on further acquaintance to be what they are acclaimed to be. But minds that esteem classics by reputation without understanding them are apt to praise copies that are not classic and to resist whatever boldly challenges the familiar.

In the arts of our own day, I think our instincts are a better guide than our studied tastes, for what the moralists of each generation would have us admire is not always what fickle posterity fastens upon: posterity may find true creativity in our blues songs and comic strips, seeking out what is vital in the vulgar and rejecting our ordered sonnets; and it may be for this reason that Yeats thought of art as a centaur, finding in popular lore its back and its strong legs. The arts of the academicians are apt to have the fatal flaw of elevation in them: that self-conscious desire to be respected for what one does, a trait that is forgivable in the individual but deadly to his art. Posterity is hard on well-meant pretense, and in the arts, at least, the making of elites can be a perilous occupation.

Taste, it has to be said, is an evanescent and unpredictable thing. It is too changy and flighty a bird to be captured by scientists or caged between measuring rods. It remains forever individual and forever comparative. Whether in painting, decoration, art or music, each age repudiates the overfamiliarity of what went before it, whose worth can only be reestablished after an intervening era. In literary styles, one generation, prizing originality, ends in anarchic oddity; the next generation pursues correctness and ends in formal sterility. By such lunges in one direction or another does the language preserve both vigor and form, and achieve a mean in theory, which, like the mean of a jiggling scale, is never visible. In décor, one generation prospers and swaggers: its drawing rooms boast with ormolu; the next generation longs to be free of ambitious encrustations and hankers after simplicity, until too much barrenness in turn produces its own revolt. And once we thus admit to fashions in taste, we have denied it absoluteness.

Some valued tastes will always be minority enthusiasms, requiring protective shade to stay alive. Others grow up in the wild profusion of the open field, indistinguishable from the weeds and undergrowth until a discriminating eye selects them out. Having lived among weeds and undergrowth, and prized wild flowers, I believe that a living society needs both the formal and the random, and that both the elite and the ordinary owe a grudging reserved judgment about one another.

19. Arts and Audiences

In this land of the carelessly free, and home of the restlessly satisfied, how fares the artist? The impact of an art on its era—and of the era on its art and its artists—is one way to measure the well-being of any society.

"Every age gets the art it deserves," T. S. Eliot once said, "and every age must accept the art it gets." Being himself so stern a doorkeeper to the classical halls, Eliot may have thought fitting punishment the art *our* age seems to have deserved and got. It cannot be said that we asked for it: but then, perhaps those times are rare, and of the highest cultural glow, when artists are in happy accord with the tastes of their own day.

The usual condition of the arts is an undeclared war between art and taste: art being what is offered, and taste the collective response to it. Taste is the buyer and sets the current market price, but cannot be the creator: sometimes it is willing to underwrite the artist's freedom but usually it hopes to command his obedience. This is harmlessly true of popular art, which seeks its own level and finds its own support, but what is forbiddingly called serious art has a harder time of it. The run of people regard art as providing the condiments of life; something at best gratefully extra, but not essential like bread and meat. In a democracy it must be left to smaller groupings to recognize and appreciate the best of the present, and to preserve and honor the best of the past.

Enthusiasm for the new in the arts is the spontaneous tribute of the young, who are apt to have dismissed, before they have learned to value, what has already been catalogued and acclaimed. Only later will they learn to isolate beauty from duty in the past. Preservation of the old has always been the special social role of the rich. "The use of riches isn't to disperse riches," remarks one of the characters in Santayana's only novel, "but to cultivate the art of living, to produce beautiful houses, beautiful manners, beautiful speech, beautiful charities. You individually can't raise the lowest level of human life, but you may raise the highest level." It is not even necessary, I think, for the rich to raise the highest cultural level (so few are equipped to)—but only to hold on to it. This role is particularly essential in America where we have embarked on the great gamble of democracy, broadening the river of culture, and hoping not to turn it into a shoreless ocean, lacking definition and variety.

My idea of a Good Society is increasingly one in which old values are preserved but in which the access to them is widened: not the keepers but what is kept is to be valued. I could understand that when I was 20—but at 20 might have swept out the keepers: only later did I realize that culture is preserved by those who live in it, absorb it and prize it. The role of preservator is in some respects a passive one. In a closed society, "good taste" frequently seems a drying up: the opera becomes something to be supported rather than enjoyed, an act of cultural piety. But in an open, undiscriminating society such as ours, I think a little taste, and a stubborn protectiveness about the old, is wanted to preserve order.

Some fortunate people have what might be called a plateau of taste that covers almost the entire landscape of the arts—whose appreciation of poetry, of design, of music, of painting, is in each sphere of the highest. Their major preoccupation is taste, and they make of it a full-time job. Such people are the fashion magazine's ideal of the Modern Woman: those who do not create but who judge and appreciate. In American society this has become largely a woman's role, a vocation for the well-to-do and a trade for others. Ours being the delegating and fragmented society that it is, even taste has become a business. We have designers and stylists for clothes and curtains, and decorators to give a harmony to our homes (the rich, who employ others to style their homes in Empire, or in Japanese contemporary, are in this sense little different from those who buy Dreams Complete, those garish bedroom sets in furniture-store windows). Beyond these dictators of style—who are really a limited monarchy, required to heed the parliament of the profitable middle—are entire regiments of counselors and consultants to manufacturers and merchants; beyond them in turn are the editors of countless magazines and newspaper home pages who advise and entrap their readers into furnishing their homes, cooking their meals and dressing themselves in one shifting fashion or another. The process by which taste spreads in America is often capricious and absurd, and a temptation to satirize—but in a democracy that is not brutishly self-satisfied any rise in the level of taste does require an act of levitation. If all American womanhood sometimes seems to be one huge gym class performing this awkward rite together, the scene is saved by the eager dedication of some, and the impish independence of others.

Those who mock the democratic process of self-improvement must ask themselves what they would substitute. None of us was born cultured; we must be instructed before we learn to discriminate. Recoiling from this democratic mass quest for culture, critics usually call up a mythology of past elites, those elites that gave the world stately homes and palaces and parks, and who bought up great art (after others had established its worth). But this answer will not do. That former day was not unerring in taste—nothing is so vulgar as a certain period of English splendor—but its fatal disability in our modern eyes is that it was part of a social system insensitive to the needs of its "lower orders" and unfair in its selection of who should enjoy its privileges. If that era had, along with much coarseness, graces which we lack and miss, entwined with them were the inequalities and selfishness that produced the century of Marx. And a pertinent question about that stately world arises when one remembers the words of the old hymn:

> The rich man in his castle,
> The poor man at his gate,
> God made them high or lowly,
> And order'd their estate.

In an age such as that, each of us may be forgiven for asking, Where would his own place have been—in the castle or at the gate? Unless he were born a Cecil, the answer might be discouraging. Perhaps it can be argued that it was better for all concerned when society was organized in such a way that everyone knew his humble place and did not yearn for what he could not aspire to. It is a thesis which can be argued—but not by an American.

The American revolution, not only of 1775 but of Jackson's day, was against the notion of elites, even of good ones. Americans started out in low circumstances, but determined to make something better of themselves. European critics who now look on in horror at the United States as a projection of what will happen to their own lands are apt, I think, to make two mistakes. The first is to assume that a previous society like their own has been wiped out in America by our masses, which is not the case. And the second is a tendency not to look at Americans as they are, but to project a vision of their own masses come to power onto their picture of the U. S.

But if there is such a thing as the American "mass," it lacks the ingrained characteristics of its European counterparts, and is not hampered by their handicaps. One measure of the difference is suggested by a remark of Hegel's. If no man is a hero to his valet, he once said, it is not because the man is not a hero, but because the other is a valet. How German a remark that is. We think of a man's present occupation not as a judgment on him but as a condition he is entitled to change, a way-station to something better, if he wishes. Is it not true that the French mass, emerging, does so with a chip on its shoulder, nursing resentments of 1789 or 1871 (and 25 per cent of them voting Communist); and that the British mass, emerging, makes economic gains more quickly than social ones, because it feels, and has been made to feel, inferior in status and accent? It is similarly in a European context that Ortega y Gasset, in his *Revolt of the Masses*, developed his thesis of an ignorant mass coming to power that was assertive, domineering and unregarding. If there are grounds to his fears, they have not nearly so much force in America, where one of the congestions of our life is in the sheer numbers of those who, not content with their own insufficient values, are eager to learn, and anxious to acquire taste.

It may be that aristocracy is by nature a better breeding ground in the arts than democracy: it is easier to serve a discriminating one than a committee of the whole. Whenever royal largesse must be widely distributed, it inevitably diminishes artistically. We cannot fashion jeweled Fabergé eggs for all, but can only provide sequins for everybody. Our conditions, then, differ from what artistic creation has faced before: where once the needs of the many were sacrificed for the pleasures of the few, the needs of the few are now engulfed in the wants of the many. In this circumstance the real artist must somehow find his own path, but the way is not impossible for him in contemporary America, I think, nor so treacherous as it is made to seem, so long as he is clear-eyed, and dry-eyed, about it.

Something in the atmosphere of each period determines its over-all artistic style, a general cultural necessity which is not to be confused with the seasonal and manipulated whims of fashion. In architecture, such homely problems as a shortage of servants and an increase in labor-saving appliances determine the size and contents of contemporary houses; the high cost of labor and the decline in craftsmanship probably influence the simplicity of our building as much as does a preferred severity of architectural taste. A society's political values are also frozen into its architecture, as when the Depression years made the well-to-do hesitant to assert their style of living too flamboyantly, and there emerged a low-lying modern house that was content to conceal rather than to exaggerate its size. The feeling that government in a democracy is ours, not above us, influenced the design of our national capital, and made our White House an intimate thing rather than a palace: its spreading size must be accomplished underground and hidden from the eye.

Art is thus always conditioned by its sponsorship and its circumstances. Berlioz' instrumental immensities, when set against Haydn's delicate chamber music of the preceding century, represents not only a difference in personal temperament and a growth in orchestral size, but a different cultural climate. What matters is that both men fashioned unique music out of their materials. Often the language of music, of painting or of architecture changes simply because it no longer satisfies those who must use it—a style becomes too rigid, or exhausts itself. But this is only the language of the arts, not what is said: men born to baroque make beauty of it as others make beauty of simplicity. "If a man's imagination is stimulated by artificial and arbitrary rules," said Valéry, "he is a poet; if it is stifled by such limitations, whatever kind of writer he may be, a poet he is not."

Every age demands beauty of its artists, but some ages are harder to oblige. For a genuine artist may accept a commission but can only speak for himself, and whatever his subject matter must declare the truth he finds in himself: if the world to him looks repulsive and deceitful his art will reflect his feeling. "I have aimed at rendering the true, not the ideal," said Toulouse-Lautrec, and would not be satisfied with prettiness. He once told Yvette Guilbert: "Everywhere and always ugliness has its beautiful aspects; it is thrilling to discover them where nobody else has noticed them." Those who are not artists may wonder whether the wish to find beauty where none did before leaves each generation with a declining field to pick over: once art sought to arrest the stillness of nature and called it beauty, then it sought the instantaneous and called it impressionism; now it seeks the fortuitous, and mirrors our times by making only fragments.

It is tempting to feel that many modern artists are only splashing out their dissatisfaction, without having fashioned art of it, or to suspect the modern poet of having taken the vows of poverty of language. But if we cannot admire, we must not complain either: art that is not a mere effort to please must follow its own necessities. When we create university chairs for poets we often make the poet more comfortable, but less of a poet; and when poetry can find no other conflict to nourish it, it will bite the hand that feeds it. I do not think that it is the duty of a culture to pyramid itself up to a point where a genius of painting or writing will crown it. Geniuses are gifts to an age, not earned, and may come along when least deserved, and may be buoyed by popularity or indifferent to it. We do not have the power to create geniuses, only the duty not to crush them, either by neglect or—in an opposite direction—by irrelevant demands upon them.

Artists by nature need to be free, and feel a need to defy: sometimes they seem to be saying, "I don't want to be understood, because I hate the values of those who want to understand." In the artist himself this impulse may be entirely genuine; resentments, even unfair ones, are often the fertile soil of art. A society may be doing most for an artist when it moves him to protest. Of course, there are also poseurs in the arts who confuse self-indulgence and rudeness with artistic integrity; and there are others who, because they cannot win popular approval, think themselves superior to it. (Philistines rightfully despise the poseur but are often not sure guides in detecting him. They think that because an artist gets paid his only desire is to make money, and any conditions on his own part are synthetic, a playing hard-to-get.)

Most of us, in our own lives, accept the duty of accommodation, and work to limit its damage to ourselves. But for artists and writers whose work *must* have an existence apart from themselves, whose work must in effect speak for itself, the accommodations that a person makes are apt to operate fatally against the work itself. He may want to establish his family in comfort and therefore will accept commissions which may not compromise his talents but do not stretch them; he may, out of vanity, for the reassuring plaudits of his immediate circle, be content to prettify and be careful to avoid the rawness and the difficulty that an uncompromising pursuit of truth requires; or he may, as most of us do, get caught up in activities which, while necessary of themselves, take too much of his time, his energy and his freshness, and are yet hard to break from.

Perhaps there is no way-station for the true artist: he must bend one way or the other: enjoy a comfortable existence and hope to maintain a decent artistic standard, or simplify his life to the point of poverty and determine to suffer no diversions from his art. To those who take this second course, the rest of us must give our respect, regardless of whether we approve the uses to which the talent is put. That man is no poseur who sacrifices comfort, even becomes indifferent to the wants and needs of his family, in a frugal pursuit of purity in his art. His quest must take him beyond what has already been done; he cannot therefore hope for popularity, or even understanding, from those who like what they are used to.

It is even a mistake, I think, to regard such artists as counting on a posthumous recognition—either the dubious compliment of those film biographies which show how a *previous* generation mistreated its artists, or the true recognition of those who learn to see with that artist's eye. Such artists are not simply seeking fame, now or later (though of course they might be grateful for it, if it did not interfere too much). Whether or not their struggle turned out "right" in the eyes of the world is ultimately a matter of indifference to them, for they are possessed of a demon within, and labor only to serve it.

Apart from this isolated kind of artist, with his blessed misfortune, there exist the creators who serve those public arts which require collaboration and accommodation—and with them the whole onrush of necessary commitments sets in. Their art may be of a second order, but their position is more difficult, for they are involved in the commercial necessity to seek the profitable middle; and after giving society the art it wants they often feel the need to exhibit their after-hours disgust in an unconventionality of dress, conversation or morality. Perhaps Shakespeare too complained backstage of those rude louts out front for whom he had to write in those painful comic scenes. Public arts have always required a price, if only in playing the courtier, whether inside or outside one's work, and this condition is not a special evil of our day. The Margrave of Brandenburg whose name was immortalized by Bach never acknowledged the concerti sent to him, or the toadying letter Bach wrote to him: "Two years ago, when I had the honor of playing before your Royal Highness, I experienced your condescending interest in the insignificant talents with which Heaven has gifted me . . ." Mozart was not fatally limited by being given only so many instruments to write for, or so short a time to finish an opera; and the greatest of Renaissance muralists triumphed over the cramped spaces left them in churches. Our contemporary art patrons, whatever their other failings, do not insist on having themselves painted into nativity scenes, in richly gowned supplication before a simple virgin and child in a stable.

All of this being true makes it no easier for a creator to bend his knee, submit to editing or be required to make something prettier in order to peddle it. Our profit-making society has developed a whole stratum of art directors, editors and script-readers to make art acceptable and profitable. They are usually sympathetic people seeking to bridge two worlds, but for all their solicitude, the accommodation usually requires an idealizing of trivial objectives, the injection of a "gimmick" or a cheapening of language and spirit. Paint your beautiful landscape—but place our monstrous automobile prominently in the foreground. Go ahead with the sombre theme of your play, but give our star a big scene in which to wear a smart gown or she won't be interested. Program directors cry for plays that are original, but would also like them to be constructive in outlook. (It is not necessarily true that art cannot be constructive, but constructiveness is a limitation, and when values that are not inherent in any material are injected into it, they often become an additive that fatally discolors.)

Not all of the hindrances that beset a creator are destructive to his art, or peculiar to our form of society. Some who think they might create better had they more time and leisure soon discover that it was the stress of circumstances that gave their work its essential tension. Under an aristocracy as in a democracy, working with others entails constrictions—propels one into rivalries, compels one into compromises. Yet, in fact, many a man is well served by advice and gains in collaboration.

Between original art and its audience lives the half-world of editors, agents, directors, backers; and the relationships are subtler than the popular view of a creator dragged down by his debasers. Directors or gifted actors often supply the artistic spark that lifts ordinary material. Agents and similar middlemen may appear to be the apparatus of corruption, but in fact exist as an apparatus of convenience. Their primary role is to be Public Facing, mindful of what an audience or a buyer is presumed to want. The creator must be both inward-looking, if he would have something original to say, and Public Facing, if he would have an audience. His motives are mixed. Is he sculpturing just to achieve a purity of shape, or does he want appreciation? Is he writing to gratify his vanity, or to move men? Out of conflicting ambitions, by some mystery of internal alchemy, come books and paintings and statues.

Those artists who will not compromise can hardly expect, though their work be better, to be as well paid as those who deliberately shape their material for reward, and who give up the precious right to speak with their own voice and to please only themselves. But it is one thing to labor to be understood by an audience, and another to shape everything—content, mood, language—to what is "sure-fire." The Public Facers are expert craftsmen; they need not be ashamed of what they do. Let them have their fame and their money, for their eventual satisfactions will be these only. They must expect to encounter resentment from two kinds of unsuccessful people—those whose art is better but more difficult and unappreciated, and those whose art is neither successful nor any good.

In art as in life there is a further conflict, that continuing conflict between the raw and the ordered, between neat minds and ranging ones. Often what restrains the creator is not the financial conservatism of his patrons, but the narrowness of their imagination: those in the arts who acquire taste often lose gusto, and are hostile to what is unexpected in the new. Commonsensical minds are necessary to make art pay, or even to organize a performance: such minds are apt to congratulate themselves on their practicality and to hold the creator in slight contempt, though each is dependent on the other.

All of these difficulties are inherent in the disturbing process that is creation; dislocation is the law of its development and the proof of its health. Some must pioneer, and others must relate the new to the old and the moving to the still, so that a culture can step, not lurch, from equilibrium to equilibrium. Those who scorn commercial necessity cannot live without it, and often gain by it—even those engaged in so private an art as poetry. Before poetry can reach its reader, someone has had to regard it as merchandise, someone to regard it merely as a job of printing, and someone else as freight—and what jewels and what dynamite thus travel as ordinary freight!

In our society a creator can usually make his way, if not at the pace he would like. If he is willing to have his difficult symphonies rarely performed, he can write as he will; he need not, like Shostakovich or Prokovicv, change his entire manner of composition, nor like those nameless Russian artists must he paint only romanticized political photostats that distort history.

Inside every artist, whatever the form of government he lives under, there wages a struggle between the need for purity in his work and the desire to have a large audience for it: he must hold in constant tension the beliefs and feelings of his essential self and the demands which are inseparable from his opportunities. But contentment was never the natural soil of art.

20. Whatever the Public Wants

It may be that never before in history has culture—music, theater, art—been dispersed so widely as in America, but it is a culture of a secondary level that gets most widely sown. When we turn, then, from the opportunities open to the creator to the cultural level of our society itself, we find, I think, a situation more disquieting.

Just as increased literacy has not given us political governance to match the days of Washington, Adams, Jefferson, Madison and Hamilton, so the praiseworthy raising of our lowest cultural level has been accomplished at the expense of the *dominance* of the top. Those powerful forces in our society who aim their arts at the most of us, at that enormous middle between low and high, have given us a waist-high culture.

The eternal optimists among us, who find us as a nation getting bigger and better all the time, point to the increased numbers of college graduates in the United States (twice as many as in 1940); to the proliferation of amateur theatrical troupes and of Sunday dabblers in paint; and to the increased sales of classical records. But if we can indeed be grateful for the numbers of Americans who escape the embrace of that which would crush them, we should admit that most of the temptations pull the other way. And those who acclaim the sale of half a million paperback copies of *The Odyssey* might remember that such an audience would fill only one row in the stadiums full of Americans reading comic books.

A cultural top does exist in America, but it does not command the most powerful facilities to spread a knowledge of itself, and even has difficulty getting heard at all above the din going on below. Sometimes it is indulgently subsidized by the wealthy middle, to claim a tax deduction or to borrow its prestige. The network that underwrote ninety minutes of Toscanini a week to offset a hundred hours of drivel was often heard to sigh over the losses incurred, but was handsomely repaid in favorable publicity, and in the use it made of Toscanini to refute its critics. The largest of phonograph record companies was lately praised for the "freedom" it gave a new artistic director: he would be allowed to issue two records to his standards of taste for every eight that were "what the public wanted." The commercial logic of such practices is self-evident—but not the right of such companies to assert that they exist only to provide the best.

For if they are to be judged by their pretensions, they have no right to plead that they are helpless servants of the public taste— they are at the controls of the most powerful engines for molding that taste. They will then be heard to say that it is the job of others —parents or teachers—to instruct; they themselves must think of their stockholders. And, stripped of all self-serving rhetoric, this is exactly the point. We have left the dissemination of culture in the hands of those who feel no ultimate duty beyond profit, and who sell the use of their government-granted channels in little fifteen- or thirty-minute snippets to the highest bidder, with hardly a thought, except a commercial one, to the balance, proportion and quality of what they provide.

The paradox is that what is most tailored to please the public often fails to. An audience can only receive, it cannot inspire: it is a blank face waiting to be made to smile or weep, and ready at any moment to yawn. Critics often shudder at the authority wielded by those who rule television, with all its resources and facilities. Yet at the center of this powerful centripetal mechanism is a fearful, fumbling uncertainty, surrounded by immense sums of money. So vast an expenditure requires an assured audience.

When producers and directors know no other standard but what has previously pleased, they are at every moment under the great risk of losing their audience through apathy. We may bestow a moment's sympathy on all who have the thankless task of providing entertainment on a scale unprecedented in history, who must fill up eighteen hours a day on three or four networks of television, and as many of radio, with what must at least seem fresh and new. One might think that with all that time and talent available, there would be endless variety, but there is not. Always there exist the standards of the implied center toward which all public facing artisans must bow in obedience, and though some get quite skilled at mixing the well-known ingredients, they have no way of protecting themselves against repetition and saturation.

The iron law of the American mass market is that every producer seeks to make his product as close as possible to what sells best. And just as all automobile manufacturers must adopt a gadget if one succeeds with it, so must everyone borrow any new magazine feature, television stunt or musical sound effect that attracts, or he will be left behind.

First comes the formula, then the satiety with it, then a desperate search for variety, until the new develops a formula of its own, and then satiety again. At certain points in this circle, producers who have become too slick must send for outsiders who resisted the system. These oddballs have their brief inning; but though isolation has made their material different it is apt to have injected a bitterness into it that disturbs the sponsor even before it annoys the audience—and back everybody goes to the old formula. Our great cultural engines, motivated by a sterile and imitative appeal to a demanding but unventuresome audience, are thus destined to saturate and bore. Then is heard the indignant cry: "Why don't they give us something good? They promised to please us, didn't they?" But the policy of formula is the enemy of the good, and the law of the profitable middle is sovereign over commercial gain but never over creativity.

But though radio, cinema and television are awash in the mediocre and the hackneyed, their impact is nonetheless more powerful than anything else around. Against their pervasive reach, the chaste virtues of education must ever be at a disadvantage, whether in inspiring a taste for another kind of art, an alternate set of values, or a different code of behavior. The only advantage education has is that for a few hours a day it can lock in the impressionable young and command their attention. Teachers are told that the reason education's values do not predominate is their fault: they ᵤhould make their instruction more interesting. But they cannot hope to match the vividness, the frivolity of subject matter or the resources of those vast organisms which do not claim to teach, yet fill the mind. Arduous routine and mental discipline are hard put to compete against the easy appeal of romances, cowboys and jingles. Once people shut their doors against the outside world's distractions and vulgarities; now these afflictions enter their front rooms, bringing sufficient benefits to lull criticism but in the end leaving a stain on our minds. We are at the mercy of our blessings, and are faced with the likelihood that all our luxuries—our cars, our television, our conveniences—will diminish us as a people, and at an increasing rate as our luxuries increase their power of saturation. We are prisoners of what we have called progress, and it would be a dangerous optimism to think that, left to its own, the situation would provide its own corrective. It wasn't so economically in the days of laissez-faire and will not be so culturally.

Those who, disturbed by present trends, despise "the masses" for being as they are, underestimate a concern that is general, and which feels itself helpless: what does one fight against, who does one fight, and how? It is a devil's bargain we have all made, with those who agree to give us only what we want so long as they are free to derive a profit from it. We are asked to fight something not hateful but seductive. And the seducers have all the organization, and we none; they have all the resources, which they can pay for in our name; they have the sanction of most of the great opinion-makers in the community, and can neutralize the rest.

Not by solemn and considered assignment of rights and duties, but by a seizing of opportunities has our society become what it is. A community organizes itself in many ways. It has churches—divided by creed but united generally by common precepts, and permitted by the state to guide only those who seek its guidance. It has schools, whose moral teachings are similar to the churches' (though watered down by secularity) and whose further duty is to teach trades. It has government, whose powers have been artfully limited. It has a press and a theater to instruct and beguile, while required to please. It has other cohesions, such as the craft standards of professional minorities, or the voluntary groupings of those with kindred hobbies or concerns. But pervading them all, and dominating all else, is the profit-making mechanism. It not only speaks to our primitive needs and to our ambitions, but does so with the confidence born of its success and the power it has accumulated. It has enlisted us all, since we must earn our daily livings. It takes from us and rewards us; it organizes our daily lives. Not all its conduct is admired by the community, but it is tolerated: many accepted forms of business behavior are not so much morally approved as philosophically consented to in the name of freedom.

It can be argued that business has become effectively tamed and socially conscious. Aware of a responsibility to the community, corporations now support charities, endow worthy educational causes and launch scientific foundations (particularly when the tax laws encourage such generosity). Corporations, in filling such needs, and justifying such idealism, proclaim a wish to keep government from expanding into these new areas. We thus have wealthy foundations to make studies of the public welfare and to encourage benevolent relationships with the Islamic or the Twi-speaking peoples. The output of these societies, though permeated with that safe knowledge of a good living that surrounds the foundation mentality, is often irreproachably worthy. Their studies have influence on national policy, though no say in it. In such random and erratic ways are the needs of the community often dealt with.

For in the end, it is the weight and force of economic power—not the power of a few overlords, but the immensely greater force of a whole intricate mechanism—that guides almost everything we do, for purposes that may be useful but are only tangentially for national ends, and confined in scope. Our society of a multiplicity of separate organisms organized for specific tasks is informally held together by our journalism, our politics, and our back-fence conversations. There is something appealingly unplanned about the way America confronts or neglects its necessities and opportunities, but in cheering how well it does, we must ask whether it does enough.

In summing up the direction we are taking as a nation, the ultimate American temptation is to return optimistic answers, aware how widespread are good intentions and how natural is the American confidence that what is wrong will inevitably be put right. But there are times when truth must war with comfort. Our society has become quite efficient at determining our wants and satisfying our needs and pleasures, but it does less to awaken our aspirations. Once this lack did not matter so much, but our increased frustrations attest to an awareness that gratification of our desires has become an insufficient response to our needs.

It is easy enough to blame all our troubles on the money-makers who debase us. Their brutal answer would be that there can be no rape when consent is given. They are not ashamed of their conduct but glory in it; they feel themselves the vital force of the nation, that which replenishes and provides for it. They would point to our material achievements which cultures with higher peaks have never attained. They would ask what other incentive would do better. They would indignantly deny that they are guilty of lowering the public taste, or of perverting its values: some among them may be at fault, but the rest are conscious of ministering to an urge for self-improvement in people. If money-makers have not provided us with the best of everything, it is because (they say) they have had to answer to the dictates of the profitable middle, which gets what it wants. And in fact capitalism's democratic referendum, just because it so effectively "satisfies our wants," makes it all the harder to rise above them, to seek our common needs.

We tolerate what contents us, placidly accept what might require too much exertion to correct, and allow a free play to ambition. The result is a society tightly organized for specific purposes but loosely controlled in general, a society which has surrendered paramount influence over itself to those in no position to encourage or require the best of it. Not profit, which admirably organizes our production and consumption, but rather the leaving to profit of duties it is not best fitted to carry out, is our difficulty. To commit to corporations or to voluntary organizations the determining of our national aims is to leave them in the end to no one responsibly. Our society must find a way first to conceive the common good, and then to honor and reward in proper proportions those activities which best serve, not individual employers, but the community's aims. It is not enough to say of a society that though it feels itself a little frustrated it is generally content, for it may be satisfied with its circumstances while unaware of its true situation.

True, a certain kind of present danger is everywhere acknowledged: our press and our politicians talk of little else but the threat of Communism. Its menace is usefully exploited to persuade us to do things that need doing, though it is also invoked in dubious causes as well. We are urged to hate Communism but to adopt its scientific and military emphasis; and we are encouraged to congratulate ourselves on how superior our own morality is. But though Communism's challenge cannot be minimized, it is not the real root of our difficulties: these would exist if there were no Russian threat. These difficulties arise from the increased tempo of our lives, from the headlong and compulsive strides of our sciences, which outwit our efforts to create equilibriums, and from the increasing capacity of our distractions to numb our energies. Our difficulties are aggravated by the fact that events everywhere are out of kilter. If a great effort must continually be made to provide against Russian assault, our real expenditure of imagination must be in lighting the chaos inside us, and recovering a clarity of purpose. Only in this way will we regain health as a nation, or hope to inspire others to admire us. The only competition that should matter to us as a nation is not with Communism but with that best we ourselves might be.

All societies create daily equilibriums, and achieve a balance amid conflicting drives. We too make a patchwork equilibrium and enjoy a fortunate civic tranquility, but I believe it to be an equilibrium out of gear with our increasing necessities. It reckons too little on the dynamic propulsion of technological changes within it, and is out of rhythm with the disturbances in the rest of the world.

We solace ourselves by regarding as progress the momentum of our technology and the increase in our comforts—but technology and comfort add nothing to our characters, and may increase our problems while weakening our ability to confront them. We must, then, seriously ask ourselves whether our society, despite its deceptive vitality, has not entered a parabola of decline, less and less able to cope with what it must face.

21. Pebbles at the Window

It is said that the Florentine artist who discovered the laws of perspective became so excited that he would waken his wife in the middle of the night to talk about his wonderful discovery. Who could blame him? To see everything in life not as all of the same worth and weight, but as modified by light and distance, and as affected inevitably by the vision of the beholder, is to receive the gift of proportion.

When I look back on my beliefs of twenty years ago, as I emerged militant and confident from college, I am not aware of despairing of America more now, but only of expecting less of it. At 21, I had heard most of the great simple ideas, but had heard also their contraries, and sometimes preferred the contraries for being more cleverly put. Growing older, I do not have the feeling of discovering unheard-of truths, but only of seeing in a new light facets of what I had first been told of long ago and only later absorbed as my own. Our minds are attics of unexamined contradictions. As our arteries harden, our imagination constricts. Narrowing our ambitions to what seems possible is called sensible; what seems possible decreases with every year. We no longer wildly dream: we accept. We no longer widely question: we avoid. We no longer justly accuse: we evade.

We set out to be good, and settle for being well-behaved. We often call tolerance what is really only the ability to hold contrary opinions so weakly that we do not perceive their contradiction. We declaim against faraway injustices and pay our charities by check so that our consciences need not travel down the back street of our own city, need not linger with derelicts or touch squalor (some give of their time, some of their money; some give of their heart, which is the costliest gift of all). Most of us, in all we do, learn to measure consequences and to ration responses, and call it practical wisdom. We contract our obligations, in order to be able to fulfill them.

Our lives, at every moment, reflect an unceasing effort to choose our own gait, without getting too far out of step with the march of society. Though insisting on our own individuality, we are none of us a new beginning or a final end, but only links in a continuing chain of culture: we are given a baton to carry forward our brief mile and then hand on. Presumably we are handed the cumulative wisdom of what has gone before, and since more is constantly being accumulated, we speak of progress. But what in fact is being handed to us is complexity, and each generation, while adding its own new deposit of discovery and complexity, must somehow establish a new simplicity.

At 21, I believed in progress and thought it easy to organize majorities to good ends; now that I am twice 21, I believe that what is amiss in our way of life is beyond writing one's congressman about.

The change in outlook may simply be the result of my own aging, though I do not think so; I believe the difference is demonstrably external. We no longer proclaim that "the world's great age begins anew." The New Deal now seems a day of confident innocence, and the optimistic birth of the United Nations—its authors so sure that they were avoiding the unrealism of the League of Nations—now seems a curious spectacle of naiveté thinking itself sophisticated. I believe that Americans have lost much of their optimism as a nation, no longer as sure as Benjamin Franklin was that theirs is the Cause of all Mankind; so confident that only their own actions in a naughty world shine with good intentions; so ready to assume that things will turn out right, or to feel that the future is theirs alone to determine. This change may reflect increased wisdom, but the nation has not yet emerged from hurt recriminations over its lost innocence, or regained a steadfast buoyancy. Still, considering the shock of the present peril and the future's awesome uncertainty, it might be argued that Americans have quickly accepted burdens that would once have been fiercely resisted: the ends of foreign policy are agreed upon; and though the demands of armored alertness may be lamented, they are generally accepted as a condition of our times.

It is a deeper level of national discontent I have sought to explore in these final chapters: to examine that widespread American sense of blighted intentions. This book began out of a growing personal dissatisfaction with the American scene—its noise, speed, hypocrisy and triviality—and a desire to stand off from it, and at a pace slower than it (in a Provençal village in the south of France) to find a new response to it. For I was conscious of absorbing, without too critical a questioning, the common indictment of the American people made by its most vocal critics, while aware of a nagging doubt about the validity of the indictment.

These critics were very sure of what was wrong and who was to blame ("I wish," said Melbourne, "that I could be as cocksure about anything as Macaulay is about everything") but it seemed to me that in returning their true bills they were much too quick to conjure up an American mass of "John and Jane Does Unknown," a mass that did not conform to my own observation. For if told about masses, I am aware of individuals—people with shames and lusts and faults and ambitions, with illnesses and deformities and disappointments, people heavy with appetite and pride or dulled by sloth and care. They are shaped into masses for single purposes—to sell them cigarettes or to fill a stadium—but they remain individual. They will remain individual, that is, if they can escape the great ooze that threatens to engulf us all, and which in recent years has greatly increased its concentration of force.

Since I no more like vapidity, mediocrity, banality and pettiness than anyone else, I have not wanted to praise what cannot be praised in the American scene, but only to separate the often-displeasing surface of American life from those who move in it. Perhaps the much-criticized American people do not need charity so much as justice. If guilty, they are not guilty as charged, and are at least entitled to the old frontier verdict: "Guilty, but not so dern awful guilty."

What has been taken to be their lack of concern is often, I think, an unconscious decision by many of them that, since their actions cannot control the world, they would live only in that world they can control. They leave it to someone else to man the gates, and if he, deceived by the quiet inside and the dark outside, thinks the peace undisturbed, they go contentedly about their own tasks —eating, working, loving, sleeping. In this they are human, but perhaps not very wise. Those who are most esteemed for wisdom in the community busy themselves in recondite tasks, withdrawing from the crowd, and sometimes despising it. They are offended by the hustle and haggle in the streets, and confuse the volume of the street noises with the size of the crowd. They do not see that others have withdrawn behind their shutters too, and that withdrawal, in one form or another, is a common practice in American life. They do not realize that those who are not members of any given crowd at any given moment always outnumber those who are. The result is that the country's decisions are taken by minorities (sometimes good minorities, sometimes bad) which get together and prevail over those who disagree among themselves, who are little interested, are too trusting, feel themselves shut out, or do not bother.

In the multiplicity of voluntary decisions open to us all, some are content to resist responsibility and tend gasoline pumps; some manufacture and some write poetry; some merely idle. Some make money by securing a better price than the value they give. Some put talent to a baser use than it was meant to serve. Many live in the society-as-it-is, and justify their own way by pointing out how prevalent it is. Some flee to a monastery—a solitary quest that must be respected even if it cannot be regarded as a universal specific. Some cultivate their gardens, or play at cults. Some think themselves above the battle, and thereby contribute to the general defeat. They do not like the dust and noise of the arena; they are willing to enter it, but only on their own terms—a favor which the great public will not concede them. They are repelled by the court of public opinion, where circumstantial evidence counts for so much. But if they would be of help, they must first submit their qualifications to the mass of men, and stand the often unfair testings of popularity and rude questioning. The good ones grow on it, for they do not waver from the standards they set themselves, and in time establish the worth of their independence.

In every community, and in every kind of society, there exist together justice and injustice, selfishness and unselfishness, greed and charity. So much then depends on which values are given the greater encouragement. What is honored in a community, said Plato, will be cultivated there. What is honored in ours? To ask the question is to be deafened by a hundred answers, but the noisiest voices, drowning out the rest, will be shouting, "Success! Money!" Though there are other ways to measure value in the community, the commonest is the price tag. The chief defect of such a system is not its economic validity but its social inadequacy. The price marks that are stamped on everything in our lives largely ignore social utility, and handsomely reward stock-market coups and amiable entertainers while regarding such useful arts as teaching and preaching as unskilled labor. The error is further compounded when the amount of one's reward is accepted as the value of his services.

To be French, English, Dutch or Italian, says the English critic V. S. Pritchett, is not felt as an intellectual elation or dilemma, a mission, or a crux, "but, whether the idea is felt to be invigorating, automatic or calamitous, to be American is also felt to be an additional fate." Perhaps this is because to be French or English is to be settled in identity, and to be free then to make one's own individuality. We seem bound to discover what it is to be an American before being sure what it is to be ourselves: our mold has never cooled, our metal never hardened.

The explanation for this continuing process of definition may lie in our history. The European values that our first settlers brought with them often proved inadequate or too refined for new conditions, and a new set of values incorporated what was learned on the crude frontier, among people who were plain, hard-working, self-confident and bluntly scornful of anything fancy or delicate. And then came those later disturbing invasions from Europe's back yards, peoples whose tongues were strange and whose manners were odd. To make them Americans too, and not just aliens in the land, was the first great mission of popular education, which had to resolve our differences and search out what we had in common. We were never made a present of our identity, and being so changing a nation, have had to find it on the run. We grew and spread so fast that what unites us has always had to outrace what would divide us: our problems, as well as our opportunities, became continental—beyond the reach of any self-constituted nucleus to control us. In fact, those who might have assumed that role became more and more convinced that their best course was to safeguard what they had, to shut themselves apart, and preserve their own values.

If, as Ernest Renan said, "the existence of a nation is a daily plebiscite," our own has often been carried out amid a hue and cry, and with many among us not paying much attention. What is a nation? asked Renan. "To have common glories in the past, a common will in the present; to have done great things together; to wish to do greater; these are the essential conditions which make up a people. . . . In the past, an inheritance of glories and regrets; in the future, one and the same program to carry out."

It may be argued that such desires still inspire us, more than they appear to. What I find most encouraging about American life today is the amount of discontent with it. But the discontent is soured by thinking itself a minority; it lacks confidence and high spirits. Intellectuals in particular are not happy warriors; the wryness of their complaints is a measure of their defeatism. If only they realized it, discontent is so widely felt in America that it exists even among those who in their daily lives do most to corrupt our ways. In other parts of their living these corrupters are alert against debasements, and make isolation booths of their private lives. They spread poppycock and eat cake (it is not a way of life I much admire).

Our difficulty, a sympathetic critic might say, is not our lack of drive but our lack of direction: we are a vital, not an indolent people; our trouble is that our strengths are continentally diffused, and our linkings are not at the highest level, but across our middles. Increasing knowledges are driving us apart: our best people form isolated pools of private conversation. These non-colliding elites, I am convinced, are more numerous than they imagine themselves to be, and their self-inflicted solitude is more injurious, and less necessary, than they realize. They tend to be elites of function—in law, in medicine, in science, in industry: if their true value is not sufficiently felt in the American consensus it is because they have let only their work speak for them. They adhere to a purity in their specialty but do not know how to develop an effective relationship to all else. For them the height of practical wisdom is to learn, like the mouse, to sneak in for the cheese without being snuffed out by the trap.

We are all now hopelessly dependent on one another, and the only question is whether we foolishly seek to deny it. The essential art in contemporary life is how to be independent of the crowd without being estranged from it. We all need to make an island of our own, and too few do; but many who make an island neglect to build a bridge back.

The impulse of scientists is to deepen their concentration on a narrow front, but we do not need burrows so much as bridges: they hesitate to come out into the light, fearing that they will be rebuffed because they do not know how to talk simply, and they find themselves baffled whenever confronted by the inexact science of public affairs. The impulse of the fastidious is similarly to isolate themselves in disapproval from our waist-high culture—but in abandoning any contribution of their own, they have forfeited the right to criticize what is done without them.

There is a discontent and a satiety with the pleasures of the middle that the producers of movies and television shows and the publishers of magazines and newspapers are well aware of. An awareness of our inadequacies may not have widened but it has intensified, brought home by shocks to our national pride; but this awareness is weakened by a feeling that little can be done about it. It is an American trait, as well as a human tendency, to dismiss as not worth the doing that which will not prove to be enough. We are under the dictatorship of the sensible, who hold responsible jobs because they have a quick appreciation of how to achieve limited goals. They are men of a narrow practicality and a self-effacing competence: they do not realize that they can be charged with failing to do what they have not set out to do. They make a success of their work, but at a too-low level of responsibility, because they conceive of their tasks in terms of the organization they work for, rather than of the community at large. They may have warm intentions, but are often satisfied merely to express them, and fail to realize that to will an end one must will the means. We live today by playing for safety, by committee decision and "sense of the meeting." It is sometimes said that all we need is leadership, and while it is true that we have lately lacked it, I believe that what men generally mean by that complaint pays too little heed to the immensity of the difficulties we face. Rather, we need a revolution of goals, a change in what we value, what we preserve and what we pursue. It may be that our discontent is what most justifies optimism. It may also be that when the younger generation is accused of lacking ambition what is really meant is that it is no longer inspired by the old standards, and it may be that this is what the "silent generation" is being silent about.

The generation of the thirties was united by government in a war against depression; the forties were united by government leading us in war; then came the unleashing of individual pursuits of comfort and leisure, with government only manning the levers of currency and credit. In that final period we have been like an orchestra playing all at once but with no particular melody and with the brasses dominating. We need not so much to abandon our fiddles and cornets, as to be orchestrated again.

What can be asked of individuals is always more than what can be required of a society. "The most radical division that it is possible to make of humanity," said Ortega, "is that which splits us into two classes of creatures: those who make great demands of themselves, piling up difficulties and duties; and those who demand nothing special of themselves but for whom to live is to be every moment what they are."

If we now return to the question of elites, that vexing problem in a self-conscious democracy, it might be said of them that they justify themselves, and are most impervious to attack, when they are a freemasonry, which any number can join, of those who set themselves higher standards. (Elites that are merely closed corporations of privilege and pleasure find themselves insufficiently armored to stand fast against the democratic assault). The argument for elites is that if there are people who feel superior responsibility, they should assume it; if they are against dead levels, they need not sink to one. They must pull away from the crowd, not because they feel above it (they may not be, in all things) but because they recognize a call to follow a superior necessity.

But I detect a hortatory note creeping into my voice. It is not my ambition to exhort, but only to examine. I do not want to smash plate glass, but only to throw pebbles at a window, hoping perhaps to awaken those who have fallen asleep with their radios on and do not hear what is going on outside. Those who have the reformer's vision must be angrier than I—and perhaps more hopeful. Their enthusiasm is praiseworthy, but their vision is often blurred by finding too much bad in others, or in demanding too much good of them. Reformers are apt to be surer than I of the efficacy of their simple remedies. They hope to "arouse public opinion" with catchy slogans and loosely defined programs, to form committees, sign manifestoes, ring doorbells. But I do not think more slogans or pep campaigns are needed, and have no desire to grab anyone's lapels. What is lacking, in this free country at this fluid moment, is the realization that if we do not like the image of America that we see about us, we need only to recognize that much of it is imposed upon us by those who have need of us; and it is further made by our own indifference, which leaves to them the field. It may be possible to change all of this, but it will be done only by a gradual reversal of what we esteem most as a society, and what we reward most; such an upheaval of values will be slow and painful, brought about —if it is at all—by a conviction that a new American outlook, even if not clearly seen in all its details, is not simply desirable but mandatory.

In America, sweeping changes of opinion begin with a rustle of discontent, which for a long time is not detected. Then it swells to a stiff breeze and sometimes to a whole gale. Newspapers hear of it, and politicians who detect and follow the public mood join it. The timid who have been afraid to speak at last find their tongues, the many who follow the wind change with its direction, and men made conscious of a discontent, and encouraged to act, begin to volunteer solutions.

Whether today's rustle of discontent will tomorrow become a breeze, I do not know, but I suspect that it would not take gale force to recapture the center of our society. It is not stoutly defended: "Troy in our weakness lives, not in her strength." The center is not well commanded: it is minded by men protecting their own interests but incapable of seeing even them clearly; they are uncertain of purpose and divided in counsel; they are listening at the door, and it is we who are still. The news about our times is that the center is empty.

The further news is that our times are out of hand, and becoming progressively more so. It may be a defect in me that I do not share the scientists' excitement in what they are about. I am not one of those whose imagination was first lit by a Bunsen burner. The genius of our times may in retrospect be seen to have been scientific rather than artistic or political. But seeing the dislocations, I begrudge even what increases my comfort and security at such cost. We are moving forward at twice the speed of sound but half the speed of sense. Progress, or at least change, cannot be arrested—who would want to resist better medicine or lighter tools?—but it must be dealt with, for the side effects of our gains often outweigh their benefits. And when we add to these derangements the disturbances that are loose in the world, the slumbering forces now everywhere awake and demanding satisfaction, it may be seen that the lazy and familiar response to our problems has been to give way to them. We have largely abandoned any effort to control events—in the name of democracy and freedom, we have often surrendered the restraint of the strong upon the weak, the good on the bad, the excellent on those who pervert—and then plead our helplessness.

The sensation of feeling our times awry extends wider than our continent: in fact, it is a view most widely held elsewhere in the world, among those who are most impatient to gain all, or most fearful of losing all. The best that past centuries have given us is everywhere threatened, apt to be destroyed in the accumulation of past neglects which are being violently avenged. We find our selves sometimes rushing to extend help to what might someday turn upon us—but we also feel the need to make a friend of the future, lest we be destroyed by its enmity. It is *our* tonic that others are getting drunk on—the right of each individual to be heard, and to have his demands justly weighed—and these others have not learned, and may not be given time to learn, a healthy moderation in the heady spirits of democracy.

Nowadays to discover what it is to be an American is only a part of discovering what it is to be modern. Others are ahead of us in disillusion; but perhaps this is because they are behind us in capacity to adjust. Europeans often dislike us because they regard us as being at the head of the egalitarian movement that is everywhere getting out of hand, leveling everything before it; yet the rest of the world too often regards us as the center of all that holds fast against what needs redressing: we are declared the villain on every side.

The whole world, I fear, is advancing toward chaos with a velocity that is unnerving, and the Russians no more than we are in control of events: they are only more tightly organized, at an inferior level, in single-minded pursuit of lesser aims. If in our own society, our dominant urge is to content the middle rather than to inspire the best, it may be doubted whether we shall be able to rise to our needs. Americans are not the inventors of the modern world's disorder, which is a universal condition; but we have been pioneers in the exploration of change and are familiar with unsettled frontiers. We are best fitted to make order out of the prevailing chaos if anyone in this day and age is: we have strength and health, and are not hopelessly set apart by faction, are not beaten, decadent or corroded; we are not slaves of a system of equality by machine gun, and can make our wishes effectively known; we are old hands, with some knowledge of the terrain, and are quick to learn. The American Experiment is still relevant to the world.

The condition of our times is so overwhelming; our own awareness of what is going on elsewhere, beyond our control, is so insufficiently vivid to our minds; and our temptation to drift is so strong, that the practical journalist in me, leery of exhortations, suspects that we will go along much as we are, deceived by small victories, and will not perceive a decline, or will think it beyond our remedying. The American in me, full of stubborn sentiment about his people, wants to believe them already astir, and conceives it always a mistake to project only the ebb and not the flow in American life, for if Americans are always slow to see danger, once they have seen it they are an awesome force to reckon with.

Sometimes I dream of a land where patriotism is not considered a superiority to others but a pride in being the hospitable center of the best from everywhere; where differences in color and race are not falsely denied but make a competition in being the best; where justice inhabits the courts, wisdom the legislatures and honor the markets; where duty is followed but in no dull way and pleasures are lighthearted; where the last is not least and the highest is not proud; where grab is despised and giving prized; where trust is unfeigned, knowing it will not be disappointed; where tranquility is to be found, but not torpor, and raucous variety also has its place; where weaknesses are not denied but excellences are exalted; where diversity roams free, and the unity of the dour and the carefree, the homely and the favored, the comfortable and the restless is in their unafraid belief in each other's freedom; where men are not angels but do not make a business of being devils; where nobility is not mere respectability and virtue does not produce a snigger; where the clang of work and the clamor of play attest to the common health; where enemies cannot reach us because our merit, and not our guns or our propaganda, has won the world to our side. . . . It is a very disturbing dream.